"This is an essential book for anyone trying to create theatre in the current environment. It's a book that opened my eyes not just to the unprecedented challenges faced by young theatre artists but to ways of addressing those challenges that aim not just to meet them but to turn them into provocations to make a new kind of theatre. New generations of theatre professionals will find it a sympathetic guide and a mine of invaluable advice."

Sir Nicholas Hytner, *former Artistic Director of the National Theatre and Artistic Director of the Bridge Theatre, UK*

INNOVATION & DIGITAL THEATREMAKING

Innovation & Digital Theatremaking introduces a blueprint for how to think differently about Theatre, how to respond creatively in uncertainty, and how to wield whatever resources are available to create new work in new ways.

In 2020, the COVID-19 pandemic had a colossal impact on theatre across the world. At a time when even the wealthiest and best-supported theatre companies in the world ceased all operations and shuttered their stages, the theatre company The Show Must Go Online (TSMGO) forged its way into a new frontier: the highly accessible digital landscape of online performance. In this book, TSMGO creator Robert Myles and Valerie Clayman Pye explore the success of TSMGO from a practical standpoint, offering insights and strategies that can help theatremakers at every level respond proactively to the future of Theatre in the digital era. Each chapter addresses a different aspect of the creative process and concludes with take-homes so readers can learn how to innovate rapidly, undertake research and development in order to create their own models, and cultivate their own theatrical communities.

Written for theatremakers, directors, producers, and creatives of all levels of experience, this book will help readers to think critically and creatively about theatre and theatre pedagogues to understand how to train their students for the theatre of the future.

Robert Myles is an actor, director, writer, and practitioner who specializes in Shakespeare in Performance, Stage & Screen Combat, and Digital Theatre. Creator of *The Show Must Go Online*, *The Shakespeare Deck*,

Fight Rep, and more, Rob is dedicated to transforming perceptions, performance, and participation in all his practice areas.

Valerie Clayman Pye is an actor, director, author, and academic who specializes in training actors to meet the demands of performing Shakespeare and challenging audience expectations about Shakespeare in performance. She is an associate professor of Theatre and Chair of the Department of Theatre, Dance, and Arts Management at Long Island University, Post.

INNOVATION & DIGITAL THEATREMAKING

Rethinking Theatre with "The Show Must Go Online"

Robert Myles and Valerie Clayman Pye

Routledge
Taylor & Francis Group
NEW YORK AND LONDON

First published 2024
by Routledge
605 Third Avenue, New York, NY 10158

and by Routledge
4 Park Square, Milton Park, Abingdon, Oxon, OX14 4RN

Routledge is an imprint of the Taylor & Francis Group, an informa business

© 2024 Robert Myles and Valerie Clayman Pye

The right of Robert Myles and Valerie Clayman Pye to be identified as authors of this work has been asserted in accordance with sections 77 and 78 of the Copyright, Designs and Patents Act 1988.

All rights reserved. No part of this book may be reprinted or reproduced or utilised in any form or by any electronic, mechanical, or other means, now known or hereafter invented, including photocopying and recording, or in any information storage or retrieval system, without permission in writing from the publishers.

Trademark notice: Product or corporate names may be trademarks or registered trademarks, and are used only for identification and explanation without intent to infringe.

ISBN: 978-1-032-26791-3 (hbk)
ISBN: 978-1-032-26785-2 (pbk)
ISBN: 978-1-003-28990-6 (ebk)

DOI: 10.4324/9781003289906

Typeset in Optima
by MPS Limited, Dehradun

*Robert Myles dedicates this book to
Sarah and Theia, Eileen & Ian:
"Up and down, up and down!"
(Theia Myles, after Puck,* A Midsummer Night's Dream *3.2)*

*Valerie Clayman Pye dedicates this book to
Thomas, Jolie, and Owen Pye:*
"Our remedies oft in ourselves do lie ..."
*(*All's Well That Ends Well *1.1.216)*

CONTENTS

List of Figures *xi*
About the Authors *xiii*

Introduction 1

1 Innovation and Theatremaking 6

2 Why Shakespeare? 34

3 Creating a Community 42

4 Producing Rapidly, Producing Regularly 64

5 Directing for Digital 120

6 The Future 149

Appendices 165

Appendix A. Sample "You've Been Cast" Email Document 166
  Appendix A1. Sample "Briefing" Email 170

Appendix A2. Sample "Briefing" Guide   173
Appendix A3. Sample Conversation Email
    Document   177
Appendix A4. Sample Props, Costume, and
    Setpieces List   178
Appendix A5. Sample Rehearsal Schedule
    Email   180
Appendix A6. Sample Rehearsal Call Sheet   182
Appendix A7. Sample Zoom Theatre Guide   189
Appendix A8. Sample Final Show Prep Email   191
Appendix A9. Sample Green Room Email   193

Appendix B. List of Creatives Involved in TSMGO   194

Appendix C. List of TSMGO Patreon Patrons   199

Appendix D. Links to TSMGO Playlist   202

Index   203

FIGURES

0.1	The Show Must Go Online QR Code	2
1.1	Image of Original Tweet	10
1.2	Thinking Differently Flowchart	21
1.3	Blocking Conventions in Two Gentlemen of Verona QR Code	23
1.4	The Letter Pass in Two Gentlemen of Verona QR Code	24
1.5	Lavinia Mutilated in Titus Andronicus QR Code	24
1.6	The Donkey Head in A Midsummer Night's Dream QR Code	25
1.7	The Cliff Dive in King John QR Code	25
1.8	Iachimo Observes Imogen Sleeping in Cymbeline QR Code	26
1.9	Leia Hologram in Shakespeare's Star Wars QR Code	29
1.10	Five-Star Chart	29
1.11	Doing Differently Flowchart	31
2.1	Shakespeare Five-Star Chart	41
4.1	TSMGO Macbeth R&D QR Code	81
4.2	Three-Point Lighting Setup	95
4.3	Amelia "Ace" Armande (nèe Amy Sutton; They/Them) as Dromio of Syracuse and Robbie Capaldi (He/Him) as Antipholus of Syracuse in Comedy of Errors	96

4.4	Shakespeare's DeLorean	99
4.5	Arrow Tutorial QR Code	99
5.1	Zoom Tutorial QR Code	134
5.2	Screen SetUp Tutorial QR Code	134
5.3	Mark Antony Speech QR Code	144
5.4	Mark Antony Text QR Code	144
D.1	TSMGO Playlist QR Code	202

ABOUT THE AUTHORS

Robert Myles is a director, actor, and writer. He is the co-creator of *The Show Must Go Online*. Over his career in Shakespeare, Rob has played over 30 Shakespearean roles in Off West End and regional touring productions. He has worked as a freelance creative lead on innovation projects for multinationals, including Unilever, Diageo, and Johnson & Johnson. He is the creator of *The Shakespeare Deck*, a powerful, portable text-work tool for actors and creatives, and host of the *Owning Shakespeare* Podcast, with guests including Adjoa Andoh and Paterson Joseph. He has spoken at Harvard University, taught Shakespeare at East 15, Wolverhampton University, given seminars at NYU London, and done Q+As with King's College London, the University of Texas, and many more. Beyond Shakespeare, Rob is also an action designer and a Certified Teacher with the British Academy of Stage & Screen Combat. He has directed several short films, documentaries, and action for the camera. He has also explored the role creative technologies can play in the future of live storytelling with Theatre Royal Bath, The Stratford Festival in Ontario, Canada, and others (http://robmyles.co.uk).

Valerie Clayman Pye is an actor, director, author, and academic who specializes in making Shakespeare accessible and training other artists to do the same. She is an Associate Professor of Theatre and Chair of the Department of Theatre, Dance, and Arts Management at Long Island University, Post, and is Assistant Faculty with Theatrical Intimacy Education, a consulting group that specializes in researching, developing, and teaching best practices for staging theatrical intimacy. Her book, *Unearthing Shakespeare: Embodied Performance and the Globe* (Routledge), is the first to consider how the unique properties of Shakespeare's theatre can help train actors as well as enliven performances of Shakespeare's plays. She is the co-editor of *Objectives, Obstacles, and Tactics in Practice: Perspectives on Activating the Actor* (with Hillary Haft Bucs) and *Shakespeare and Tourism* (with Robert Ormsby). Her essays have appeared in *Shakespeare, Teaching Shakespeare, PARtake: The Journal of Performance as Research, New England Theatre Journal, Theatre Topics,* and several essay collections. A 2018–2020 LabWorks Artist at the New Victory Theatre in NYC, Valerie has been developing "Shakespeare's Stars", an immersive, multimedia, multi-sensory performance for babies and their caregivers, along with Spellbound Theatre (www.valerieclaymanpye.com).

INTRODUCTION

In March 2020, the World Health Organization declared the spread of COVID-19 a pandemic. Quickly, unprecedented lockdowns followed across the globe. Lockdowns prevented mass gatherings in public spaces, and theatres were among the first to be shut down. These lockdowns were essential: the virus went on to infect over five hundred million people and kill over six million worldwide (at the time of writing; Source: Wikipedia).

Producer Sarah Peachey and Artistic Director Robert Myles have lived itinerant existences with portfolio careers, having worked together in theatre first as actors and later as producers and directors, but also variously for multinationals including Unilever, EA Games, General Mills, Diageo, Johnson & Johnson, Bayer, Telefonica, and more on innovation projects as a producer and creative lead, respectively. This seemingly random combination of work and life experience gave them an ideal context to respond to the impending crisis.

Only six days after the WHO declared COVID-19 a pandemic, Sarah and Rob had co-founded *The Show Must Go Online* (*TSMGO*), cast, rehearsed, and broadcast their first production of *The Two Gentlemen of Verona* – a digital, performed reading of the play featuring an international cast, broadcast live to YouTube and performed on Zoom, utilizing improvised costume, props, and blocking conventions.

TSMGO quickly became a global, volunteer-led, and values-led movement dedicated to creating **Shakespeare for Everyone, For Free, Forever.**

2 Introduction

FIGURE 0.1 *The Show Must Go Online* QR Code (bit.ly/smgo).

Between March and November 2020, *TSMGO* cast, produced, and directed a Shakespeare play every week for nine months, broadcast live on YouTube, completing the entire *First Folio* plays in the order they were believed to have been written. In addition, *TSMGO* worked with Quirk Books to produce short excerpts of New York Times Bestseller Ian Doescher's Shakespeare's *Star Wars IV: Verily, A New Hope*; *Mean Girls*, *Clueless* and *Back To The Future*.

In that time, *TSMGO* worked with over **500 actors and creatives across 60 countries.** It attracted over 250,000 views and 6,500 subscribers during its initial run, with more in legacy and over 7,600 followers across our social media platforms. We raised over £25,000 through our Patreon hardship fund, which was distributed to actors and creatives who opted in to receive a share at the end of each month.

TSMGO was featured twice on the BBC's flagship news and current affairs show, *Newsnight*, as well as in The Guardian, The New York Times, and across the global press. *TSMGO* won three awards from OffWestEnd, including their special OneOff Award, and was nominated for Digital Project of the Year at The Stage Awards alongside the most established and best-resourced institution in the UK, the National Theatre, despite not existing before lockdown.

Artistic Director Rob Myles worked with Dr. Jeffrey Wilson of Harvard University to develop an education initiative centered around the work. *TSMGO* was featured by the Folger Shakespeare Library in Washington, DC, the Shakespeare Birthplace Trust in Stratford upon Avon, and more.

Once the First Folio Series was complete, *TSMGO* continued to produce new work from under-represented directors and creative teams, constantly pushing the frontier of digital theatre and early modern texts through a combination of passion and perseverance.

TSMGO **consistently sought to uphold progressive values** through casting and productions, including all female and non-binary and all Global Majority casts; an on-going commitment to race-conscious casting, especially for key productions like *The Merchant of Venice* and *Othello*, ensuring not just representation but culturally intentional casting and storytelling, valuing principles like the wisdom of crowds and flattened hierarchies.

Put another way:

> *Come what may in digital theater, The Show Must Go Online will always be a landmark production, the first to take all of Shakespeare's plays online. What stands out even more is that the series transcended the world of Shakespearean theater to become a global community for art, conversation, and human connection during a time when everyone was isolated, exhausted, and anxious to know how our moment fit into the larger course of history. Bridging performance with scholarship, and Shakespeare's time with our own, the series outmaneuvered the polymorphous challenges of corona-times to create a space for laughter, reflection, pathos, and learning more about ourselves and others. Perhaps most importantly, The Show Must Go Online set a standard for future theater that is radically inclusive and committed to progress toward more truthful art and a more just society.*
>
> Dr. Jeffrey Wilson, Harvard University

When we set out to write this book, it was to be a story of *TSMGO* – an aide memoire for a unique time in theatre history, seen through the lens of one of the most prolific creators of digital theatre in pandemic times.

This book is not that.

This book has become **a survival guide for making theatre in times of crisis.** Theatre. On whatever stage, in whatever age. It is a book about how to *think differently* about producing theatre, by leading with values and process.

While we wanted to memorialize and offer the many lessons *TSMGO* discovered along the way, we realized through the early stages of writing this book that the things that *TSMGO* taught us could be applied in a much broader sense. Through writing, we returned again and again to a desire for this to be *useful*; a forward-facing piece, not a retrospective. This was more aligned with our values – to emphasize *how TSMGO* did what it did, so you can too, in new and unforeseen ways.

A survival guide is useless unless the contents are applied in context, and the same is true of this book: **your participation is required.**

The methods, insights, and lessons contained within require you to engage with them and try applying them. For that reason, **it's good to have a project or challenge in mind** as you read. Apply the ideas contained to your project *in parallel* to your reading, and compare what you had at the beginning with what you had at the end. In some cases, the idea and your plan for its execution will have evolved beyond recognition. As you will find, there are no shortcuts.

Throughout, we will refer back to *TSMGO* as a case study, using the project to highlight the principles that made it a success, the lessons learned along the way, and how to take them on into the future.

What happened to us, and what we did in response, is one small example in a storied history of the challenges theatre has faced over the millennia. We must stress: **this will happen again**. And again. Perhaps sooner than any of us realize.

The 2020 COVID-19 pandemic brought theatre to its knees, and at the time of publication, much of it remains there. While the headline commercial productions may be back, they are far from safe, the Daniel Craig/Ruth Negga *Macbeth* (on Broadway) and the Kathryn Hunter *King Lear* (at Shakespeare's Globe) both missed shows due to COVID-19. In the industry beneath that lofty ceiling, things continue to be much more dire. Investment in arts and culture in the UK was slow to come, insufficient when it did, and lacked a long-term vision in how it was distributed. There is a talent drain in progress in the theatre industry as talented theatremakers migrate toward higher-paid work in other media and industries, driven in part by the ways in which theatre has responded (or not) to the challenges of the age.

So how can we better respond to "build back better"? A phrase frequently uttered as the reopening began, but that has yet to be felt significantly by audiences or theatremakers in the years since.

This book does not have *the* answer. In fact, our intent is not to give you *any* answers but instead **a sequenced series of *good* questions to ask – a process of inquiry** that will empower you to generate new answers to new challenges.

What You'll Get from This Book

In the **Introduction**, we've provided the origin story for *TSMGO*, which serves as the spine running through much of the rest of this volume.

Chapter 1: Innovation & Theatremaking will offer original thinking on how the innovation process can be streamlined and applied to the process of creating your own work, taking the proven tools of business success and applying them to the creation of art.

Chapter 2: Why Shakespeare? In this chapter, you'll understand some of the reasons Shakespeare has been repeatedly leveraged by new creators in tumultuous times and how the constant reevaluation of this work both enlivens it and puts it in conversation with theatre's past and future.

Chapter 3: Creating a Community will put what it means to be a part of something under a microscope, understand what matters to you, find the people who care as much as you do about it, and start creating the change you want to see in the world.

Chapter 4: Producing Rapidly, Producing Regularly will show you how we delivered the work, using "formula as a friend", optimization techniques, and calculated risk-taking to create a unique body of work that constantly improved upon itself – and how you can do it even better next time.

Chapter 5: Directing for Digital will examine how to meet a previously unexplored medium on its own terms. We will demonstrate how the same set of tools (outlined in Chapter 1) was used in execution as well as in the conceptual stages. Simply, how to get shit done and then do it less shitly.

Chapter 6: The Future assesses the shit we're facing as an industry and society, throws down some gauntlets to the world at large, and invites you to pick them up. What do we need to do differently in the future, and how can we start doing it *now?*

The Appendices provide an archive of useful links and examples of the materials deployed throughout the run of *TSMGO*, giving you a starter pack for Zoom theatre creation. This will include information on streaming Zoom to YouTube, actor tutorials on blocking conventions and interacting with Zoom's tools, setting your screen up for optimal performance conditions, prop tutorials, and more. Essentially, how the sausage got made.

1
INNOVATION AND THEATREMAKING

How can the principles of innovation intersect with best practice in theatremaking? How do the tools honed to a keen edge by the forces of capitalism get reappropriated for the creation of art? The formation of a community? The delivery of meaningful experiences?

A common phrase echoes through countless theatre rehearsal rooms: "specific is universal". Shakespeare understood it. You understand it. We do too, which is why we'll use *The Show Must Go Online* (*TSMGO*) as *a specific example* to illuminate the principles that informed its success and inspire you to use them in the creation of your own work, wherever and whenever that might be.

This chapter will share the principles of innovation best practices as viewed through the **creation** of *The Show Must Go Online*. The chapters that follow will examine the **execution** of *TSMGO*. At all times, this book will be as transparent, self-reflective, and transferable as we can make it.

The first question to ask yourself before you begin is: **what makes theatre theatre?**

Some starter prompts to get your juices flowing (hint: disagreement is good):

- Theatre is a "feeling box" to safely explore the dangers in society and in ourselves
- Theatre is a physical place where people gather in person, pointed at a stage. It has a red curtain and a lighting rig
- Theatre is an act of communal storytelling
- Theatre is a space for embodied stories and experiences

DOI: 10.4324/9781003289906-2

- Theatre is professional wrestling with better talking and worse athletics
- Theatre is …

Another, more helpful way to phrase this question might be – what makes theatre unique? What differentiates theatre from other media?

In 2020, the pandemic tested our definition of theatre as never before, and consequently our idea of what is and isn't theatre fractured and diffused.

However *you* go on to answer that question, it may inform how you create future work in unexpected ways.

An Overview of Innovation Best Practice

Many books have been written on this discipline, and although these actions have been practiced by the authors, we claim no ownership or authority over them. Instead, it is useful to signpost to the clearest and most succinct definitions available.

Producer Sarah Peachey worked at? What If! Innovation with Matt Kingdon, co-founder of the company and author of *Sticky Wisdom* and *Science of Serendipity,* both of which will allow you to trace the roots of the thinking as it was applied in our case. Sam Conniff's *Be More Pirate* is an excellent and eminently readable book about social entrepreneurship, and his *Uncertainty Experts* no doubt dives much deeper into some of what will be covered here when it comes to the "in times of crisis" portion of the thinking. If you seek further inspiration, this is where to find it.

In the interests of keeping this book accessible, we have further simplified, unified, and synthesized these processes for theatremaking, with a specific focus on **the need to do something you've never done before.**

Our innovation process breaks down as follows:

Part 1: Thinking Differently

1 Get curious
2 Find clues, have hunches
3 Imagine new possibilities

Part 2: Doing Differently

1 Rapid prototyping
2 Stretch and build
3 Go again

Why Have a Process?

When we are faced with an existential threat, our bodies go into a fight-flight-or-freeze response, in which adrenaline limits our brains' non-essential functions and pushes us toward intuitive, rather than analytical, processes. This results in our falling back on knee-jerk decision-making, based on what we have done before that helped us survive – our *most practiced* response.[1]

Applying this in a behavioral context, the practice of being a theatremaker is a constant work in progress: always striving to become a better person, a better citizen, and a better artist. We examine our own ideas and behaviors, and we change them as we grow; we are always looking to shed unhelpful inherited ideologies and societal conditioning. If all this is true, it necessarily follows that our *best* response to a situation cannot therefore be our *most practiced* response. Whatever is most practiced quickly becomes outdated, especially in a society that evolves as rapidly as ours does. We want to come up with our latest, best response as our latest, best selves, not fall back on our earlier, less evolved response based on our more primitive experiences.

By committing to process, we can limit the impact of our human foibles.

Paradoxically, if we can embrace process *as* our *most practiced* response (while honing and evolving that process as we work), we can ensure we find new answers to new problems, mitigating uncertainty in a proven way without stagnating. It gives us the confidence to *not know* what the hell we're going to do when, for instance, we are first faced with an unprecedented global-level crisis, because we know *how* to find a way through.

Producer Sarah Peachey and Artistic Director Rob Myles' *practiced process* created this slice of theatre history; it enabled them to take to a new stage *in response to* the age.

To get a handle on how this process works, we'll use *TSMGO* as an example.

Part 1 – Thinking Differently

Get Curious

The most important aspect of responding creatively to a crisis is curiosity. It is the first casualty and the most necessary to protect. Researching the problem thoroughly through multiple angles and extrapolating from that along a number of different lines is the best possible starting point for innovation. You'll read it throughout this book, but we believe in standing on the shoulders of giants. Sometimes, you'll stand on the inspiring work you discover to elevate your own work. Sometimes, you'll stand on the dated, the problematic, the flawed things you encounter to rise above it. Both ways are valid, but neither is possible unless you *get curious*.

If you are looking to *get curious* as a theatremaker in crisis, there are key actions you can take to fuel and inform that curiosity.

Look at the Wider Theatre Industry: this is sometimes called competitor research, but we eschew this definition because art isn't a competition. Simply, find out what other people are doing! If we're innovating theatre, we can look at other theatremakers, producing houses, different types of theatre, and different types of offers (e.g. NT Live) to determine how others are responding.

Look at Related Worlds: what is *sort-of like* the thing you're interested in? If you're a theatremaker, look at industries that share commonalities but are fundamentally different. People would often think of Film, TV, or Radio, but entertainment can also mean restaurants, dance, travel and tourism, professional wrestling, zoos, etc. A major trend during the earliest days of the pandemic was quizzes – people gathered to do things online that they had previously done in person.

Ask the Audience: what do people want? What do they like, and what do they dislike?

There are, in brief, two ways to glean insights from people. Called *quantitative* and *qualitative* research, they essentially break down to talking to lots of people while asking simple questions or having an in-depth discussion with a small number of people around complex questions.

How Did **TSMGO** *Do It?*

When we **looked at the wider industry**, the picture was grim: every theatre was shutting down, consumed by the incredible red tape of furloughing or laying off staff, securing their venues, and the like. There were some murmurs of institutions releasing archived content to fill the void left by the lack of in-person theatre.

When we **looked at related worlds**, we had a prior advantage: we had already been working with globally distributed teams through our innovation and creative work with multinationals using the then-obscure Zoom platform, which we watched become exponentially more popular for quizzes.

When it came to **asking the audience**, we took the simple route, with two implicit questions: if we were to stage readings of Shakespeare's First Folio, would you want to do it? Would you want to watch it?

Aside: it is worth noting that this was not the first time this idea had been attempted – Rob had unsuccessfully tried to create an in-person reading group in Glasgow several times to work through the complete plays, based on Jonathan LeBillon's model in London. The alchemy of success depends on kairos, or 'the opportune moment' – doing the right thing at the right time.

This was the first and most important question, and the answer determined whether it was worthwhile to continue. It may not have been. But in this case, it was.

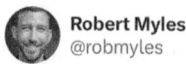

Robert Myles
@robmyles

In response to #Covid_19, I'm going to set up an online #Shakespeare play-reading group via Zoom or similar. Once a week, evenings UK-time so US people can join during the day as well. We have to do what we can to stay connected and creative over this time. Anyone interested?

3:12 PM · 3/13/20

79 Retweets **23** Quotes **372** Likes **7** Bookmarks

FIGURE 1.1 Image of Original Tweet.

Aside: *After that, we would go on to ask the audience many more questions, some more explicit and some more implicit. We asked for their questions during the Q+A, which illuminated how the production had landed with them, we interacted with them on social media, and most importantly, every decision we made was tested in a live environment and our metrics were the kind of thing that TV producers would pay market research companies huge sums for – instant quantitative feedback. A big reaction meant a moment was successful and it worked. A muted reaction or no reaction, and we knew the approach had failed. This allowed us to move toward what worked and away from what didn't.*

What's more, we received qualitative support through in-depth discussions with specialists – for this we must single out Dr. David Sterling Brown as a shining example, who supported our exploration of a consciously cast, diverse production of Othello that preserved the central character's apparently anomalous Blackness.

Outcomes

From our initial exploration, we sought to identify a series of insights from what we could see around us.

> **Pain Points** – *what sucks about the way things are right now?*

For this, we had to look at the problem from two sides – **what sucks about theatre** and **what sucks about lockdown**.

Theatre

- **Expensive Tickets** – for generations, the commercial economics of the medium has been a major barrier to access to theatre. Lest we forget, rising ticket prices were part of a larger swathe of reforms in America, emulated elsewhere, designed to remove the working class and minoritized groups from theatres; the same behavior that led to the Astor Place riots and dueling productions of Shakespeare plays, among other things
- **Limited Seating** – exclusivity is a palpable economic driver and means only a certain number of people can attend
- **Geolocated** – theatre, especially large-scale theatre, tends to be concentrated in centers of economic and political wealth
- **Bad Viewing Angles** – even for those who are able to attend, theatre has historically favored some over others; all views are not created equal. Restricted view seats, "cheap seats", "in the gods", and other such well-established colloquialisms betray an expectation of a diminished experience for many attending

Lockdown

- **No Gathering** – people couldn't physically be in the same place at the same time in groups larger than two during most of the UK pandemic response, and similar restrictions were in place abroad. Even as restrictions eased, groups couldn't be inside, couldn't be without ventilation, and couldn't be as close together as typical theatre seats
- **No Sense of Community** – with everyone isolated in their homes, individuals – who are by their nature social animals – were restricted from being with those with whom they shared ideologies, preferences, cultures, and proximities

- **No Touching** – the sense of touch was essential in pre-pandemic theatremaking, to the extent that we never even considered it until it was taken away. How could we connect with such a distance between us?

> **Rule Breakers** – *is anyone in your industry already defying the usual expectations and conventions?*

Theatre

Site-Specific Theatre – the team had experience in site-specific theatre, which responds to the unique parameters of the space it finds itself in, taking theatre out of the proscenium arch and into the world itself. This form of theatre would prove a powerful inspiration for the work *TSMGO* would undertake.

Gaming – livestreaming of computer games and Dungeons & Dragons were both drawing huge numbers of people together *before* restrictions prevented in person gathering.

> **Aside:** *Stage Manager Emily Ingram later described how the disabled community had already been investigating digital theatre as a medium of performance to mitigate limitations of access to venues for both performers and audiences. This did not initially inform the creation of this project, but is worth acknowledging here so you have a further lead to investigate.*

Lockdown

While innovation tends to prize exceptionalism, this is an example where that isn't the case. The extraordinary thing about lockdown was that people overwhelmingly demonstrated solidarity by *following* rules that negatively impacted them in the short term to protect those most vulnerable.

> **Improvements** – *what are people doing to make a positive difference to their audience/consumer/users?*

In the case of both theatre and lockdown, there were no incremental improvements to discover, as the innovation was happening in the days leading up to lockdown in anticipation that what had happened in

China and Europe would reach the UK. Everyone we could look to was doing their best simply to limit the damage done.

> **Gaps** – *you may find nothing, and that's exciting too! Don't be afraid of space.*

Theatre and Lockdown – the gaps were overwhelming. No new productions, no existing productions, no work for actors, no government support for the industry, and no end in sight.

As you can see, getting curious about these three simple things – the industry, related worlds, and the audience, all empowered us to identify **opportunity areas**.

So, the process again:

- **Look at the wider industry**
- **Look at related worlds**
- **Ask the audience**

And take away:

- **Pain points**
- **Rule breakers**
- **Improvements**
- **Gaps**

And from these, identify and zero-in on:

- **Opportunity areas**

For that, we need to **find clues, have hunches**.

Find Clues, Have Hunches

In order to **find clues**, actively reflect on research you've undertaken. A useful rubric the director Jack Stigner shared with Rob for longform improvisation and Valerie has been using for reflections on practice is: I see (the facts), I notice (the observation), and I wonder (the inquiry).

- I *see* that theatres are shutting down. Let's dig into that **(clue)**
- I *notice* that they are suggesting streaming archival content **(clue)**

- I *notice* that there's a gap in *new* productions **(clue)**
- I *wonder* if anyone is responding by creating new work? **(hunch)**

The beauty of this is that it allows you, as Marie Kondo suggests, to follow your joy. What surprises you? What sparks your interest? *Why* does it?

Another essential practice is note taking. Writers are fantastic at this, but all artists can benefit from this practice. The mind-body connection, the magic of writing, is real. Capture your thoughts *as you have them.* Create the rubric of fact > observation > inquiry and fill out the blanks to save mental space. Underscore the compelling ideas and takeaways. When it comes to the questions you ask or the discussions you have when exploring an idea, listen to what people say, but importantly, listen to *how they say it.* Don't attempt to translate the data you're receiving, as the magic is in knowing how your audience or your collaborators frame it – what language? What shared references? What ideas?

From there, it's time to have hunches. Some believe that a process like this might flatten intuition or turn creativity into a formula. Far from it – you find the spaces your creativity can fill.

First, start to think about the *implications*. Our simple thinking is framed as: **if *this* (the clue), then *what* (the hunch)**?

What's the next step that no one has talked about? How could the success of something be taken further? What problem hasn't been solved?

What's more, use your innate superpower. We are gifted (or if we become entangled in conspiracy theories, perhaps cursed) with **the ability to make connections** between disparate pieces of information. It's even considered the fundamental basis of what is unique about humanity.[2] As we research the areas in Get Curious, we will naturally start to see trends emerging, a sense of direction in which most work is flowing, or a link between two successes that otherwise appear to have little in common. This is when your brain will start fizzing with possibility, and that's when you may be on to something.

Finally, ask **how can this serve my work**? Always ground these explorations in action – in formal innovation there is a distinction between an idea and a hunch. An *idea* is defined as something actionable and executable – something that can theoretically be made or done. **If it can't be acted upon, it's not an idea**. It's a hunch.

When articulating your hunches, start with *"wouldn't it be great if ... ?"*

- Wouldn't it be great if we could still make theatre during the lockdown?
- Wouldn't it be great if audiences still had new productions to watch?

- *Wouldn't it be great if we could have mass gatherings legally, ethically, and safely?*
- *Wouldn't it be great if we could use the tools of multinational capitalism to make art instead?*
- *Wouldn't it be great if we could reimagine how a theatre company runs?*
- *Wouldn't it be great if we could do things differently from how the industry has excluded us in the past?*
- *Wouldn't it be great if someone could watch the show one week and be in it the next?*
- *Wouldn't it be great if we could replicate the conditions of the old repertory system, and have less experienced actors, even amateurs, working alongside and learning from industry veterans?*
- *Wouldn't it be great if our casting pool was not limited by geographical boundaries?*
- *Wouldn't it be great if I could be the youngest, fastest person to direct the complete First Folio plays?*
- *Wouldn't it be great if we could hybridize what we know from working in theatre, film, TV, and radio to tackle the unique demands of a new medium?*
- *Wouldn't it be great if …*

So far, we'd asked a simple question on social media, and we'd reflected on our lived experience and that of others through social listening. Our clues, which emerged from the extreme duress of the pandemic, were mostly negative. Therefore, our resulting hunches were mainly problem-solving exercises. It's important to point out that clues don't always have to be *bad* things – you can steal good things with pride and build on them, but that wasn't our case. It was time to turn our specific clues into hunches.

TSMGO's *Clues to Hunches*

Clues: for these, we aimed to crystallize exactly what we were facing. We did so by creating pull quotes that people did, or might feasibly, say, in response to our social listening.

- **Exclusion** – "Shakespeare isn't for the likes of me". "I don't go to the theatre" (due to my disability, living in poverty, no opportunity due to lack of shows, or my location being too far away from a theatre)
- **Isolation** – "I'm stuck at home". "I can't see my friends". "I can't do the things I normally want to do"

- **Shutdown** – "I can't do what I love". "I lack purpose, direction, momentum"
- **Uncertainty** – "I don't know what's happening, when, or even why"
- **Danger** – "Being in large groups is a threat to my health and life, and others' health and lives"
- **Fear** – "We've never been through anything like this". "I don't know what's going to happen". "How long it will last". "Will theatre die?"

Hunches: for these, we simply flip-reversed the problems we'd articulated to imagine what their opposite would be, again, in a humanized way, as a potential participant or audience might phrase it.

- **Inclusion** – "wouldn't it be great if I was given permission to be a part of something?", "Wouldn't it be great if there was active facilitation of my involvement?" "Wouldn't it be great if I felt invited?", "Wouldn't it be great if I saw a demonstrable commitment that People Like Me are welcome?"
- **Connection** – "wouldn't it be great if I could meet new, like-minded people with similar passions from around the world?" "Wouldn't it be great if I could feel a part of something?"
- **Productivity** – "wouldn't it be great if I could still do what I love with theatres closed?" "Wouldn't it be great if I could hone my craft, and actually learn new skills?" "Wouldn't it be great if I could engage with works I've never seen, in ways I'd never thought about?"
- **Reliability** – "wouldn't it be great if I had something to rely on when everything around me is totally unpredictable?"
- **Brave space** – "wouldn't it be great if I could explore something new in a playful and inventive way, even take risks, where the only pressure is how much I want to commit to the experience?"
- **Hope** – "wouldn't it be great if I could help to create something that benefits others in their time of need, while I get a kick out of it too?" "Wouldn't it be great if I could overcome the restrictions placed on me, without putting anyone in danger?"

You'll notice that each statement is simple and in the first person. That's because all innovation thinking is meant to begin with empathy – **putting yourself in the position of the people who you're trying to create for**. In theatre, we'd call this an "audience focus".

Aside: one of our favorite stories is of Jordan Peele directing "Get Out" by telling the actors what he wanted the audience to shout at the screen for each beat. This is a gift to any artist; to imbue the work with the reaction you wish to provoke.[3]

With your hunches in place, it's now time to **imagine new possibilities**.

Imagine New Possibilities

When you are coming up with ideas **the most important thing you need to do is be playful *not* practical, be creative *not* critical.** There is **NO A) RIGHT** or **B) GOOD**. It's also important to mention that at this stage, **you don't have to know HOW to do them.** All that comes later, so park those instincts for the time being.

The most poisonous thing to do is to try and find the shortest route to the "right" answer. Unfortunately, due to the way western education has been formatted, this unhelpful behavior is of course the singular pursuit we are most rigorously trained in. In his book, *How to Think Like Shakespeare,* Scott Newstok articulates this argument well, alongside education luminaries like Ken Robinson, that our education system shifted its focus from creating "good citizens" to creating "productive members of society" in the Industrial Revolution, and so agency, argument, free thought, critical analysis, and indeed creativity have been swept aside. To quote Yoda, you must "unlearn what you have learned", and allow space for the mind to wander, and allow flights of fancy. Get carried away.

When looking at related worlds that are not directly in your industry, steal their solutions and apply them to yours in novel ways. This can be stretched extraordinarily far: a classic example of these apparently "random links" is **the apocryphal tale of the nose and the printer**. Let's say a major brand in the paper printer industry was looking to innovate their product to be more effective for customers. A key pain point was that printers often got paper jams, which slowed everything down while the jam was being repaired. The innovators give a simple brief: **imagine other things that get blocked up**. Among many other ideas, the nose gets mentioned. The nose has two nostrils so that if one is blocked, there is another to breathe through. This inspired the printing company to develop a printer with not one, but two paper feeds. In the event one became jammed, the other could be deployed in the interim while the problem was resolved, increasing efficiency.

During the process of generating your ideas, here are useful concepts to apply:

What shares the same problem/opportunity, no matter how laterally? For us, creating theatre in lockdown shared a lot of the same challenges as working with globally distributed teams and clients.

Define the rules in order to deliberately break them – the world exerts pressure on our creativity at all times through consensus. Rail against it. For instance, what if bread *didn't* come in loaves? The rule of lockdown *and* theatre was to shut down and isolate, so we opened up and connected.

Tweak something that exists to make it a little better – Apple is notorious for creating the *minimum viable product* – what's the least we can do to improve the thing so you'll buy a new one? Dyson now has a cordless vacuum cleaner because the cord is a pain point, and "stole with pride" the idea of a battery from a mobile phone. In *Atomic Habits*, James Clear tells of The British Cycling Team and their quest to win the Tour De France. Known commercially as Team Sky and led by Dave Brailsford, they discovered the exponential impact of what they called marginal gains. Rather than try to make a revolutionary paradigm shift in cycling, Dave and his team sought to improve every tiny aspect of their training by just 1%. Before this approach, no British cyclist had ever won the Tour de France. In 2012, just three years later, they won, and went on to win *every* year until 2018, making six consecutive victories in total. The point is – you don't have to completely transform the way theatre is made to make something extraordinary – just make small tweaks everywhere you can. We applied this every week to our work, as you will see.

Aside: though this isn't about directing, this is precisely how I had to approach that discipline with only two and a half days of rehearsal – if I could sharpen everyone's performance by 1%, make every beat 1% crisper, the dramatic arcs 1% clearer, the textwork 1% more audience-focused, the dramaturgy 1% more compelling, then I knew I was bending the arc of our time toward quality. This is also great insurance against becoming one of *those* auteurs who leave no room for co-creation.

If there's a gap in the market, how can you fix it? Novelty infomercial homeware products like the *Slap Chop* go crazy in their pursuit of this, and the film *Joy* (2015) charts the rise of one such success, the creator of the self-wringing mop. Another great example is the peer-to-peer short-term room and home rental service *Airbnb* – their offer of a platform for unique, local, spare rooms answered two simultaneous needs: the rising need for accommodation and the rising need to monetize any available space, especially in sought-after areas. The self-catering style suited many more than traditional hotels, and the unique and distinct properties available played to a growing need for authentic experiences in the travel marketplace. By identifying these two needs and simply (but elegantly) drawing a line between them, *Airbnb* has made billions. They created little more than an *opportunity* in order to make their money. Our market was full of gaps – we couldn't find anyone creating anything, and while streaming services had no shortage of entertainment, none of it was *live*. This matters, as we'll cover at the end of the chapter.

Throughout your ideation (a portmanteau for "idea generation") session, try and answer all your hunches in as many ways as possible. Challenge yourself to imagine *all* the ways your hunch could be realized, and don't let feasibility hold you back. Again, follow your joy, your excitement, and choose the ideas that are really fizzing most to share back with a small team of like-minded individuals, colleagues, or co-creators. If you have people involved at the earliest stages of your project, then invite them to do this exact same process too! It's essential to use the **wisdom of crowds** at every opportunity. The more brains you have working on the problem and imagining new solutions, the more possibilities you have to find the very best idea.

> **Aside:** *the best idea doesn't have to be yours. You're all working toward the same goal, but you have to be open enough to allow for the possibility that others can better realize your vision – trust enough in your taste to perceive what makes an idea the best, in order to go with it. This comes with time and practice.*

Once you have your ideas, it's time for …

Yes and! Great news, theatre people! The founding principle of improvisation is also one of the core directives of innovation. Namely, once you have your ideas, share them back with a small, hand-picked team and ask others to **yes and**! them. Conversely, if your team has ideas, *accept the proposition* and build on it, take it further, and imagine new branches. Any idea presented is a *seed*: we don't know what it could become at first sight, so we need to feed and nourish it to find out – the really exciting idea might not be the actual seed – you just might find it on the end of one of the branches, but you won't get there if you crush that seed under your boot. So get carried away.

After a thorough session of getting carried away, it's time for another round of reflection. What are, genuinely, the best ideas? The strokes of genius? How can you tell?

A good way is to **vote**. You may not wish to make things purely, anarchically democratic. It's ok to keep your hand on the wheel and steer the ship if you need to. Have you ever flipped a coin to make a decision, then defied the rule of chance once the result was known? That's because role-playing an outcome can be invaluable in helping us sharpen how we feel about a potential route forward. By giving everyone 3–5 votes to place behind their favorite ideas, you'll quickly get an understanding of what ideas have the most energy in the room.

Aside: *This is meant to serve as an indicator of where the energy lies – a fast, first form of market research in which your creative team and other participants vote as if they were the audience. In the unlikely event you're in disagreement with the wisdom of crowds, you clearly feel passionately about a given route, so make the argument for it. Power dynamics still exist in this process and you will not always be responsible to those participating to follow up on their ideas. But, if you can bring the team with you, you have a better shot at creating cohesion around it. Of course, this should be a rare exception, and check yourself if the hill you're willing to die on is your first idea – this is a red flag.*

From Hunches to Ideas

For *TSMGO*, we looked at each of our hunches (see page 16) and decided on the following routes – if you're familiar with the work of *TSMGO*, much of what it became can be seen to crystallize at this stage.

Inclusion: design the sign-ups so as many people as possible may apply to take part, design the process to do whatever is possible to enhance accessibility (for both watchers and participants), and make a point to champion underrepresented artists.

Connection: do it online, encourage globally distributed casts, time the shows and rehearsals so people in Europe and North America can take part, wield social media to communicate with audiences, and create a sense of audience togetherness in isolation via a live chat.

Productivity: deliver on a weekly schedule, make sure "everyone leaves with a biscuit", offer responsive working solutions for different schedules, and use guest introductions.

Reliability: make the weekly schedule "appointment viewing" for audiences – an anchor in the maelstrom.

Brave Space: do it online! Create and evolve a set of rehearsal principles and best practices then live by them, curate the live chat to minimize toxicity, and use introductions to offer content disclosures.

Hope: develop an optimistic tone of voice and progressive principles that strive for utopia, make it free at the point of use, make archival recordings accessible to anyone, anywhere, anytime, and in legacy.

"That strain again":

Innovation and Theatremaking **21**

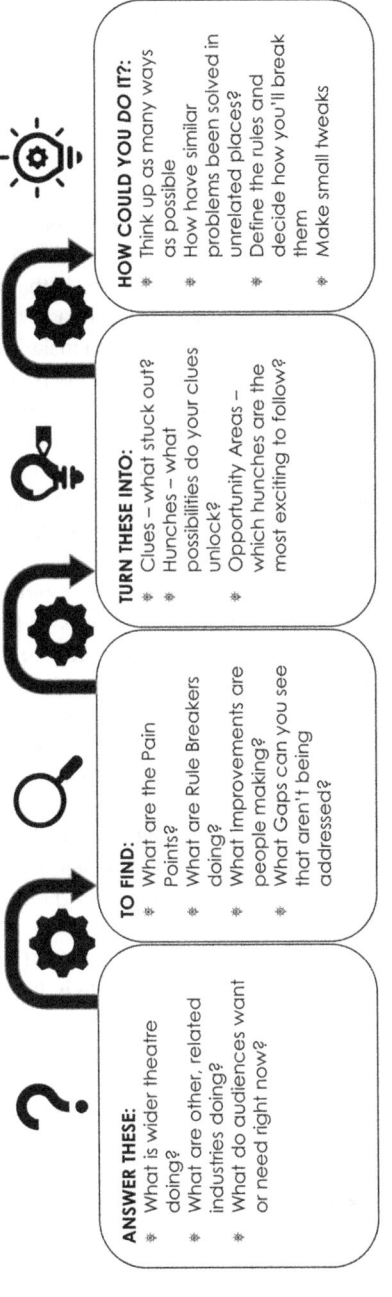

ANSWER THESE:
* What is wider theatre doing?
* What are other, related industries doing?
* What do audiences want or need right now?

TO FIND:
* What are the Pain Points?
* What are Rule Breakers doing?
* What Improvements are people making?
* What Gaps can you see that aren't being addressed?

TURN THESE INTO:
* Clues – what stuck out?
* Hunches – what possibilities do your clues unlock?
* Opportunity Areas – which hunches are the most exciting to follow?

HOW COULD YOU DO IT?:
* Think up as many ways as possible
* How have similar problems been solved in unrelated places?
* Define the rules and decide how you'll break them
* Make small tweaks

FIGURE 1.2 Thinking Differently Flowchart.

Now that we've done our *thinking differently*, it's time to begin **doing differently**. Once you have established the routes, you're most excited about, you figure out *how* to do them in **rapid prototyping**.

Part Two: Doing Differently

Rapid Prototyping

This is your opportunity to create a rough-and-ready version of your idea to see how it survives contact with reality. The result will never be what you intended, and that's ok. The most important thing is that you should be building this prototype for your end users – in our case, this was our participants and our viewing audience. We wanted to make sure the viewing experience had as little friction as possible, and as most people were not yet familiar with Zoom, we decided YouTube was the most ubiquitous platform for the general audience. Zoom, by contrast, was the tool we were most familiar with from our innovation work and had the perfect blend of options to replicate a stage environment (see *Chapter 5 – Directing for Digital*).

We wanted to get something up as quickly as possible, but *how* quick was "as quickly as possible?" It turns out, six days. With encouragement from Ben Crystal and others, we realized that only a rapid response would be effective enough in lighting a beacon to push back the encroaching darkness of lockdown. Fortunately, we were used to these kinds of unreasonable deadlines. We created the initial sign up form and distributed it to our rapidly growing mailing list. We cast our first crop of actors, rehearsed the show, and established many of our foundational conventions. In design thinking, this is known as a **bias to action**, and you'll see this time and again throughout this book. We weren't creating the perfect form of our art, we were creating *any* art at all, which was better than none – and some of the very earliest art to be created in this way. This is also articulated as ready, fire, aim – make a start, and find your course as you're on the journey.

When you are creating your prototype, **it is important to find the best tools available without spending money to execute it**. If you're creating a set, build it from some household LEGO. If you're composing blocking, scrawl it on scrap paper. The storyboards for *Knives Out* are a brilliant example – the simplest possible line drawings a child could do, on a multi-million dollar hit movie with an astonishing ensemble cast. Alternatively, see your prototype, and your journey to creating it, as the *Iron Man* Mk. 1 suit. You are in a cave, with a bunch of scraps. Only **ingenuity, resourcefulness**, and **vision** will get you out of that cave. But if Stark had spent his time refusing to create an exoskeleton without his high-tech lab, cutting-edge materials, and hot-rod-red paint, he'd have died in the cave.

Our first show, *Two Gentlemen of Verona*, was in many ways our first rapid prototype. By committing to putting on a show, and putting it out there quickly and publicly, we learned more than we ever could by theorizing, or holding ourselves back until we had a "perfect" show. Many things remained from those initial explorations: watch this show in contrast with *The Tempest*, the last show of the run, and see how completely the seeds flourished in unexpected directions.

In short: **do it**, and don't be afraid to change! If you attempt to create your idea in the simplest form and it can't work, this will give you invaluable direction to take with you into the future evolution of the concept. If it *does* work, *ish*, you can begin tweaking, molding, and iterating the next, and the next, and the next version. What's more, you have a proof of concept that can help others understand what you're doing and why, so they can help you explore how to do it better.

Rapid prototyping, followed by iteration of incremental improvements, became the basis of our ongoing work (see *Chapter 4 – Producing Rapidly, Producing Regularly* and *Chapter 5 – Directing for Digital*).

A brief history of the innovation of the form follows, for those intrigued by how this constant tweaking can create a snowball effect.

Blocking Conventions in Two Gentlemen of Verona

We started with the head-and-shoulder shot and created an autocue system for actors with the camera as their eyeline, but immediately began to toy with proxemics and costume, with Julia disguised and hidden behind foreground objects.

FIGURE 1.3 Blocking Conventions in *Two Gentlemen of Verona* QR Code (bit.ly/2gent1).

24 Innovation and Theatremaking

The Letter Pass in Two Gentlemen of Verona

We collapsed the "fourth wall" of each actor's space by allowing objects to pass between them using forced perspective. This later became known as "pass the parcel" by acting teachers trying to teach actors how to perform on Zoom.

FIGURE 1.4 The Letter Pass in *Two Gentlemen of Verona* QR Code (bit.ly/2gent2).

Lavinia Mutilated in Titus Andronicus

After *Two Gentlemen of Verona*, we rapidly began to understand how the camera could play a role and staged Lavinia's torture in *Titus Andronicus* as evidenced through Chiron's phone recording of the events. The importance of sound design was pushed here and remained integral throughout the series.

FIGURE 1.5 Lavinia Mutilated in *Titus Andronicus* QR Code (bit.ly/lavmut).

The Donkey Head in A Midsummer Night's Dream

Soon AR became involved, allowing us to do things that were impossible in an in-person theatre, such as Bottom having a 3-D model head that could be puppeteered by the facial expressions beneath it.

FIGURE 1.6   The Donkey Head in *A Midsummer Night's Dream* QR Code (bit.ly/botdonk).

The Cliff Dive in King John

We then began to explore how the multi-camera setup of Zoom could allow for the same action to be seen simultaneously from different perspectives. In this case, this also allowed us to bend time, stretching out the moment in a cinematic way.

FIGURE 1.7   The Cliff Dive in *King John* QR Code (bit.ly/kjdive).

Iachimo Observes Imogen Sleeping in Cymbeline

Toward the end of the run, this multi-camera approach combined with remote operation of multiple devices to create a four-camera shot progression in a single scene, designed to ramp up the audience's complicity with Iachimo's invasion of Imogen's privacy.

FIGURE 1.8 *Iachimo Observes Imogen Sleeping in Cymbeline* QR Code (bit.ly/cymb).

This brief summary of invention skips out the many intermediary steps that took us from one to the next, as new things were tried and discovered with every production, but from the most rudimentary to the most sophisticated, *none* broke our requirement of needing to be achieved using only the readily available tools in the time available. The creative constraint of rapid prototyping forces you (and we discovered, your audience) to ramp up your imagination – which, of course, is entirely Shakespearean.

Finally, you should develop more prototypes than you intend to use. During ideation, you will doubtless have thought up multiple routes to execute the same moments or multiple concepts through which to express your vision. This is good – you won't know yet which will be the most successful. Writers know it's important to kill your darlings – the things that excite you but don't serve the piece as a whole. Having multiple prototypes will allow you to select the best ones. Every execution listed above had multiple prototypes.

The journey continues as you share your prototypes with your team to **stretch and build**.

Stretch and Build

Once you've developed your prototypes, it's important to **share them with your team.** This can be done in several stages – whether that team is your internal artistic team, a small sample of your target audience, or in our case, everyone everywhere forever, it's an important phase of development.

We are fortunate in that theatremaking is an intrinsically collaborative art, so we will all have experienced a member of the team bringing a novel interpretation to the table – of the text, of a note, of a design brief. We know that many minds make bright work. So once you have a prototype that can help others grasp your idea in execution, allow them to get carried away with it and help to expand its horizons.

When sharing internally, there are two different directions one can take: **an open route and a closed route.**

In an **open route**, you simply get honest first impressions and reactions and capture them in as much detail as you can. Have conversations, ask open questions, and follow up on things people say (or how they say them) that make you curious. Capture everything, freely, and without judgment. How you choose to proceed depends on the alchemy of how your team works together, but you'll want to reserve time to establish a critical distance for reflection before you start to compose the actions that will come from this process.

In a closed route, it's important to state up front what kind of feedback you're looking for. Feedback that is **constructive** should be a given, so focus instead on what your intention was, what you hope the effect will be, elements of the prototype you encountered difficulties with, and where you want to get it to in the next phase. Typically, designers will time this very carefully because **what matters is the first impression** – the longer we have to scrutinize in a critical mindset, the more any piece of work will fall apart. The first wave of feedback, and the direction that emerges from it, will be taken away to be worked up.

Whichever route you choose, capture the feedback given, *in the terms it is expressed*. The *way* people articulate their thoughts can be a crucial insight. You can then categorize that feedback into **themes**, to see if you can identify a given trend or consensus in the thinking that is shared by different members of the team.

From here, you'll start to gain clarity on what the next set of opportunities are for refinement – convert these opportunities for growth into the actions needed to seize them – and gain consensus from your team on what they are. Now is the right time to decide who on your team is best to execute this next development – it may not be the person who originated the idea. This happened often on *TSMGO*, as anyone could pitch ideas for any aspect of the production. New eyes, and different expertise, can all help.

Whatever comes out of these processes, you can use the learning, inspiration, and prismatic cascade of insights to inform the next round of development and the next. Remember: failures are useful! They tell you what avenues are worth exploring by eliminating those that aren't – it's still progress, even if it might not feel like it or look the way you expect it to. In short, **improve it or lose it**.

With *TSMGO*, we opened the process such that all team members could pitch creative routes forward for moments identified in the script as good candidates for setpieces.

Everyone was encouraged to bring ideas to the R&D session, or alternatively come up with them in the room, and demonstrate their rough concept. Others could build on them or simply offer their reactions as sample audience members. We would align on what the strongest executions were.

When choosing the route forward, we had a subconscious understanding of **What Success Looks Like**, but you can absolutely define it.

For us, they might be codified as:

- **Novel** – we could use the same tricks, but not in the same way. We strove to "surprise and delight" audiences with something new every week
- **Achievable** – does it use readily available, inexpensive materials or items/technologies we have existing access to?
- **Impactful** – we strove for disproportionality: simply, that our devices needed to have the greatest impact for the least effort. This agnostic term is helpful because the impact can be further defined as funny, moving, upsetting, etc
- **Sophisticated** – we wanted to wow audiences, so we would often combine multiple elements into a presentation (camera position or movement, blocking, proxemics, props, etc.) to give the beats richness. This often resulted in a sense of magic – "how did they do that?" Notably, when Leia appeared as a hologram in *Shakespeare's Star Wars*, the live chat was frenzied with speculation as to how it was achieved, which proved we were on to a winner
- **Value-Aligned** – does the execution deliver on, progress, or enhance our values (described in summary in the Hunches section)? Does it run counter to them?

Innovation and Theatremaking   **29**

FIGURE 1.9   Leia Hologram in *Shakespeare's Star Wars* QR Code (bit.ly/leiaholo).

If you wish to formalize your process, you can **rate each idea against your five criteria out of five using a five-star chart** to help you evaluate them. For instance, an idea might be harder to achieve but more sophisticated, or less novel but most impactful. Being able to see this data and compare it at a glance may help you decide between competing routes forward. The biggest and most symmetrical star represents the thing that has reached the highest ideals of all your priorities. Most ideas won't reach these heights, but you can very quickly compare them visually to aid decision-making.

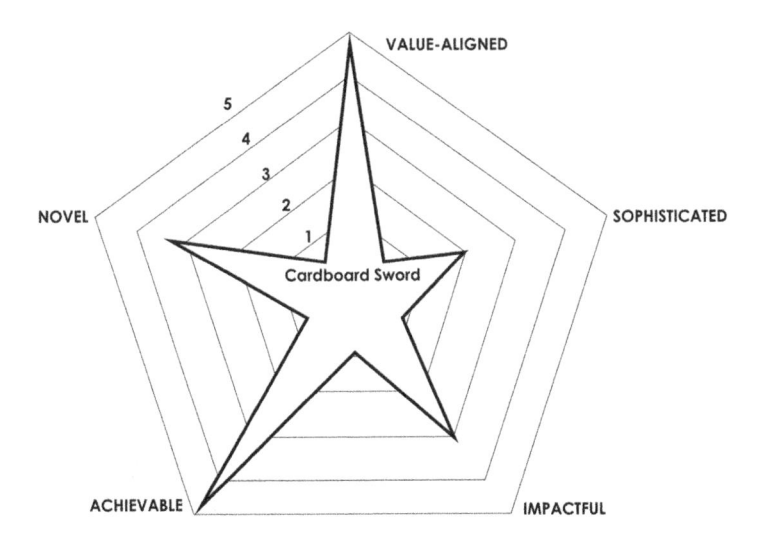

FIGURE 1.10   Five-Star Chart.

This method will tell you which prototypes are the strongest to take forward for further development. Once you know how you're going to develop your prototype into something more refined for your audience, it's time to **go again**.

Go Again

Back to step one of **Doing Differently** we go, but this time with fewer, stronger prototypes to develop and take forward. We're no longer creating our prototype, we're optimizing it. This is called **iteration** and may involve several different attempts at optimization to determine which path is the best way forward. We keep iterating and refining until we optimize our execution, or we run out of time and budget. Try to do the first before the second.

"That strain again":

Innovation and Theatremaking **31**

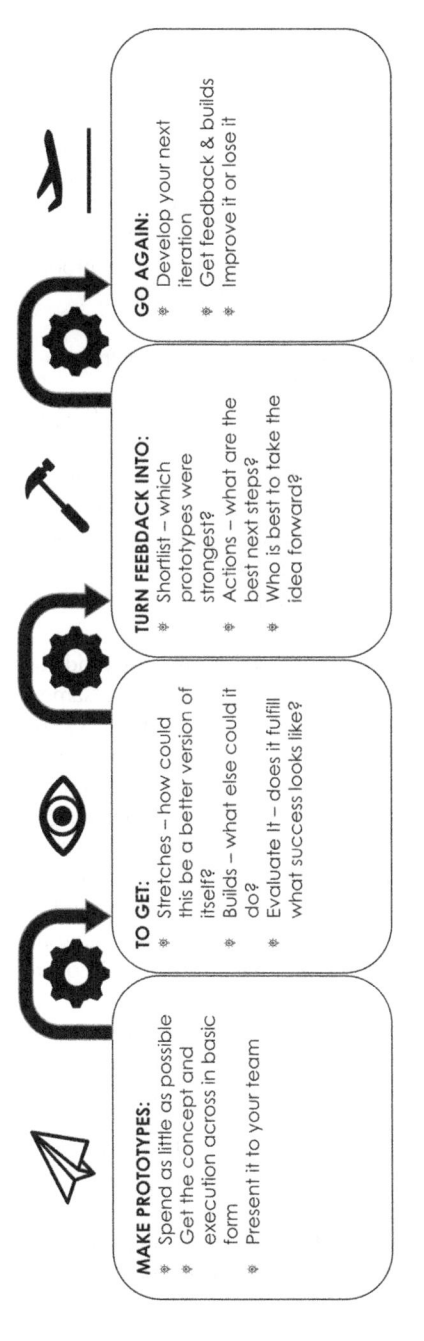

MAKE PROTOTYPES:
- Spend as little as possible
- Get the concept and execution across in basic form
- Present it to your team

TO GET:
- Stretches – how could this be a better version of itself?
- Builds – what else could it do?
- Evaluate It – does it fulfill what success looks like?

TURN FEEDBACK INTO:
- Shortlist – which prototypes were strongest?
- Actions – what are the best next steps?
- Who is best to take the idea forward?

GO AGAIN:
- Develop your next iteration
- Get feedback & builds
- Improve it or lose it

FIGURE 1.11 Doing Differently Flowchart.

Wrapping Up

So, returning to the very first question asked: **what made theatre 'theatre' for *TSMGO*?**

Liveness was absolutely essential. In a world filled with blockbuster streaming options, the fact that the show began and continued uninterrupted until the story was told, for better or worse, was the key differentiator of our work that could mitigate the lack of budget or production value in comparison to the work being produced elsewhere. For us, liveness was further broken down to mean:

- **A Simultaneous Experience** – the original audience are watching at the same time as it is being performed
- **A Communal Experience** – the audience can share their experience with one another
- **Shared Space and Shared Light** – the performance is taking place in the same conditions as those the audience find themselves in
- **Storytelling and Invention** – the "surprise and delight" we promised enabled us to live more fully whilst upholding our civic duty to one another to remain in lockdown

Theatre is a living art. An ephemeral event. It reminds us, among other things, that others are existing, right now, in the same circumstances, place, and time. In Shakespeare's case, it reminds us that people have always lived, in far-flung places and times, with similar fundamental challenges. In these times, it is an extraordinary act of solidarity, defiance, optimism, and communion. It is people telling one another stories, using their humanity to explore humanity.

"It's on a stage with a red curtain" appears nowhere here. While there will always be places with spaces, curtains, and rows of seating, we must not limit our imaginations to *only* this – and those very same places could be enlivened by what has been discovered in the time they were denied us.

This chapter, now concluded, provides the frame for the picture that the rest of this book aims to illustrate. We hope it has shown why *TSMGO* set about doing what it did and started to answer the question of how we began doing it. More excitingly, it shows that by following a process like this, you will inevitably come up with completely different results for yourself because each artist, each set of circumstances, and each set of resources are always different. Following this path, you will never replicate *TSMGO*, nor should you. You'll begin to create something new, urgent, wonderful, and needed now. As it should be.

The Take Homes

- **Use Process** – process can help you find new answers to new problems, overcoming the tendency to fall back on our most practiced responses
- **Cast a Wide Net** – to innovate you need new knowledge, which comes from novel stimulus, which exists outside your existing context.
- **Innovation is not Invention** – it's combining existing elements in novel ways. What connections haven't been made that need to be?
- **Get Carried Away** – don't block your inspiration by focusing on execution too early in the process. Leave the critical brain for later
- **Define What Success Looks Like** – use this to evaluate your ideas against, so you understand which will be the most exciting to develop further
- **Wisdoms of Crowds** – co-creation puts more processing power behind ideation, problem solving, and evaluation
- **Keep Tweaking** – even the idea you decide is best isn't finished. How can you elevate it?

Notes

1 https://www.ncbi.nlm.nih.gov/pmc/articles/PMC5146206/
2 https://www.ncbi.nlm.nih.gov/pmc/articles/PMC4141622/
3 https://nofilmschool.com/2017/02/get-out-jordan-peele-interview-allison-williams

2
WHY SHAKESPEARE?

We will look first at **why Shakespeare was a good choice** – the *prescriptive* portion of the chapter.

Then, we'll think about **why those qualities helped make *TSMGO* a success** – the *descriptive* portion of the chapter.

Finally, we'll seek to **extract some more universal principles** from these two areas to help you think differently about what content you choose when developing theatre in times of crisis.

> *Aside:* This is not about Shakespeare in Lockdown – for that, see *Lockdown Shakespeare – Allred & Broadribb (2022)*. This is not about Shakespeare and plagues – plenty has been written about that in academia and journalism. This is about what we can *learn* from **why** Shakespeare was a good fit for the pandemic, and what that tells us about what makes for good content in times of crisis.
>
> We will not venture into the larger questions of whether or not we should continue to produce Shakespeare, or argue for (or against) why Shakespeare should still be performed, studied, or interrogated. There are a lot of other books that are happy to take that on.

Why We Chose Shakespeare

For *TSMGO*, Shakespeare was the perfect source material as Rob was a highly specialized practitioner (see author bio). He already had the skills necessary to work with the text and experience creating work. Sarah was also experienced with Shakespeare, and with project managing large-scale, long-term projects. This positioned them in a state of **readiness**. The quality of "overnight success" – a show being produced in a new medium in six days and receiving over 20,000 audience in the first five days – was *in part* due to over a decade of preparation. But this is only one factor, as this chapter will make clear.

> **Aside:** The lessons in this chapter are about **reflection, *not* intentionality**. We chose Shakespeare because we were good at it. We must always remember that the success of *TSMGO* was a phenomenon in the scientific sense of the word – an observable event to be interrogated. As artists we need to believe our ideas will find their audience, resonate, and grow beyond us, but that is never a guarantee. We betray our fellow artists when we claim authority from our successes.

Why Did Shakespeare Make for Good Content?

As we begin to consider why Shakespeare was especially well suited for the pivot demanded by pandemic digital theatre, we return to the age-old inquiries at the core of any project: **why this?** – and **why now?** For pandemic Shakespeare, "why this?" comes down to three fundamental ideas: Shakespeare is familiar, Shakespeare is malleable, and Shakespeare is resilient.

Another valid reason was that there was **a community that believed in the value of such an undertaking** and rallied behind it – without a strong initial response, the project would have gone no further.

We could reasonably expect that an audience would show up. Even if you don't *know* Shakespeare particularly well, you still know Shakespeare (sort of). Even without being a Shakespeare aficionado, you probably recognize that Shakespeare is very broadly something we're *supposed to* appreciate (even though it may be difficult to understand or even, dare we say, boring). As the most frequently produced playwright in the western world, we are familiar with Shakespeare as a recognizable entity, as a known quantity in the theatrical canon.

Shakespeare is nothing if not malleable. Shakespeare lends itself to innovation – not only because **it's free** – but because, just as Shakespeare relied on generating new work from established works, Shakespeare's canon carries with it the cache of being a known quantity, of having an established track record of "success". We know that Shakespeare has been adapted, appropriated, and stretched in countless different ways by a continuing line of practitioners across 450+ years. From the drolls of the interregnum that included *Bottom The Weaver*, to impresarios Killigrew and Davenant adapting the plays during the Restoration (among others, to give *King Lear* a happy ending), to Garrick claiming Shakespeare for the Victorian agenda, to *10 Things I Hate About You* and Punchdrunk's *Sleep No More*, there is an unbroken thread from first performance to today.

Shakespeare was perfectly suited for a changing landscape during the pandemic because its **familiarity** served as an anchor to the production and performance practices that were emerging, **balancing novelty and cognitive load**. It is too daunting for audiences to experience novelty across *all* aspects of a project; similarly, for producers, exploring new ways to create and collaborate during a time of crisis is enough of a cognitive load to balance – doing so with Shakespeare allowed for a fixed, reliable entity with which creators could explore. *TSMGO* could take all of the energy that might have been spent on creating and curating new, original content and channel that directly into creating the systems of producing digitally with a new creative team each week.

Beyond being free and familiar, Shakespeare's theatre was also **economical in its production**: it is a theatre of imagination – of empathy, of the human experience, and of resilience. The Chorus in *Henry V* famously asks the audience to "piece out our imperfections with your thoughts" – the work was designed to be done with minimal staging and production value.

Beyond this, **Shakespeare's work was innovative in its own time.** At the time the plays were written, playmaking was, for the first time, a capitalist venture in the most nascent "experience economy". Shakespeare was *thinking differently* about theatre – about its power, perhaps, but also about its execution and delivery. Shakespeare himself leaned on familiar stories and reimagined them in ways that hadn't been considered before. Shakespeare and his early modern contemporaries were writing in a shifting paradigm as the playing companies migrated from a patron-sponsored endeavor to a public-facing model.

Shakespeare's company needed to evolve, to create systems in order to produce regularly and rapidly. Early modern playing companies had to consider their aims – in this case, to provide entertainment on demand to a public, paying audience. The Lord Chamberlain's Men needed to examine ways to shortcut and systematize processes so that they became a repeatable function of their day-to-day existence: actors played familiar archetypes, known as character "lines", for example, and those stock characters helped to reduce the cognitive load of both the players and the playgoers. That shorthand enabled playing companies to understand the *kind of* story that was being told so that they could maximize output value with minimal effort. These **Original Parallels**, a concept we'll return to elsewhere in this book, made Shakespeare's text well suited (though, we stress, not *exclusively* so) to the challenge ahead.

By pulling from stories that were familiar to him, from sources such as the Roman comedies or Hollinshed's Chronicles, Shakespeare could focus on improving what was already in place within the dramaturgical canon. Shakespeare used the material he had the privilege of being exposed to through a grammar school education and democratized it through popular entertainment; he leaned on stories he knew so that he could focus on the execution of those stories. Like all creatives, Shakespeare was responding to the world around him and creating in response to it. If he could rely on an existing plot, he could focus his attention on something entirely novel for the time – character development, for example. Throughout Shakespeare, we see examples of these models of innovation over and over. If people loved Plautus' *The Menaechmi* featuring a set of twins that are separated and mistaken for one another, then they would surely be delighted by *doubling* that confusion. Shakespeare's *The Comedy of Errors* would not exist without Plautus having previously laid the groundwork. Shakespeare was clearly looking to the world around him and figuring out how to do things differently, **how to improve on what was already in practice**. We couldn't arrive at the smartphone if our primary means of communication across distance was still the letter.

Shakespeare has become the cultural inheritance of *our* education as the Greek and Roman plays were his.

Why Shakespeare Helped Make *TSMGO* a Success

Deciding to make something is one thing. People deciding, consistently, to show up for it, is quite another. Why did this idea resonate with its audience?

Shakespeare is familiar. That familiarity brings with it a sense of consolation. At times of upheaval, there is a certain comfort, a reassurance, from Shakespeare, which has withstood and survived other, critical moments in history.

March 2020 demanded that kind of reassurance.

The start of the pandemic brought about catastrophic feelings of upheaval. It isn't hyperbole to say the world came to a crashing halt in those early days when we sheltered in place and nearly everything we understood (and took for granted) about our daily lives changed in what felt like an instant. In such times, individuals are often pulled to make meaning in order to understand the world around them. This period plunged people into solitude and isolation, which activated within the global consciousness a need for hope and resilience. Shakespeare's malleability invites those of us who engage with it to use it as a framework to experience delight, explore, and interrogate our own experiences. If Shakespeare's works could survive 450+ years of pestilence, violence, and war and continue to thrive, perhaps we could, too.

In this way, Shakespeare embeds us in a cyclical experience where our contemporary plight finds connection with what was happening at the time Shakespeare was writing the plays.

If we consider how theatre was made during a period of extreme overwhelm – the COVID-19 pandemic lockdown – then it's easy to understand how Shakespeare was particularly well suited for this moment, and how Shakespeare's constancy allowed for other forms of innovation to emerge.

So, *why* did so many choose Shakespeare, for so long, as a companion through these difficult times?

During the Covid catastrophe of March 2020, both mainstream and social media reminded us that "Shakespeare wrote *King Lear* during the plague". Why? What messages did that send, either intentionally or not? On the one hand, it aimed to promote the hopeful, though pollyannaish, idea that we are capable of positive things in the worst of circumstances – that each one of us can be master lemonade makers from the bitterest lemons life has given us, if only we believe we can and if only we are positive enough. It also aims subliminally to entice us to believe that we may be rewarded with an unexpected prize if we "hang in there". Had there never been a plague in which Shakespeare wrote *King Lear*, there would be a *King Lear*-sized void in our culture. We cannot necessarily understand an event while it's underway but often can identify unexpected benefits once the moment has passed. We might discover something we couldn't have anticipated if we simply continue to move forward, even though it feels as though the world is falling apart, or has come to a grinding halt. Which, it did, actually.

While there was justified eye rolling around the pressure of creating a masterpiece with this pandemic-imposed windfall of time (which disregards the inequities in available time for many; those juggling caretaking responsibilities, for example), some could still aspire to create something new; new things *did* come to fruition. We can say that without a doubt this book would not have existed without Covid. *TSMGO* would not have happened. Rob and Valerie would possibly never have met or collaborated. We can confidently say that the place that Zoom would assume in our daily lives would likely have not happened. Zoom existed before the pandemic; it was not a new technology, but *because of* the pandemic it began to be used differently. In February 2020, the idea that people would get married, grieve and attend funerals, graduate, celebrate, and mark other life events (both big and small) through the screens on our devices would have been surprising. And while there was certainly digital theatre before Covid, the moment that Covid brought us, within the context of an innovative technology that became ubiquitous, created a perfect opportunity for new things to happen.

And second, the tale of *King Lear* in lockdown also helped to implant the idea that things will eventually be okay. Even if we are not creators, we could be reassured that we are not alone in our isolation; that others before us have also endured similar experiences. The "*King Lear*" shorthand reinforces the notion that "everything happens for a reason", which is meant to satisfy, but also to silence or suffocate the uproarious need for understanding that, at times, cannot be made material.

The phenomenon of the "Shakespeare salve" is not unique to our time: we saw it in the Robben Island Shakespeare. When imprisoned on Robben Island, Nelson Mandela's fellow inmate Sonny Venkatrathnam concealed a contraband copy of Shakespeare's Complete Works by dressing it as an Indian Holy Text, and asked his fellow inmates to sign their names by their preferred passages, essentially animating the "works" through its own form of performance – claiming a piece of Shakespeare in response to the moment, and entering a dialogue with others through this act of choice. In this case, the object "Shakespeare" performed on a daily basis as religious scripture. While this exchange of one illicit object for a sanctioned one may be nothing more than necessity, bringing with it a sense of stolen pleasure during a time of injustice and hardship, it tells a particular story to an outside audience. As all audiences are primed to construct meaning from what is before them, the story the Robben Island Shakespeare constructs is that if Shakespeare could help Mandela endure, it surely could help us do the same.

What, besides familiarity, gives it that quality? Shakespeare is known for arguing earnestly from all perspectives present on the stage, for a universalizing abstraction that displaces the concerns of his own time into distant settings, and for using poetry and pith to try and encapsulate certain thoughts, feelings, and sensations. A preoccupation with grand themes, contrasted with low jokes, wrapped in characters that feel "lived in", and the ability to ask hard questions from a safe distance, all contribute to its enduring quality.

Ultimately, Shakespeare is as valid an object of meditation as anything else, and if "the more you seek, the more you find" is true of all things, it is certainly true here. That continuing reward is enough for many.

The Take-Homes

Here are the characteristics Shakespeare had in this circumstance that will help you choose material to face future circumstances. You don't have to decide on the same core values, but decide what values *will* make the work sing to the time, and evaluate potential material against them.

Balancing novelty and cognitive load is something we come back to again and again, and it has validity here too. **Familiarity** does little, in fact, to diminish our enjoyment of story. The strict conventions of Romantic Comedy plots, or the touted eight million+ covers of The Beatles' *Yesterday*, can attest to this, and so can Shakespeare. Which is not to say we cannot, or should not, be original. Instead, giving the audience a degree of safety somewhere in the production can enable them to engage with more adventurous choices in other aspects. Think *Bridgerton*: an original take on Jane Austen engages interest that an expected interpretation doesn't.

Politics of respectability too plays a role. In rhetoric, we call this *ethos* – the reputation of the speaker and why they should be listened to on the topic at hand. From where does the material derive its authority in the here and now?

Design is a key factor – has the work been made, either intentionally or through fortune, to operate successfully within the limits you must deliver the project?

Parallels – does the work, or the conditions the work was made in, parallel the time it's being reproduced in? What is required to highlight these parallels?

Affect – if "comfort" was the key word for the intended impact of choices in the lockdown moment, what affect are you looking to deliver now, in this moment? Better yet, what affect are people seeking? What works will help to achieve this?

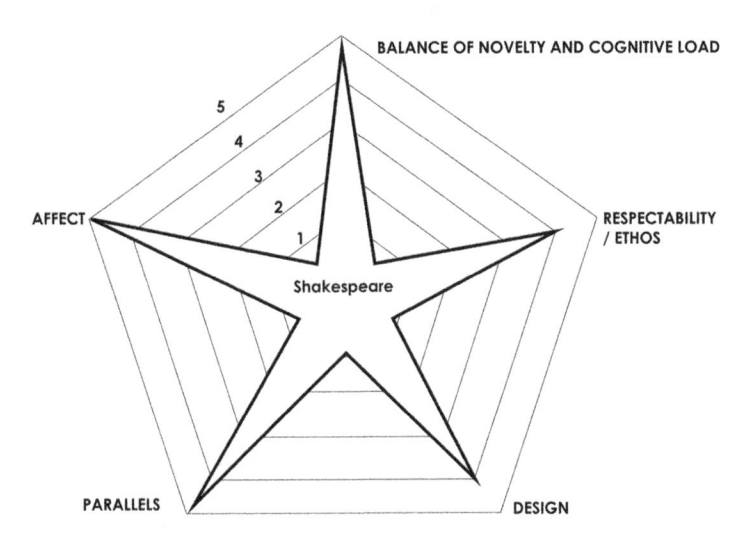

FIGURE 2.1 Shakespeare Five-Star Chart.

3
CREATING A COMMUNITY

Like all healthy relationships, communities require commitment and reciprocity to thrive. We'll be looking at what being a part of a successful community *gives* you and what it *takes* to create and maintain a successful community. Some of these lessons were learned the hard way, and some were only ever distant aspirations we couldn't fully realize. None of that should stop you from benefiting from what we've learned, so hindsight will be just as powerful here as any foresight we may have had.

Community brings people together through common purpose, shared values, shared passions, and shared needs. These knit us into a whole greater than the sum of our given parts.

The Show Must Go Online was built on community. With no financial resources or institutional support to draw upon, impassioned commitment and values-led practices were the only currencies *TSMGO* had to work with. *TSMGO* cultivated an international audience through grassroots efforts alone.

In this chapter, we'll explore the ways that makers of all kinds can create a strong community by focusing on two critical components: **finding your focus** and **finding your people**.

This chapter takes the lessons we learned along the way about how to propel artists and companies at all stages of their development, so you can benefit from an approach to community that is both strategic and responsive.

Part 1 – Finding Your Focus

What Do You Do Especially Well?

When thinking about community, it's important to figure out what your role will be within it. Whether an individual or a company, what is the offer you can make that will be uniquely valued by those who take you up on it?

Ask yourself:

- What makes you happiest?
- What do people you love and trust think you're good at? What do they think you're better at than they are? (***Aside*** *a great question for the panel in interviews is "why are you excited about the possibility of me working here?" the answer allows you to play to those strengths, and if they can't answer, you know they haven't invested in you the way you have in them.*)
- What common themes connect the things you enjoy, in your work, your social life, and hobbies?
- What was the best thing about the last piece of work you created? And the one before that?
- Imagine a company headhunted you for a project, saying "you're the perfect person to lead this!" – what do you imagine the project needed?

Take these answers and list three-to-five strengths and features. Many, including your authors, may cringe at a positive and optimistic self-assessment like this, but it can be crucial to see how you might make a positive difference for others. After all, the reason to join or form any community should be about being a positive part of something greater than yourself.

It also helps you identify what help you might need from a community without criticism – if something simply isn't a top strength for you, rather than calling that a weakness, you can find someone for whom it is right, who has answers around what makes them happiest.

Most of all, this process can help you *relax*. You can find your place in a group. Knowing what you contribute can abate feelings of being in deficit, which can make us try too hard or act out. Centeredness is hard to find, but knowing where your ethos (in both the modern and rhetorical sense) comes from can be a valuable anchor.

What Is a Meaningful Purpose for Your Art?

Having gone inward, reverse the focus. What do you want your community to **say, think, feel, and do**? In design thinking, this is known as an **empathy map**. The same question can (and will) be applied to your audience, but it's worth reframing your audience as part of the community that includes your cast and creatives.

As practitioners and theatremakers, we often focus on the aspect of what our audience "feels". But what a *community* feels is very different from what an *audience* feels. A community is *active*, not passive, especially if you begin asking yourself what you want them to *do*. An audience might feel the emotions of a character in a story (or not), but a community can feel, process, interpret, criticize, and respond. An audience may applaud a point well made, but a community can take your message and turn it into action. Rho Chung's *TSMGO* production of *Gallathea* was a crystalline example of this: creating queer theatre with queer makers for a queer audience and, importantly, focusing on the sense of gender *euphoria* brought cohesion to the cast, crew, and creatives. This cohesion then enveloped the queer *and* non-queer audience in its warm glow, helping people who have gone, *and who will never have to go*, on that journey, to experience the joy of discovering their identity. The community was able to understand something unique about the lives of its marginalized members through artistic expression.

Answering the *think, feel, and do* questions can get you thinking about what the community will *need* in order to make those outcomes a reality – and these outcomes, of course, are all changes. Put simply: what difference are you hoping to make?

Understanding these things can help to identify what success looks like for the community you're looking to assemble. What is its **purpose**? Why does your community exist?

We are at our most focused when we are **intentional**.

TSMGO was *intentional* about creating an optimistic vision of what theatre *could* look like, having experienced first-hand the setbacks and frustrations of a system that facilitates the supremacy of artists of a narrow, privileged background (read: *Culture is Bad For You*, O'Brien et al. for an exhaustive, and exhausting, breakdown). We started with our casting, as many companies have done (as this was the most apparent to audiences) before expanding into our creative teams.

TSMGO was *intentional* about creating an equitable system of redistributing donations through the *TSMGO* hardship fund, consulting with Equity in the UK to arrive at a fair model for distributing the funds (one share per person, per show).

TSMGO was *intentional* about completing the entire First Folio plays (despite occasional balking from outside observers), and later, in expanding the pool of early modern texts we covered.

Intentional communities are burgeoning globally. The Foundation for Intentional Community offers various definitions,[1] but this one feels most useful:

> a group of people living cooperatively, dedicated by intent and commitment to specific communal values and goals.

By their definitions, *TSMGO* would constitute a **public intentional community;** one dedicated to public service, outreach, education, and events.

Their advice on starting a successful intentional community also rings very true to what we found in practice:

- Don't underestimate the scale of the undertaking
- Start it with at least four other people who share your vision
- Acknowledge and engage with the necessity for personal growth throughout
- Seek expertise from others and make training a core part of the work

This is certainly what we did (and you can see more of this in Chapter 4, producing rapidly, producing regularly). In particular, **personal growth is driven by the inevitability of your ideas coming into contact with reality.** If you are creating art, you are creating something that will impact others' lives. If you are impacting others' lives you should want that impact to be positive. If you seek to positively impact others, you will almost certainly need to change yourself. More on this later.

Part 2 – Finding Your People

Now it's time to think about how your strengths, intentions, and purpose interact with people's wants and needs. How does this go from personal to interpersonal?

When it comes to **purpose**, The Foundation for Intentional Community asks quite simply: **why does your group exist?**

When setting out to find the purpose of your community, consider the **satisfying tension between challenge and skill.** Mihaly Csikszentmihalyi talks about this in his influential book *Flow*. Csikszentmihalyi identifies that flow is about getting fully absorbed in a task that is satisfying because it's just challenging enough. This definition is also useful when you set about discovering the purpose of your next artistic undertaking. A shared purpose is a key driver in community cohesion, so you will need something challenging enough to unite people, but not so impossible that it puts people off. John F. Kennedy famously committed to putting humanity on the moon without knowing how NASA would do it. But he did so when we had *already been* to space – had William Taft done so after the Wright brothers flew for the first time, it would not have been the rallying cry history now remembers.

For us, we made that very clear from the outset, but our initial claim gained nuance with time as more people contributed and co-authored what *TSMGO* could be.

In the very beginning, *TSMGO's vision* was to read the complete First Folio plays in order (a huge challenge, but achievable) over lockdown to stay **connected and creative**.

In time this evolved to create **Shakespeare for Everyone, for Free, Forever** – arguably our best-known calling card.

At the conclusion of the First Folio, our purpose evolved again into championing the perspectives and contributions of emerging and underrepresented artists. The common thread through it all was centered around **inclusivity**, and that aspiration drove much of this second generation of our work.

How did we arrive here?

We were influenced by the concept of **purpose architecture** – something we thought of as a purpose *vector*. In purpose architecture, you must start with a compelling why, which in turn informs the how, which finally arrives at the *what*.

Ikea's flatpack furniture is an expression of their purpose to make design more accessible. Their website claims their purpose (the **why**) is to "To create a better everyday life for the many people" and their business idea (the **how**) is "to offer a wide range of well-designed, functional home furnishing products at prices so low that as many people as possible will be able to afford them". This means Ikea does not limit themselves to one type of furnishings (the **what**).

And how did this purpose vector evolve for us over time?

Why: to stay connected and creative during lockdown.
How: online via Zoom.
What: performed readings of Shakespeare's plays.

Which became:

Why: to create freely accessible performances of all Shakespeare's First Folio plays.

How: by amassing a global cast, crew, and audience every week.
What: performed readings on Zoom.

Which became:

Why: to give a "franchise" platform to underrepresented artists.
How: by inviting directors and creatives from those backgrounds to create *TSMGO* performances.
What: performed readings on Zoom.

As you can see – the why is infinitely more interesting than the what or how – it's more compelling too. By front-loading purpose, we were able to inspire meaningful participation without defining the product in a way that limited us.

The change in our purpose was, as previously mentioned, a result of *our ideas coming into contact with reality*. We knew what we wanted to achieve, but it was achieved in dialogue with all those who sought to achieve it together.

Back to Ikea again, and founder Ingvar Kamprad, "IKEA is not the work of one person alone. It is the result of many minds and many souls working together through many years of joy and hard work".[2]

So, our advice is to draft what we'll call a **first purpose** as an individual artist – your own personal mission statement – and be open to how that mission can grow with the benefit of others' influences. But *whose*?

Who Is Out There, Where Are They, and What Do They Want?

In British Sign Language there are many regional and cultural variations, and so there is a sign that indicates you are "tuning" to new people, as you get to know their method of expression; it's a wonderful concept. When you set out to begin community building, tuning for resonance with one another is a valuable process.

Based on your purpose architecture above, what are the key words or concepts in your idea that you can use to test for resonance with potential community members?

For *TSMGO*, our focus on Shakespeare created what social media experts will call a **"niche"**. We immediately had one important pool from which to draw our potential community – although of course, this was perhaps the *one* pool that we hoped to invite more people to, through the work we were creating, and how we set about creating it.

Within that pre-existing pool – let's call them the "Shakespeare people" – there are multitudes, almost certainly including factions who would not be welcome: the intolerant, for instance, or authorship conspiracists.

And so we sought to frame our community in such a way that it would resonate with those who shared our values and naturally deter those who did not. In short, we were *intentional* about who we sought out to join us.

Other circles can be added to your Venn diagram – for us, it would include "theatre people" including performers, creatives, and audiences; "neophiles" – lovers of the new who wanted to see how something old would translate into this new medium; "excluded audiences" – those for whom traditional theatre spaces and prices proved an insurmountable barrier to culture; "randoms" tossed at us by YouTube's "Featured" algorithm; "educators & students" who were seeking online resources to aid them in their studies during a time of unprecedented challenge, and so on.

Another way to look at this is – what problems do I want to address and how can I purposefully cultivate my community to do that? An early challenge for the very first *TSMGO* show was that of **accent**. Accent homogenization in UK theatre has been an ongoing project, conscious or otherwise, for generations. Driving everyone toward the fundamentally *un*real RP of the ruling classes contributes to the sanitizing of what theatre is and who it is for – it creates tacit endorsement for the privileged and their privileges, and for a more unequal society. So when *TSMGO* created its very first show, we knew we wanted to maximize the sound palette of the show, as an open invitation to people from all corners. We had a variety of Brits, we had several North Americans, and we had a few European accents in the mix as well. By purposely curating a soundscape that dismantled the elite hierarchy that is often associated with Shakespeare, *TSMGO* demonstrated a commitment to conscious inclusion. Eliminating received pronunciation, and adopting a spectrum of voices, set us apart from the vast majority of work heretofore produced. It also helped *TSMGO* establish a small seed of a core value that grew through the whole run – **respect Otherness**.

Aside: Although there is power in community, there is also danger. It's clear to see from this exploration that a community, no matter how inclusive by design, is **inherently exclusionary.** The very nature of a defined community preferences those within and disregards those without. You must reckon with this early on, and understand how your borders are drawn. For instance, we learned most people with access needs will prefer to see the limitations of your access honestly acknowledged and easy to discover. If you claim universality, it will only serve to spring traps on people once they have become involved – traps you may or may not even be aware of. Take time to catalog your access limitations. The act of writing these limitations out requires you to actively engage with them. This proved to be a helpful ongoing process of critical reflection that we discovered as we built our community, which in the future could be engaged in from the outset. Seek to find your blindspots and points of bias, for you cannot change what you are unaware of.

Our group was of no interest to those who actively dislike Shakespeare, unappealing to those afraid of it, or simply boring to those uninterested in it. We sought to lower the barriers to entry for those afraid or uninterested, but those who hated it could not (and should not) be our focus. Similarly, **codes of behavior** can dictate who is *out*; a proto-culture quickly formed in the live-chat, which became self-regulating over time. (More on that later).

Once you have a list of existing groups who might wish to be a part of your community, **identify what they might need and want** from what you're creating. Your community has to fulfill at least some of people's needs and wants in order to make it worth their becoming a part of it. See how many of these priorities can sit harmoniously alongside one another without coming into direct conflict. When there is a conflict, you'll need a structure to determine which needs and wants are in, which are out, and why.

In considering how to evaluate the needs and wants of your community, a useful, lighthearted framework for decision-making can now be found in *The Good Place* and *Parks & Recreation* Showrunner Michael Schur's book *How to Be Perfect,* imperfectly summarized here, as it relates to our community. Though not the framework used (the book had not been published at this time), Rob and Sarah took a lot of inspiration from its author and report of how he ran his shows. The clarity of *How to Be Perfect*, his self-described "exit interview" for *The Good Place,* cuts to the center of how *TSMGO* sought to operate. Two ideas in particular were critical in establishing which needs and wants would be prioritized.

1 **What do we owe to each other?** The idea is to live by rules others wouldn't object to as unfair. Would your intended audiences be able to reasonably reject the way your community runs and operates?

   For instance, we believed that no one could reasonably object to the practice of putting those who had applied most and cast least at the top of our casting sheet, as this transparently strove for equity of opportunity.

   For instance, we believed that no one could reasonably object to our aim to cast a range of experience levels across each show, giving equity of opportunity to all who were interested in participating (largely resulting in saving the lead roles for professional actors or those who had shown themselves capable in a previous performance).

2 **Imagine the result of what you're going to do** – how many people will be made happy, and how many made sad? *How* happy or sad will they be? How quickly will they be affected? And for how long? Does this equation allow for sufficient net-positive happiness for a sufficient number, at an acceptable "cost" (which you must decide; our tolerance for inflicting misery was understandably very low, but it can never be zero), to justify the energy a particular action requires?

For instance, we understood that many more people would be made sad by the fact they *weren't* cast on a weekly basis than those made happy by being cast. However, when we were able, we invested energy in contacting people to let them know when a decision had been made and invited them to apply for the very next reading.

For instance, we saw that open captions reduced the visible field of the Zoom window on screen in later performances and made the character names harder to read. This was overborne by the benefit to those who needed live captioning for access reasons and for those studying the play who could read along at home.

When it comes to ascertaining the needs and wants themselves, this can be done **directly or indirectly**. At first, we responded to our social listening – what we were seeing on social media, conversations with our friends and colleagues, and so forth. As our community began to establish itself, people were able to communicate with us directly, as both participants and audience.

The audience for the very first week asked for a naming convention to identify characters on screen as well as the actor's names. Within the very first show, the convention can be seen taking hold and is formalized in the weeks to come. This raises an important point: **listening in action** is the only listening that matters.

The "reasonable rules" for our community prioritized accessibility and safeguarding.

Everyone's participation began with consent. Specifically, for *TSMGO* to use the recorded shows in perpetuity, in keeping with the mission. This was a requirement of signing up to get involved – informed consent.

Your intentionality can be reflected in something as simple as the design of your sign-up form, using accessible fonts (as we have aimed for here), and researching how to phrase questions to mitigate unintentional harm. We were fortunate to benefit from expertise in this regard, and our question "do you have any access needs?" was repeatedly referred to in applications as helping people with traditionally excluded characteristics feel encouraged to sign up. We got better at accommodating these needs with time and experience, but we started with a stated willingness to try and did our best to follow up on that in action.

Like your purpose, your community rules *should* change, and as a leader in that community, so should you. Michael Schur once again has a useful rubric for this. In reflecting on our actions, we ask the cornerstone questions: what am I doing? Why am I doing it? Is there something I could do that's better? Why is it better?

In our view, these simple questions can apply just as well to your community guidelines and processes, and inviting the community (whether that's your cast and crew, or your audience) to reflect on these can open up new avenues of insight in action.

We encouraged our participants to communicate with us about their experiences and to flag any concerns they may have through an anonymous reporting form for any incidents that may have occurred within or outside of our space that could affect our productions.

In particular, we were contacted on several occasions by actors who came forward with allegations of historic improprieties and predatory behavior from individuals who had been cast in our plays. Having engaged with the dialogue emerging from the #MeToo movement, we considered our priority to be safeguarding the community.

As we understood it, our job was not to establish guilt or innocence, that is for the law. Our duty was to mitigate risk to the community. Our duty was to **believe those who came forward** with such allegations, and our commitment to listening in action meant we removed those accused from our productions.

The risk of leaving these people in place outweighed any potential impact on the production of losing them. Because we were not providing a contracted role, the negative impact on the person accused was also limited, in the statistically unlikely event that the accusation was untrue.

With our short turnaround times, this solution was the cleanest and safest for all. The people accused were also ruled out of casting for the remainder of the run of productions, as the risk remained. In other professional settings, nuance within safeguarding may be appropriate, and mitigating steps short of termination may be considered if they are considered acceptable by the accuser. For institutions with the resources to do so, engaging with the restorative and/or transformative justice framework is sure to be recommended.

Our community grew thanks to **the amplification of key pillars within other, related communities**. Critically, Kate Morley PR agreed to freely distribute press releases to media outlets. *The Guardian, The New York Times*, BBC Newsnight, *Playbill, The Stage,* and others all ended up featuring *TSMGO* in both its infancy and during its run. The Folger Shakespeare Library promoted us, wrote articles about us, and had us on their podcast. The Shakespeare Birthplace Trust featured us on their podcast and in their email newsletters. Sarah Ingram, an early supporter, went out of her way to contact networks of higher education institutions and tell them about the work we were doing and how it might be of use to them. Lucy Aarden created viral content from moments of the show to convert longtail interest into views. *The New York Times Bestseller* Ian Doescher was an early supporter and spread the word via his Shakespeare 2020 reading group on Facebook, which had over five thousand members. Many other similar interest groups disseminated our existence and drew participants to us. What's more, peer-to-peer sharing of an exciting opportunity coupled with an ambitious goal, a novel execution, and the relative poverty of opportunity elsewhere all combined to ensure new people were constantly discovering us. This peer-to-peer sharing was leveraged primarily through social media, where bios of all participants were shared to showcase their involvement, giving others in their network permission to feel like they, too, could be a part of this if they wished.

In this way, attracting the attention and earning the respect of influential first followers is a key part of building your community from among pre-existing communities. You need ways to reach people where they are, and influencers, as maligned as they may be on Instagram, exist everywhere, and can have a genuine impact on your success.

Aside: This raises an interesting point about the exceptionality of our circumstances. There is only so much that can be learned from success stories, and you'd be right to be cautious about overextending what you find here as universal. Unusually, not *one* of the impressive list of people and institutions above had a pre-existing relationship with Rob, Sarah or the team. Instead, all were inspired by the creative response to a crisis – it was *kairos*: doing the right thing at the right time (and doing it well) – that drew their support for previously marginal artists. If there's a lesson to take, it's in trying to maximize your resonance with the current moment to get what business calls *earned media*. Earned media is money-can't-buy advertising and promotion, when a company enters the conversation in a meaningful way.

Cultivating Your Community

A community should enrich the lives of those who are a part of it, and being a part of it should reflect positively on each member. For those within it, the *TSMGO* community was a form of international arts service, free at the point of use; a volunteer initiative that was creating connection, entertainment, and culture. Anyone who gave their time and talent freely to participate in such an endeavor could feel good about having done something meaningful with their time in lockdown – something that would have a lasting legacy.

What's more, a community can only thrive if there are multiple ways for people to meaningfully engage with it, and multiple types of rewards for doing so. Below, we'll look at how we used different channels to communicate different aspects of our communal identity to the world, and what the fundamentals were that informed that approach. Rewards needn't be capitalistic in nature. Within our vibrant community, a sense of belonging is a reward all its own. This was nowhere better evidenced than in the live chat of "digital groundlings" that massed every week to watch each performance.

The Live Chat

The Live Chat was an anarchic and eventually self-regulating arena where participants became known as "Digital Groundlings". Like the groundlings of Shakespeare's theatre are thought to be, they were rowdy, rambunctious, there for a good time, and not above wandering concentration. Within this microcosm, a culture naturally formed that allowed people to find a sense of immediate community and feel a sense of being part of an audience, rather than a lone auditor in their homes.

Within this, some were cheerleaders, some jokers, and some fans, whereas others sought to find a sense of stature within the community. Some delighted in having a captive audience for their own commentaries, while others delighted in fan-fic style speculation. Still more enjoyed the opportunity the live chat provided to "vocalize" their own reactions and see others do the same. Debates about dramaturgical choices were conducted, questions were asked, and emojis flooded in at points of high impact. The live chat was immediate and unfiltered.

Social Media

We used social media to make regularly scheduled updates that all became part of the **ritual of participation** for audiences. The publication of the cast for each week's performances, the preview of our guest introducer for the week, and later an introduction to the production director all helped build anticipation and opportunities for engagement.

Beyond this, we created "special events" around the shows that included home dress-up themes, signature cocktails, and even recipes that allowed people to feel even more of a part of a "party atmosphere".

On different occasions, we created gif reactions to the plays as a live tweet along, aiming to contemporize reactions to an antiquated text. We also distributed original content that aimed to expand the world-building of the play, describing fictional events as real – a practice that dates back to Orson Welles' *War of the Worlds*.

Patreon

Throughout the run of the plays, Patreon (an online platform that allows creators to take donations from fans for a percentage fee) was a critical tool in our arsenal. We set up the Patreon Hardship Fund, an opt-in fund that those taking part could sign up for to receive one share per person per show. Over the run of shows, this generated more than £25,000 in donations. In exchange for these donations, we created exclusive content – interviews with makers, behind the scenes vignettes, production diaries, and even festive musical numbers. The Patreon supporters would get access to our ticketed shows as part of their membership, and the Sonnet Project saw alumni create short videos interpreting the sonnets in all manner of creative ways. This was a way for us to stay connected with supporters who had the financial means to support the project.

Participation

The practicalities under which *TSMGO* operated meant that, by signing on, participants consented to entering a community with established values. This understanding enabled large numbers of new members to be integrated in a short period of time, which suited the unique rate of turnover we experienced as whole casts changed week to week. Those who participated agreed to do so on the basis of upholding the values we demonstrated. In turn, this created a social contract that bound the leadership to live up to those same values in practice.

> **Aside:** In different circumstances, establishing agreements together, as a community, is an incredibly valuable practice, and we will offer ways of doing that at the end of this chapter.

Similarly, we aimed to make expectations as clear as possible up front for those taking part and created a whole host of resources geared toward helping people get up to speed with what was required as quickly and easily as possible (more on this in Chapter 4: Producing Rapidly, Producing Regularly). By standardizing this approach, and making sure we addressed as many of the potential barriers as possible before the first day of rehearsal, we were starting on the same page. Similarly, as we moved through the canon, we began to include a discussion of the play in the first session, to give participants an opportunity to flag their thoughts and feelings about it and note any possible issues of interpretation. This allowed everyone to align around the vision before we began to rehearse in earnest.

Moderation

In rare instances, breaches of our community values did happen. We always sought to respond to these on a case-by-case basis, but with decisive swiftness. One exchange, in which a commenter on *Hamlet* sought to undermine the merit of visiting scholar Dr. David Sterling Brown's work on race in *Hamlet*, saw us draft a response as a team which you can still read today.

What's more, when inappropriate, abusive, or derisive comments were made by trolls in the live chat, we made sure to ban them. This became less and less necessary as the community began to self-regulate. Anyone who skirted close to the lines of what were acceptable modes of address was firmly warned by other members of the live chat that regressive attitudes and abuse would not be tolerated.

This, we believe, stemmed from the strength of positivity in our culture. Our tone of voice in social media posts and the way in which we encouraged participation, criticism, and debate through our Q&A sessions was an ongoing process, but one that consciously sought to frame the nature of our interactions as productive, positive, and reciprocally respectful.

Leadership

Facilitative leadership is a concept worth familiarizing yourself with if you haven't already. The Systems Thinker has a wonderful summary of the concept, which offers compelling keystones for this practice.[3]

The objective of this style of leadership is to "[use] processes and tools to maximize the collective intelligence of individuals in a group to determine the right course of action and to then build a template for acting on the choices they make".

Facilitative leaders:

- Make connections and help others make meaning
- Provide direction without totally taking the reins
- Balance managing content and process
- Invite disclosure and feedback to help surface unacknowledged or invisible beliefs, thoughts, and patterns
- Operate from a position of restraint

Viewed from the perspective of *community* leadership, especially under the constraints of a project as simultaneously ambitious and resource-scarce as *TSMGO*, facilitative leadership provides a valuable way of working that is crucially more energy-efficient for your leadership team, and empowering for those your community relies upon to survive and thrive. There are simply too many plates, spinning too quickly, for you to be solely responsible for them all, so this redistribution of ownership can help you lead more effectively.

Within this framework, there are three **metaphorical roles** you can switch between as a leader that can provide enough structure for your community to thrive, without throttling it or sending it into anarchy.

Canvas-Maker: rather than try to be the artist, try to be their canvas-maker. A canvas maker defines the limits of the art, they create the **frame** of the piece, the dimensions in which creativity is expressed. This framing may be physical (you have a webcam's width to play in!), practical (we use *this* visual grammar), or perceptual (consider the character's needs), but these useful limits will ensure your artists' creativity is being siphoned in the right directions, without reducing things to paint-by-numbers. From here, the sandbox in which we play is set, and we must navigate it together.

Navigator: when you assume a position of leadership you will inevitably have to make decisions, yet in the current culture, the implications of our decisions are scrutinized at a level heretofore not seen. Without help, this can cause a paralysis in leaders, afraid to act for fear of the punitive consequences of mistakes. In this case, your role as a navigator or guide can help you steer clear of these dangers, and help others to do the same. First, you must have a **Compass**. In *TSMGO*'s case, the team always had their established *values* to judge their decision-making against. But it is not enough to hold the compass, you must share the bearings – to model how decisions are being made so others within your community can make them in a similar fashion – be the guiding light out of choice paralysis and into **exploration**.

Gardener: Once your community is exploring, the leadership team must at some point be responsible for the larger vision, especially in theatre practice. As such, you'll need your **Sprinklers** and **Shears**. The sprinklers are always first, because you must encourage ideas to grow to see what they become. If there are unruly weeds choking out the balance of other elements, or if they are encroaching on a neighbor's patch, you can use your shears to prune them. With gardening as with theatremaking, the overall vision for the end result must be the guide along the way. Of course, there are many ways to shape a garden; your 'taste' develops *as* you sprinkle and shear, and so will your trust in your ability to do so.

Behaving in this way and on these terms does not immunize a leader from error, and as essential as it is to set your leadership up for success, it is also essential to be prepared to fail. For an insight into *TSMGO's* failed leadership preparedness principles, we head back to Michael Schur, with a little bit of Stephen Colbert.

Stephen Colbert, on the secret to a happy marriage, said "Do not hesitate to say 'I'm Sorry'. Because you don't lose anything ..." and that goes for any relationship built on trust. Consequently, Rob apologized multiple times for instances where *TSMGO*, regardless of intention, failed to live up to its values. This is the right thing to do and signals to the community that leaders are holding themselves accountable to the social contract they've entered into with their community.

There is a great deal of advice out there about how to make effective apologies, and this is a hybrid of several (which we have discovered in the writing parallels the work undertaken by Theatrical Intimacy Education, among others).

- **Apology** – it is essential to start by saying "I'm sorry", or otherwise clearly frame your intent to apologize directly without couching (not, "I *want to* apologize" and certain not "I'm sorry, *if/but*"). Anything else you elaborate on needs to be contextualized within the apology itself.
- **Active Reflection** – it is possible to explain your *intent* without making excuses for the *impact* you caused. The best possible assessment you can give yourself in an apology is to understand how your intention itself, the execution of it, or a combination of the two, was flawed and led to an outcome that caused pain. In short, what did you do, and what was the outcome?

- **Acknowledgment** – take the time to really sit in the *impact*, and try and understand it as un-subjectively as you can.
- **Action** – explain what you're going to *do* about it, ideally both in the singular instance, and moving forward. The more concrete you can make this, and the more explicit the investment of energy in repairing the damage done, the better.

For an imperfect example, you can critically reflect on Rob's apology for a proposed casting award at the *Groundling's Choice Awards*.[4]

In *How to be Perfect*, Michael Schur suggests that being a good person is like a job or a puzzle that never gets solved.

In other words, you should develop ways to find satisfaction in the *attempt*, and like Edison with the lightbulb, confront the inevitability of attempting and failing.

With practice, this will cultivate **adaptability** – the chance to fluidly take on new parameters and respond to them positively and pro-actively. The emergence of stating one's pronouns, of non-binary identities, of differing access needs were all outside of the *TSMGO* founders' experience at the time they decided to create a community. Adaptability comes from owning your ignorance and biases, and from being able to step outside oneself to see the situation from the perspective of the Other. If what they're asking of you is free from bias, hate, or harm, then strive to meet that person where they are and action their request, be it practically, perceptually, or behaviorally, rather than seeking to dismiss them or center your own beliefs. The process of building and maintaining this community was a process of growth for each individual involved – for both the founders and the members, who all shared a mindset of self-development. That individual commitment to personal growth ensured the community continued to grow – we strove never to turn inward, to never say "we've had *enough*" to the next challenge of leadership, inclusion, or progress. It would be heartening to consider the assertion that your leadership capability is directly, perhaps *only*, limited by your capacity for personal growth. Growing pains of the emotional, psychological, and behavioral variety will surely be encountered, just as your muscles get sore after exerting yourself. But the soreness you experience leads directly to growth and results; your muscles build back stronger, and so does your empathy.

Reframe failures as **opportunities for growth**. You *do* get to give yourself points for effort, and you will feel a particular sense of reward when, after many attempts, you find a solution for one piece of the puzzle that really works. But part of this process includes discovering the best approximation of what is "good", and then rediscovering it. Essentially, what we've been doing as a society since the beginning. If the arc of time bends toward Justice, as Dr. Martin Luther King Jr. put it, try to be on the leading edge of its curve. Or as Spider-man put it, with great power comes great responsibility.

First Followers

To end, we'll look at those in the audience who had a disproportionate impact on the community's culture through their contributions. These "first followers" helped to set and maintain a positive, supportive, uplifting tone.

Ksenia Nemchinova created GIF threads every week, immortalizing small moments from the plays on social media.

Debbie Gilpin from Mind the Blog reviewed a huge number of the shows, offering critical insight into how audiences were receiving the productions, and getting fresh eyeballs on what we were creating.

Carly Sponzo created fan art almost every week, bringing the characters to life and exploding the world and atmosphere of each production with her imagination. These were later part of the online merchandising store.

Annabelle Higgins produced fan art every week, rendering the characters, moments, and key lines within the given play before the production went live, giving the audience a final piece of regular content to look forward to.

Ian Doescher created original material, from sonnets to a Muppet Show Theme Tune that we used for the Groundlings' Choice Awards. Ian also curated a Shakespeare Facebook group with thousands of members, and created our first partnership, with Quirk Books, to produce excerpts of his work.

Eugenia Low coined the immortal term "poig" from an accidental typo, indicating a poignant moment in *Henry IV part I*, gifting the group their own in-joke.

Dominic Brewer offered insight and camaraderie to all who used the live chat, week in and week out, in addition to performing.

Tamara Ritthaler, Emily Carding, Danielle Farrow, and many others who regularly kept the chat buoyant, engaged with social media posts, promoted the show beyond its own borders, and used their own influence within Shakespeare companies and communities to endorse the work we were doing.

The Next Steps

In looking forward to how future projects can be *more* successful than the one on the title page, we'd like to turn to the principles we've learned that can help other organizations thrive. **Community agreements** are growing in popularity and show a definite trend toward "governance by consent of the governed" and flattened hierarchies in rehearsal spaces. Community agreements generate responsibility and buy-in from participants and establish a sense of shared commitment in collaborators, who co-author the governing principles of a space or collective.

Defining and adhering to parameters of accountability helps all those involved understand expectations and achieve shared goals. This kind of consequence systemization can also be seen in Montessori practice, to take the emotion out of disciplining children. If you use this item inappropriately, it will be taken away – it's ok to be upset, but it remains taken away for the rest of this playtime. In the same way, it can help to take the ego out of conflict resolution.

In theatre training, we intentionally cultivate spaces where theatremakers in training can exercise their ability to take risks and create by establishing governing principles that maximize one's ability to be brave in a space. This is useful for all collaborations, but particularly so when a primary goal is process over product or growth over results.

Ideally, this is done at the highest, most encompassing level first: across an entire company, a department, or a production, where a deliberate culture of place is established.

In turn, that culture informs the spaces that make up the overall organization, structure, or collective. While the governing principles established at the highest level establish standards of behavior that all agree to follow, the agreements that are made on the subsequent levels help to identify what is needed in a particular context in order for those individuals to thrive and meet the particular demands of that subcommunity. In this way, the smaller spaces – which may be rehearsal rooms or studios, or even a particular production – establish further agreements that are significant to those smaller communities, ensuring that both the overall values are respected as well as the particular group's agreements to hold each other accountable.

In order to establish these, we might begin by asking:

- What do we need in this space in order to thrive?
- What do we need from one another in order for us to do our best work here?

- What will help us fulfill our greatest potential?
- How will we hold each other accountable so that we can all grow and thrive?
- What will we do when someone fails to uphold their agreements?

For example, if a group decides that in order to thrive, support one another, exceed expectations, and hold each other accountable, they need to cultivate a space in which they can fail, offer feedback constructively, avoid censoring, and reward creative risk-taking, all while repairing harm through apologies, their agreements will look to align with actionable items that bring about these desired results.

The sub-questions might be:

- What does thriving look like? What actions support or encourage that result to come about?
- How can we fail productively? What does failing productively look like?
- How can we communicate more effectively? How do we offer feedback or criticize in a way that centers growth and reduces the likelihood of judgment or harm?
- When harm is done, or mistakes are made, how will we handle it? What does that accountability look like? How can we establish those practices before we need them so that we understand how we will respond when a response is needed?

It's important to acknowledge that even under the best circumstances, and with clear agreements in place, boundaries will be crossed and harm might be done because communities are made up of people and no person is perfect. Even if a group has the best intentions, mishaps will happen. Since you can't guarantee that they *won't* happen, it's useful to understand how wrong-doing will be handled in advance so everyone involved is clear about the steps that will be taken to rectify harm and realign with the community values. You can use the apology practice above as a guide.

Whether for community agreements or apology practices, there are two primary governing principles: **respect** and **action**.

How do we cultivate respect?

What actions do we agree to follow when we gather together?

How do we benefit from being a member of the community, so that we are in a mutually reciprocal relationship?

Asking these questions provides an exciting opportunity to democratize how we create the work we create, especially if we allow the exploration of these questions to inform the definition of **goals** and **roles** – how might the function of a director, for instance, shift, if examined through these lenses? This informed consent, self-regulation, and collective responsibility should allow us to better create brave spaces.

Legacy

It is valid to also consider the *dispersion* of a community. Communities of the "mission" variety have a shelf life. What is left to keep people together once the mission is complete? Are you able to wind down your community in a way that will allow them to feel fulfilled in going their own way?

A useful piece of advice is to **envision the end point from the start, and hold yourself to it** – every artist needs to know when to put the last brushstroke on the canvas. It truly is better to end on a high than fade away. Due to the unending nature of the pandemic, we were unable to establish what this might be, and *TSMGO* managed to continue thanks to the efforts of the core team despite Rob and Sarah welcoming their first child in 2021. The *Month of Marlowe*, which saw new directors, new casts, and new concepts explored, did wonderful work, but led to attrition – the people pushing the community forward could push no further. *The Two Noble Kinsmen* was, at that point, the last Shakespeare collaboration stone left unturned, and Matthew Rhodes, an emerging Canadian theatremaker who had risen to become essential to *TSMGO*'s existence over the run of the shows, was yet to direct a show. It made perfect sense to end with Shakespeare and conclude the journey with Matt at the helm.

As the world opened up, in-person *TSMGO* collaborations and encounters have increased in frequency. The cascade effect of bringing over 500 people together from 60 countries, all of whom share certain core values and attitudes, is bound to help new artists to collaborate on new projects well into the future. This proliferation of collaborations outside the *TSMGO* banner reflects positively on exactly what it was that made the community work; how the participants aligned with the overarching principles enabled them to flow into new relationships, behaviors, and expressions. This is where being a "values" community can give an affiliation long-lasting benefits, even once the work itself has come to an end.

The Take Homes

Be Intentional: think about what sets your community aside and lean into the elements you can cultivate in order to strengthen your intentions and your ensemble.

Be Facilitative: use your energies to activate, guide, and cultivate others, not to control or dictate.

Lead with Integrity: how can you shape your environment through your decisions and your actions? How can you hold space to evolve those decisions and actions?

Flatten the Hierarchy: how can the community forge forward with agreements that guide everyone's participation?

Don't Let Ego – yours or anyone else's – **Impede on Your Agreements:** apologize when you are wrong. Help others to do the same. Extend grace, when it's possible to do so.

Remember What You Are All There to Do: live in and through your values.

Notes

1 https://www.ic.org/what-is-an-intentional-community-30th-birthday-day-13/
2 https://www.ikea.com/gb/en/this-is-ikea/about-us/the-ikea-vision-and-values-pub9aa779d0
3 https://thesystemsthinker.com/the-art-of-facilitative-leadership-maximizing-others-contributions/
4 https://twitter.com/TSMGOnlineLive/status/1367521020819742728

4
PRODUCING RAPIDLY, PRODUCING REGULARLY

Although creativity thrives under constraints, the same may not necessarily be said of logistics. Anyone who has ever put on a show can tell you that it is an incredibly ambitious undertaking to manage the spinning plates of cast, crew, venue(s), design, performance, and more. It is, essentially, a miracle any piece of work gets made, and even more remarkable when that work achieves its artistic aim and the audience's experience resonates with the creators' intent.

Running *The Show Must Go Online (TSMGO)*, we learned valuable lessons about optimization in almost every area of production, and we did so using a variety of tools, including "what if's", "rule breakers", and other ideas taken from innovation; a data-driven approach to casting, and resourceful ways of distributing creative tasks (among other things) to create an infrastructure that could sustain the relentless, weekly production of a brand new show.

In many ways, the wrangling of a weekly live production calls to mind television institutions like *Saturday Night Live (SNL)*, where formula is a friend.

A *TSMGO* show was akin to an *SNL* show where the *whole cast* was guest stars. This meant that the success of each cast was *iterative* – with a new configuration every week, many of whom were performing for the first time; there was nothing for the majority of the cast to build on from their own experience. Instead, they had to stand on the proverbial shoulders of giants and benefit from the best practices of those who came before them, which was codified over time to help with the baton-passing.

DOI: 10.4324/9781003289906-5

A representative weekly schedule of Jobs To Be Done looked something like this, with some flexibility. Since some of the production schedules varied, we will refer to these days throughout as Day 1, Day 2, etc. to accommodate for these variables.

- **Day 1 (Thursday):** Read and edit the play | Cast the play
- **Day 2 (Friday):** Confirm, finalize, and brief the cast | R&D the play | Create the rehearsal schedule based on cast availability |
- **Day 3 (Saturday):** First cast meeting | Music and sound development | Props development | Create ensemble track for next week's play | Finalize rehearsal schedule
- **Day 4 (Sunday):** Rehearse setpieces | Rehearse the play | Aesthetic tutorials distributed | Email casting form for next week's play to subscribers | Announce cast via social media
- **Day 5 (Monday):** Rehearse the play | Develop VFX for scene transitions etc. | Loop in guest introducer
- **Day 6 (Tuesday):** Tech run-through and cue programming, prop and costume triage
- **Day 7 (Wednesday):** Close casting applications for next week's play | Prepare and execute live show

Aside: There was also a short period in which we were running two shows a week, creating productions of excerpts from Ian Doescher's works for Quirk Books, but this schedule is representative of the majority of the First Folio run, and serves to orient the reader for the coming chapter.

While our casts were always changing, our core producing team remained much the same for the duration, which allowed us to make *cumulative* progress, where our confidence, our techniques, and our approaches expanded and refined week after week, while the number of unanticipated challenges we had to navigate, on average, reduced.

This systemization was a critical component of our success, as the weekly to-do list was comprehensive. Over the coming chapter, we will take you on a tour of that to-do list, giving you a detailed understanding of the scope of this undertaking and the lessons learned by the team in each of our various departments. Each of these contributions has been led by the person chiefly responsible for that particular role in the core team during the original run, in order to maximize the depth and breadth of insight and perspectives available. These include:

- Producing a Play in a Week – Sarah Peachey (page 68)
- Read and Edit the Play – Rob Myles (page 76)

- Research and Develop the Production – Rob Myles (page 76)
- Casting a Show in a Week – Sydney Aldridge (page 81)
- The Use of Data in Casting – Ed Guccione (page 86)
- Props, Costume and Visual Identity – Emily Ingram (page 91)
- Music and Sound – Adam Gibson (page 99)
- Curating Guest Introductions and Creative Producing – Ben Crystal (page 103)
- Community Engagement Using Social Media – Ruth Page (page 107)
- Reinventing *TSMGO* for Sustainable Working – Matthew Rhodes (page 111)

We covered all this in seven days, every seven days. To make all this possible, we had to rely on the philosophy best expressed by the Pareto principle: 20% of the effort results in 80% of the progress, and most efforts after this initial 20% result in ever more diminishing returns as perfection is impossible. We would strive to create the very best show we could in the time we had, and then optimize what we discovered in order to yield the best results we could on a consistent basis.

In most cases in this chapter, we will describe where we ultimately *arrived at* in terms of our best practices, so that we pass the baton of our processes on to you to take forward into your own work. Occasionally we will sketch out the *journey* this process went on, to extrapolate useful ways to think about optimization. Where relevant, we will also describe how the values informed the evolution of our approach.

In Shakespeare's writing, time plays many roles. Among young lovers, for instance, time moves quickly when they are together and slowly when they are apart. This **"accordion of time"**, time's ability to compress and extend, is a phenomenon of our perspective well represented in the plays. This **accordion of time** also offers a useful framework in this context, to illustrate that when we don't have a lot of time, we must move slowly. And spending that time well enables us to go more quickly when we have to.

> **Aside:** It feels necessary to acknowledge that we worked on a relentless schedule that became a feat of endurance for all, and relied on practices that were unsustainable. While it did "make possible things not so held", it is not to be replicated in and of itself. We'll be covering this in the final chapter in greater detail.

Starting with the "why": it is a worthwhile question to ask before you plunge headlong into the ridiculum of *what* we did to ask *why we did it in the first place*. Typically, the values of the project and the parameters of the time it was responding to coalesced to determine that this labor-intensive approach would be the best way forward.

In responding to the pandemic, we realized that the core offers of the project had to respond to the core challenges of the time. These have been outlined in the introduction, but the key factors *here* were **productivity** – the ability for people to come together and practice their vocation for the benefit of an audience – and a **brave space** – an environment which encouraged creativity and collaboration during a time when most people didn't have the energy to get out of their pajamas.

By holding to a weekly schedule, we offered a refuge from the tedium, and the amorphous nature of day-to-day existence during the pandemic, and of lockdown in particular. By offering **appointment viewing** at a time when the last bastion of such, arguably *Game of Thrones*, was off the air for good, we gave our audience a reliable anchor in a time of so much uncertainty. The safety of a regularly scheduled time and place for a community to gather meant audiences had something they could rely on. *SNL* proved that for all its faults and fluctuating quality, *liveness* is always exciting, even on screen. *Game of Thrones* proved that appointment viewing could still be successful; in an on-demand age, appointment viewing set *TSMGO* apart. In both cases, the release schedule was weekly, so we went weekly.

What's more, choosing to do the First Folio plays in the order they were believed to have been written **saved cognitive load** at a time when we would be pushed to capacity. We used this formula to systematize our practices and alleviate weekly decisions about what would come next. There was no curation of the plays needed after that point, and while the plays sometimes interacted with the unpredictability of life in jarring ways (most notably *A Midsummer Night's Dream* in the height of the Black Lives Matter outcry following the murder of George Floyd, and the fantastical story of *Cymbeline* being realized in the fraught energy of US Presidential election night 2020) it offered many a predictable point of connection for which we were all starved while maximizing opportunities for performers and creatives to practice their craft at a time when doing so was all but impossible.

This regular schedule also encouraged audiences to join for plays they were less familiar with, being introduced to new worlds and characters, enriching their knowledge of the plays, meeting new performers, and finding surprising parallels between the plays and our lives.

To commit to appointment viewing was a huge commitment up front. It was the first question journalists asked about the project: "will you *really* do all the plays?" At that time, it was thought the pandemic would last no more than a few months, and that the world would reopen by summer, at which point there would be no appetite for the work.

Our response at the time was based on a couple of ideas, the first best summed up by Charlie Geller in Adam McKay's film, *The Big Short*, "People hate to think about bad things happening, so they always underestimate their likelihood" (IMDB).

In Stoicism, there is a technique called *negative visualization*: you take a few moments to sit with the notion of the worst that could happen. When you then return to the present moment, you do so with a new appreciation for everything that exists that is better than that alternative. When we created this project, the pandemic very much felt like it was the worst thing that could happen, and yet as history shows, governments and the media consistently underestimated it.

We did not.

If we expect that things can get worse, we are ready when they do, and pleasantly surprised if they don't. This is not pessimism, but preparedness.

If one important factor of the schedule was what it could do for the audience, the other was what it could do for us. It's important to remember that creativity thrives in constraint. We know that Shakespeare's company had as many as 40 plays in repertory at once – a feat that feels unbelievable to modern actors familiar with modern processes. The movement known as "Original Practice" has once again sought to replicate the conditions of the early modern period by rapidly raising a Shakespeare play, with projects like *60 hour Shakespeare* and Bard City's *Shakespeare in a Week* based on the approximate amount of time the early modern actors were thought to have to prepare a piece for performance.

The best thing for any project is a deadline. In a pandemic, especially when focus was hard to come by, an external pressure that could crystallize it and funnel energy toward an end goal was hugely useful. It also meant that progress, not perfection, was our aim. The first show could not be a masterpiece because it was our first rough sketch on that canvas. Our audience knew this and were along for the ride. For those performing the plays, it was a short-term commitment. Hundreds of actors cut their teeth in apprenticeship on the digital stage, week after week.

This myopic state also kept our attention on what was immediately in front of us and prevented us from being swallowed up by the enormity of the task we were undertaking should we take a longer view.

Now that we understand *why* this work came to be done in this way, we can allow our attention to be spent on the what, the how, and the lessons learned.

Producing a Play in a Week (Sarah Peachey)

Let's start with an overview of a week producing *TSMGO*, as it provides a context and framework for much of what will follow in this chapter. In this section, I will discuss production practicalities such as timeline organization, people management, and briefing preparation, all of which reduced error rates, and some general lessons that emerged from a continually evolving process over the initial nine-month run, including how to give yourself the best chance to get the best out of everyone who takes part.

Production Process

Assembling and Preparing a Cast

Although the shows ran on a seven-day timetable, production started during the week of the *previous* show, in order to get everything in place and ready to begin on day one of the next rotation.

First, our Mailchimp account was updated weekly with all the new sign-ups who wished to receive casting notices.

Once this was done, the email with a link to the casting form was sent out, usually on Day 4, and a second reminder on Day 6, with the deadline being midnight UK time on Day 7 of the previous rotation.

This ensured we had a complete list of applicants by the morning of Day 1 when casting would begin. Overnight, our Associate Producer, Matthew Rhodes, would manually go through the list and color-code applicants to assist with the shortlisting process, highlighting Global Majority actors, actors for older roles, actors for child roles, and more, based on the data they submitted about themselves.

Once the cast selection had been approved, an invitation email was prepared and sent out to the prospective cast. When accepting their role, all actors were required to send a headshot and Twitter-length bio to our social media manager, Ruth Page. Offers were valid for 24 hours, after which if we had not received confirmation of acceptance, the role was offered to another actor. This was made clear in the initial offer and happened with increasing regularity as the world began to open up during the summer months. Typically, we'd secure two-thirds to three-quarters of our first offers in a given week, making a second round of offers necessary. As part of the casting process in the latter half of the shows, we regularly had multiple names beside the principal roles for this purpose.

The casting invitation email included:

- A breakdown of the ensemble roles to be played by each member of the ensemble
- Link to the *TSMGO* theatre guide pdf and video tutorial
- Cast list (including emails and pronouns)
- The overall structure of the rehearsal period
- Request for availability update
- A link to the PlayShakespeare.com character list and script
- A link to the LitCharts Shakescleare thought-for-thought transliterations

The email usually went out at the end of Day 1, and all actors were given 24 hours to accept their part. Once they accepted their roles, they were sent resources with which to familiarize themselves with the script, story, and their character and work through the digital theatre tutorial materials ahead of the first meeting on Day 3. The master script with edits then followed in the main briefing email once the full cast was solidified, giving us time to finalize the cut.

Once everyone had accepted their roles, confirmed their availability for the coming week, and necessary recasting had been achieved, the main briefing email (sent once the cast was confirmed) was then usually sent out on Day 2 or Day 3.

The briefing email included:

- A reminder of the briefing guides sent in the first email
- The edited script and a fresh link to (or attachment of) the Shakescleare translation
- Updated breakdown of ensemble roles (incorporating any changes from Day 1's read-through and edit)
- Final cast list (including emails and pronouns) – this also included a timeline of the scenes which showed which characters were in each scene, so people could see at a glance which scenes they would need to rehearse
- Zoom links – one for rehearsals, and one for the performance (we used a separate Zoom link to connect to the YouTube livestream)

Following the read-through on Day 1, a copy of the edited script, including highlighted production elements (props and key costumes, actions, implicit stage directions, sound, etc.) was prepared and sent to the core team in preparation for the research and development (R&D) on Day 2.

During the R&D on Day 2, notes would be taken on props and costumes, to create a briefing for the actors which would be sent to all those who had confirmed their roles, allowing them as much time as possible to prepare what they'd need in time for the dress rehearsal.

The rehearsal schedule was sent in a separate email later in the week, which included instructions on joining the Zoom (see below) and a link to a time zone calculator (all times were written in GMT/BST).

Scheduling

The biggest task of the whole cycle was to build the rehearsal schedule. This was not dissimilar to a Rubick's Cube in scope and challenge, as it involved resolving complex conflicts including multiple time zones, access needs, large group scenes, individual availability, and prior commitments. Because our performers volunteered their time and talent, we always strove to make the schedule work around what participants were capable of giving to the process, and most of the time, we succeeded.

In my role as an innovation project manager, it's very typical to have to arrange workshops or meetings at short notice around clients in multiple time zones and with extremely limited availability, so it was a familiar challenge for me; one for which there is *always* a resolution. There is almost always a need for speed and hyper-efficiency when working on innovation projects, which served us well on *TSMGO*.

To facilitate the construction of the rehearsal schedule, we standardized the amount of time needed for each scene. This was based on Rob's (some say anomalous) average of being able to cover eight pages in one hour. Some scenes would require more time if they involved big set pieces or complex issues. Other scenes may be quicker if there were large sections of fast-paced dialogue between two characters. This elasticity meant we could flex around this robust outline once established.

My approach for tackling the schedule was to start with the actors with the greatest restrictions – those in the furthest time zone from the UK, those with access needs, and those with the most limited availability, as they had the least amount of flexibility. Once their scenes were plotted out, this would then form the foundation of the schedule, around which I would need to fit the remaining actors and their scenes.

Next, I would prioritize those in primary and secondary lead roles; those with the most scenes, or carrying the greatest load in performance.

It was essential that they rehearsed all of their scenes with Rob. For more minor or ensemble roles, if it was impossible to schedule one of the scenes at a time they were available, we would record the rehearsal for them to watch back with a swing standing in for them and being noted in the same way. We then encouraged them where possible to arrange time outside of rehearsals to work the scene with their colleagues.

Action sequences and set pieces were rehearsed in a separate block. This required more flexibility from the actors as it was difficult to predict how long the cast and creatives would need to negotiate these physical sequences, particularly where cross-screen interaction, props, and complex timings were involved. This dedicated block gave the actors maximum lead time for complex business and gave us maximum flexibility in the schedule to accommodate the degree of flex required.

Running the Rehearsal Room

As the time constraints typically only allowed for scenes to be run twice, we encouraged actors to arrange to meet scene partners outside of scheduled rehearsals to work their notes – the Zoom rehearsal link remained open 24 hours a day for anyone who needed it, and we would also provide breakout rooms during scheduled rehearsals so people could work their notes alongside the main schedule.

Actors were asked to join the Zoom at least five minutes early with their script and performance space setup and ready so that we could start promptly at the call time. Either Matthew Rhodes or I would be on the call at least ten minutes before, taking note of actors as they arrived and sending chasers via email to anyone who hadn't joined by five minutes before.

As the schedule allowed us no time for delays/do-overs, we sent out daily call sheets each morning which detailed what scenes were being rehearsed at what time and who was called for each one. It also indicated any known absences and a request for swings to read in for those parts at those times.

Given the number of people involved in each show, in order to minimize communications getting lost in email threads, we setup a separate email chain called "conversation" where actors could discuss costume/props or scene ideas, and ask general questions, while the main "show" thread was preserved for essential communications from the production team.

Following the dress rehearsal on Day 6, a Final Show Prep email was sent out, which included the separate performance Zoom link and details on the following:

- A reminder about optimal lighting and sound setups
- Guidelines to boost your internet connection
- Protocols for swings
- Instructions for how each person's name should be presented to audiences during the show, i.e CHARACTER NAME (Actor Name)
- A list of entrance/exits
- Directions for turning off device notifications and other operating system sounds

I also provided my contact number in case of any major issues during the show.

Meanwhile, for our guest speakers, a similar briefing email was sent out with Zoom links, advice on setup (for good lighting and sound), and directions to help boost their internet connection. We also asked for a short bio and any social media handles so we could announce them on our profiles. Occasionally I would need to jump on Zoom with them in advance to support them with their setup. Otherwise, we would ask them to join at the half and spend a couple of minutes explaining how the introduction would work.

Other pre-performance tasks included setting up the YouTube livestream link with cast/production team lists (including social media handles), organizing content warnings, our speaker's bio, and links to last/next week's shows.

In Performance

In the half hour before the show, the full cast was called to the Zoom, and we would ask everyone to turn their cameras on so we could take a cast photo – this was then shared on the Facebook alumni group, where we'd congratulate and welcome the cast into the rest of the community, and in the Green Room email, which got sent out with a congratulatory note and links to social media after the performance.

Stage Management

In most cases, stage management was led by Emily Ingram during the performance and by Matthew Rhodes during rehearsals. During rehearsal, the need for specific stage management cues would be established and captured. These would be practiced during the tech on Day 6 and then distributed to members of the team to execute during performance. Stage management duties during the First Folio series typically included:

- Checking that actors' names were properly presented and correcting them when necessary (this was especially important for Ensemble members who had multiple character name changes during the performance)
- Remote camera kills for swift or sudden exits that left actors away from their keyboards or for actors who failed to make their exits on cue
- Camera start requests and microphone unmute requests in the event that actors had missed a cue
- Stage management would frequently cover their own cameras with a post-it note, which would create an even canvas upon which to "project" Zoom's virtual background (VBG) feature, allowing us to play scene-change videos, include static images, and other special effects in the playing space, often renamed as relevant (such as "ACT IV SCENE II" or "YORK'S HEAD")
- In rare cases, controlling actors' devices remotely to start and stop cameras using Google's remote desktop feature (remotedesktop.google.com/)
- Calling for "RADIO SILENCE" in the Zoom chat during the show for actors with complex camera choreography or live cues to coordinate their movements*
- Posting additional show-related material in the YouTube Live Chat

***Aside:** In Romeo & Juliet for instance, we were unable to predict if the two actors would be oriented in the Zoom window on one side of each other, or the other. As we wanted them to turn to face each other, this risked them turning in the wrong direction. To combat this, we had to rehearse the camera moves two ways, and then live cue on the night which direction they turned to face, based on how they appeared on YouTube.

In reality, these duties were sometimes distributed among the core team – multiple simultaneous remote camera kills would be handled by two people at once, for instance, as would multiple simultaneous projections, or specialist use of things like SnapCamera (an augmented reality filter app that allowed us to project 3D objects on top of actors, such as Bottom's donkey head), which requires higher baseline hardware, would be run by those whose devices had the processing power required. Similarly, cues that required highly practiced timing would be done by whoever was most familiar.

Distributing Contributions

At the end of each month, I would reconcile the Patreon donations, accounting for any expenses such as Zoom and Mailchimp subscriptions and the occasional prop. I would then send out an email to all the actors and creatives involved in the shows that month, informing them of the total amount donated and roughly how many people were eligible to apply for a share. They would then complete a Survey Monkey form which captured the shows they were involved in and their preferred payment details. A deadline was given to complete the form – after this time, I totaled the number of acceptances and divided the money into the number of shares required at a flat rate of one share per person per show. I would then make the transfers.

Producing Tools

When processing a lot of information, for a lot of different people, spreadsheets are your friend. They are by no means the perfect solution, but almost all operating systems offer software for free that creates files compatible with various devices and allows you to present information in a way that is clearer than a dense block of text in a Word document or email.

Be conscious of colors and font types as some people find some choices more difficult to read than others – it's worth confirming dyslexia-friendly fonts and color-blind-friendly colors. Some people who aren't familiar with Excel struggle at first to parse information presented in this way, and this is particularly common with actors/creatives. A brief explanation of how to navigate the information, essentially teaching people how to interact with it, ensured that most could navigate the schedule effectively.

Templates are hugely beneficial when needing to share a similar set of information on a regular basis. This ensured we had covered all the necessary elements in a way that was well presented, while only needing to amend the particular details for each weekly show. These templates would be updated and optimized when new information or inspiration came to light, but we always had the best version of our templates available.

Mailchimp is a simple platform for creating engaging content – it allowed us to do weekly callouts for casting and promote audience attendance for the shows while keeping our database updated and tracking engagement.

Patreon is a great way of engaging supporters with regular content and allows you to track donations (as well as any increases, cancellations, etc.). The fees are quite high, and some users found the signup process a little complicated, but overall it was a positive experience, and at the time of publication, no other platform provides a better service for a smaller fee.

Lessons Learned

When you have to provide a lot of information to a lot of people, it is valuable to present it through **different touchpoints and in different formats**. For those who struggled to navigate the details of the rehearsal schedule, the call sheets gave them another opportunity to ensure they knew when they were called. This level of attention is particularly important when working at speed, as it's very easy for mistakes to have a snowball effect.

Language is key when managing a lot of people from different countries, all with unique ways of processing information, some of whom may be neurodiverse. When creating training materials for innovation workshops, we take a lot of time to fully consider the choice of words to ensure there's minimal chance of confusion. **Making things memorable** is also very important – if people have to engage a lot of effort to remember the term for something, it complicates the process and causes frustration. **Clarity and simplicity win.**

Spending time up front **setting up templates** for sharing information is a huge time saver. It's also important to do this when setting up processes – having a way of doing things means everything is generally more predictable, and we were able to **set clear expectations from the start for everyone participating**. If people couldn't or wouldn't accept working according to those expectations, then we consequently may have to consider replacing them. This very rarely happened, but this encouraged everyone in our shows to be fully on board and pulling in the same direction.

Innovation processes rely on **incremental improvements** – it's not necessarily about doing something completely new but improving something so that it solves a pain point. Changing too much in one go risks being too disruptive, so it's important to keep change incremental. This also allows you to properly test the effectiveness of new ideas. These incremental changes can make a huge difference, spotting opportunities or challenges, and being prepared to try something new in order to improve, allowed us to gradually build up a system that worked smoothly. The call sheets, for example, were a very positive introduction, as they massively reduced the instances of actors missing rehearsals.

Read and Edit the Play (Rob Myles)

Beyond the architecture of how the week was run, the foundation stone for what we did in that week was built from the play itself, which is the next essential step to cover. Here, I will explain what tools and techniques I used to read, understand, and edit the play. I will also explore what these processes enabled us to achieve in the rest of the week and in the long-term production process.

Every play had to be approached as blank slate and tackled from the ground up. This was by far the toughest part of every week for me.

Editing Process

In order to produce and direct the play, both Sarah and I had to read, parse, and understand the play, sometimes for the first time ever.

Editing as we went, the objective was to keep the shows to a maximum of two and a half hours (which we discovered was around 21,000 words in a verse-weighted play at the maximum pace Zoom would allow) and to make them as clear and accessible as possible without gutting the poetry of the characters and story. To achieve this, we had guiding principles:

- Don't cut any scenes outright – internal cuts only
- Try not to cut ensemble characters outright, or flag early if you're consolidating two characters
- Preserve female characters' lines where possible to redress the balance of line loads to the extent that we can
- Cut obscure Latin/Greek passages and allusions that create a barrier to understanding
- Cut racist and other insensitive language when it is not part of an explicit theme of the story or character(s)
- Where the speech is long, excise excess examples of the argument without skipping over the character's journey through the dilemma

Every one of these principles had exceptions, but they gave us guidelines to target our proverbial red pen as we worked. Early in the process, Jeremy Mortimer volunteered his time and talent to suggest cuts for editing several of the plays and quickly became a de facto supervising editor for a team of academics and performers (including Gemma Miller,

Dan Beaulieu, and Dominic Brewer) who offered to go through the plays and highlight possibilities for cutting based on the principles above. With this initial pass done, we would use this candidate text and implement those cuts we agreed with while making a strong argument for retaining material that had been put on the chopping block, forcing us to find further cuts to offset those.

Multiple editors and multiple sources all helped us understand the play as deeply as possible as quickly as possible and allowed me to get to the heart of what I wanted to say with the play and what I felt the dramatic intentions of the piece were.

As we went through the text, producer Sarah Peachey would highlight lines that had implicit stage directions such as "here, on my knees" to cue the actors that there would be business at these points and highlight props so actors would know they'd need items on hand, as well as costume changes, moments of action that would need to be staged, sound cues, and more. A color-coded system was deployed so we always knew *why* a highlight was present in the text and *what* to do to action it quickly and efficiently – another example of **streamlining cognitive load**. Whenever we found what we called a "setpiece", a key moment in the text that required a novel solution or theatrical innovation, we would make a note of it as something to workshop in the research and development phase.

While this was happening, we had to consider the casting brackets for each character – while PlayShakespeare.com provided character descriptions as a separate resource to the texts, the relationships were not always obvious, and details around age and other character traits would often become clear in this first reading (such as the thinness of the Bastard's brother in *King John*). Since casting was taking place simultaneously, all of these tidbits would be sent immediately upon discovery to the casting director, in case they changed what we needed for a given character.

Editing Tools

When reading the play we used the text from PlayShakespeare.com, in contrast with Bate and Rasmussen's *RSC Complete Works*, and triangulated these with the LitCharts "Shakescleare" thought-for-thought transliteration. In this way, we could use PlayShakespeare.com data-rich text with act and scene titles that could be used for navigation to save time in rehearsal, benefit from contextual footnotes in the RSC edition, and use LitCharts to help us untangle some of the knottier expressions of thoughts in Shakespeare.

We used the PlayShakespeare.com texts because their team had embedded data into their work like no other product available and made that data open source. Using PlayShakespeare.com's texts as our "base layer" ensured that the text we used conformed to this data, allowing us to automate and graph out who was present in each scene. This in turn ensured we could create tracks for ensemble characters and keep from casting people in conflicting roles *(see:* Casting Using Data).

Using three sources prevented me from treating any one as definitive – I frequently disagreed with our two supporting texts and regularly changed pronunciations, and even lines or passages from the PlayShakespeare.com text, depending on how the quarto and folios had been reconstituted and according to what we determined was the best sense of the line and scenes.

Lessons Learned

Use productive disagreement with (and between) the sources to find what you believe the text must mean faster than starting from scratch: it's always easier to build on an existing theory, and we are fortunate that Shakespeare has a huge ecosystem of supporting resources built up around it.

Use what's readily available, and define your position in response to a continuum, rather than try to new-mint the choices driving your production in a vacuum.

Read the plays on their feet, out loud, and in full. Make sense of the text *in delivery* in order to make every decision. **Embody the text.** It will enable you to get inside the play very rapidly and fully prepare you to navigate difficult passages in practice (which otherwise may have remained theoretical) so that the play is directable come rehearsal time.

This is a huge energetic investment up front, and this process paid dividends in every other area: creating a vision for the play, for its moments, and being able to support the actors in eking out clarity and sense. The play will have **a lived-in familiarity** by the end of Day 1 (sometimes late at night, and occasionally on the morning of Day 2 when the play was mammoth and other complications had absorbed too much time). Often by this point, there were masses of notes that would inform the rest of the production.

Research and Develop the Production (Rob Myles)

This section focuses on how we systemized the process of identifying and exploiting creative opportunities within the play, both at the macro scale in terms of the overall approach as well as the micro scale of specific moments, with a focus on how to generate the greatest number of ideas in a compressed timeframe.

R&D Process

Research consisted of me reading the introductory essay on the play in question in Bate and Rasmussen's *The RSC Shakespeare: The Complete Works*, analyzing the themes as identified by LitCharts, reading the character descriptions given by PlayShakespeare.com, and then making the most of JSTOR's 100 free articles a month to look up critical reception and literary insights. In this, I made a point not to read anything before 1970 and strongly preferred work created in the last 10 years, to try and avoid being influenced by the typically male, pale, and stale academia that has defined Shakespeare in culturally imperialist terms. While there are incredible works available before this period, narrowing the sphere of influence to a more contemporary time frame enabled me to enter into a more direct dialogue with where Shakespeare studies are *now*.

I would then synthesize this information into notes and generate provocations for the R&D session so I was able to take in other perspectives and contexts from the room. We would then unify these into a codified aesthetic and approach to the show. This would form the beginning of the R&D, where we would talk about the global approach to the look and feel before diving into the specifics.

R&D Tools

I then generated a Google Doc with a scene by scene summary in plain English (the whole creative team did not always have time to read the full play in detail), followed by a breakdown of the common "opportunity areas" in each scene, namely:

- LIGHTING
- PROPS
- COSTUME
- SET PIECES
- WHAT CAN WE RECYCLE?
- MUSIC
- ATMOSPHERE

This "opportunity map" gave us a standardized framework by which to explore, scene by scene, what the show required. It simultaneously created a comprehensive briefing for the various members of the creative team, so everyone could find what they needed from a single source and capture their own tasks for the coming week. When pressed for time, this required an additional process of filtering out everyone's separate work streams, which Rob and Sarah facilitated.

By using this framework to discuss the scenes, we were able to "audition" different approaches. Perhaps the most interesting provocation above is "what can we recycle?" As we progressed through the run of the shows, Shakespeare recycled dramaturgical devices in different contexts, and we were by and large able to do the same. The "double exposure" method we used for ghosts in *Star Wars* and *Julius Caesar* was again deployed for the air-drawn dagger. Originally, the idea was to try and use the silhouette of a dagger that could move across Macbeth and their background, but finding tightly focused light in order to accentuate the shadow with sharply defined edges using only home-made found materials proved too difficult. So, this "recycling" provided a safe, known approach as our fall-back option if our more ambitious designs fell short.

Lessons Learned

One of the main advantages of the R&D was creating such a thorough exploration of multiple routes forward to stage the different moments in each play.

It was easier to improvise off the back of a detailed plan gone awry than to show up and simply try to "find it" in the moment. Even when we had prepared elaborate stagings that for one reason or another were not possible with the actor's home setup or capabilities, we were much better able to adjust our approach in the moment for having gone through this explorative process in advance because we had a fuller understanding of the sandbox of possibilities.

You can see an R&D document here:

FIGURE 4.1 *TSMGO Macbeth* R&D QR Code (bit.ly/macrnd).

In the case of *Macbeth*, the opportunity areas are well-worn territory to theatremakers, and finding novel ways of interpreting these classic features of the play while also bringing the uniqueness of the medium to bear provided an opportunity to push ourselves to what were then our limits.

We "swung for the fences" with this production, and in doing so, we redefined for ourselves how far the medium could be pushed in service of immersive production values. For most weeks, progress was more iterative – one or two new things – but this show attempted to combine more existing and new ideas than ever. The result meant we did not achieve everything we wanted to the extent we wanted to, but ended up further along than we'd ever been before. **Sometimes the attempt yields its own kind of progress.**

Casting a Show a Week (Sydney Aldridge)

I cast a different show every week without the benefit of auditions, and responding to this challenge evolved my thinking about the project, casting as a whole, actors, and creative partnerships.

According to the UK training organization *Screen Skills*, "Casting directors find the stars to bring the characters in a film or TV drama to life. They are hired by the production company to match actors to roles".

They didn't mention theatre. As a casting director who has worked in theatre, I relish the opportunity to work on Shakespeare. One of my last jobs before joining the team at *TSMGO* was to cast a team of actor-musicians for *Twelfth Night*.

I have worked in casting since 2015, and it's relentless. I primarily work in Film, TV, and Commercials. At the start of 2020, I was working on five commercials a week and that was just about manageable. Commercials are quick turnaround projects. I could normally complete one in just over a week and the shortest amount of time that I've turned one around is three days. It turns out that this mindset and practice of working quickly came in handy for what was coming down the road as March 2020 hit, and Rob and Sarah created this project.

For the first time in my career, I had little else to do, so I thought I'd watch *TSMGO's Taming of the Shrew*. One of my favorites! And I was curious to see how Shakespeare could be adapted to this medium.

Watching, I found myself asking, "How did they manage to get so many people from around the world all together for this?"

Rob saw that I had watched the show and messaged me the next day, saying that the endeavor was a 24/7 job and they were looking at ways to bring people on board to help with the process. Casting was one of the big jobs that took a long time for them, and could I possibly come and lend some expertise and time? I jumped at the chance.

Casting Process

We had a meeting where Rob explained the process they were using, which consisted of a mailing list with a weekly signup sheet for the next play in the canon. Actors would upload their headshot and express any special skills they had that could aid the production. They would explain their level of experience with Shakespeare and a CV, if applicable. Finally, they would express a preference for a role or roles that they would like to play in this week's show. Soon, we asked people to confirm that they had a strong internet connection, a working camera, and microphone. Everyone's submissions were then collated into a spreadsheet.

Inclusion is a huge part of my work as a casting director and this was something I found was integral to the *TSMGO* team as well. The production team had guidelines we would adhere to for each production to make it as inclusive as possible. These included gender and historically excluded identities, together with levels of experience. Rob, Sarah, and I would look at which characters would best be played by actors of another gender so that we had an equal and inclusive gender representation. We then sought to maximize the inclusion of people of color, disabled people/people with disabilities,[1] those with access needs, as well as those with specific identities applicable to the play in question. Finally, we wanted a good mixture of experience in each cast; roughly ⅔ professionals or recent graduates, with ⅓ experienced amateurs or beginners.

Part of the reason I love to cast Shakespeare is because I believe that anyone can play any role, but there were times when specificity was called for, and we strove to achieve this. In *The Merchant of Venice,* where antisemitism is prevalent, we ensured that we cast Jewish actors in both Jewish and Gentile roles across the piece, in both leads and supporting roles, so that their voices, perspectives, and lived experiences could be integral to the rehearsal process (this extended to the creative team, in which Israeli fight and intimacy coordinator Yarit Dor was consulted during R&D, before the cast was set and before rehearsals began, to ensure we had a perspective informed by lived experiences, and that we had an opportunity to consider at least some of the unique history and context of Jewish identity from the earliest stages). This company also included people from diverse and underrepresented backgrounds including Global Majority and Disabled actors, who have experienced systemic prejudice.

Another element that had become integral to the project was its global focus. Each week we aimed to have as many different countries represented as possible. Actors based in the US told me they felt Shakespeare was inaccessible to them. *TSMGO* gave international actors a chance to explore these characters, including those for whom English was a second language. Rob always found such fantastic ways of explaining and dissecting the text to make it as accessible as possible to the audience and actors alike. *TSMGO* prized accent diversity and aimed to shake off the notion that RP (Received Pronunciation) was the only acceptable way to speak this language.

Combining this many values, a global distribution of talent, alongside a variety of experience levels, identities, and genders, was a little like solving a Rubick's cube against the clock – these considerations aren't in place for every project, but they certainly made this project so much stronger for it.

Preparing for the First Casting

My first production was *Henry VI Part II* – not a particularly well-known one, so I wasn't expecting huge amounts of applicants. I felt a little daunted because I didn't really know the play. I'd never seen this one performed but every week, I'd prepare by reading the relevant text and I watched Rob's production of *Henry VI Part I* so I had a little bit of an idea of how I wanted to proceed with casting.

I made a note of all the characters in the play with a little description and, in this case, how they are related! PlayShakespeare.com was a great resource for this kind of information, having character biographies for all the characters in a given play. For this particular play, there were 55 roles. I was awaiting news on which roles were going to be doubled/tripled (one actor playing multiple parts) but for the time being, that was all I had to go on.

Casting the Roles

Day 1, when we had received all the applications for this week's show, was always a long day for me. I looked at every single applicant who applied, every single week. This was an important part of my process, honoring the effort people had made to apply and the values of inclusion to leave no stone unturned in the casting process.

First rehearsals originally began on a Sunday morning, so I had to get the final draft of casting done by the evening of Day 2 for approval by Rob and Sarah, so offers could be made then and there, or by the morning of

Day 3. It was fast, but it was also exciting to cast this way. I didn't need to watch someone "audition" for a role. I made snap decisions on who I thought would be best in the lead roles and the ensemble, based on the information they provided, which might include a showreel or list of roles they'd previously been cast in.

I looked at every single applicant and made a note of people who matched our guidelines. For *Henry VI Part II*, we had 19 roles to fill but I made a note of 25 names for leading roles and 12 names for supporting roles – this longer list offered some flexibility in creating the right *combination* of talent to live up to the project's values, and providing alternates in the case of drop-outs when offers were sent out.

It was also important to take note of how many times people had applied and how many times they had been cast. For example, if someone had applied three times and been cast twice, I was probably going to give someone else a chance. If someone had applied every single time but never been cast, I wanted to reward that person for their support and find a place for them.

This was how I worked every single week. It didn't matter what the play was, we had the same principles in place for each individual show. This really helped me to not get too attached to the idea of the applicants being disappointed. It's the worst part of my job telling people that they haven't got the part. But with this, we were able to genuinely say "Try again next week!" and what a blessing that was. This company was going to complete the canon. We all knew it, so people were able to deal with the rejection of not being involved with *Richard II* because *Romeo & Juliet* was coming up the following week.

A Unique Approach for TSMGO

One of the questions I get asked the most from working on *TSMGO* was "Was it different to how you normally work?"

The biggest difference is that with *TSMGO*, we didn't audition anyone. We had one moment while casting *Hamlet* where Rob and I could not decide between four candidates. It was such a pivotal role that we decided, on this occasion, to ask them if they wouldn't mind sending a tape of them reading one of Hamlet's speeches. They were all up for it, and actually, it made the selection process a lot easier. This was the only moment in the casting of 21 shows where I felt like it was similar to my normal practices as a casting director. We never asked people to audition at any other time, primarily because this was an unpaid opportunity, and actors invest time, energy, and care in making their submissions the best they can be. This *could* result in people taping potentially every week, which quickly shows how unfair it could become. With so many actors underperforming in auditions, it could also become a barrier to access, in a project that was consciously trying to be as inclusive as possible.

The rest of the time, I had to make decisions based on the data that I had in front of me. I found casting from data a refreshing and liberating experience. Casting is so often based on how well a person reads for a role, their star power, or their relationship with a director. With *TSMGO*, we had an entirely stripped-back casting process and we looked at several factors that were not considered under normal circumstances. This experience allowed me to make daring and bold decisions that fulfilled me creatively and also gave the audience a fresh and exciting take on the play.

It's also rare that I get to make any sort of final decisions on casting under normal circumstances. The director always chooses the final cast of actors. Whilst Rob and Sarah had final approval, it was rare that someone was swapped out of where I had originally put them. We were so often on the same wavelength with casting, often discussing the decisions as they were being made in real time, that we were aligned throughout. The timescales, the trust, and the communication broke down traditional hierarchical structures that might be present elsewhere.

Casting Tools

To cast the shows, we had a complex, interactive Google Sheet that was designed to help us resolve the many priorities we wanted to achieve. This will be described in detail by Ed in the subsequent section, The Use of Data in Casting. I remember first seeing this spreadsheet and feeling a little overwhelmed by how many people wanted to be involved. It made complete sense to me because, just like myself, in this feeling of hopelessness, people wanted a project to work on. We had around 200 applicants for this production, which led me to wonder "How many are we going to have for *A Midsummer Night's Dream*?!" Spoiler alert: we had around 600.

Lessons Learned

If you have time, take it. I genuinely believe this experience has made me a better casting director. It's also made me work more quickly, which isn't always beneficial! With a new play every week we simply didn't have the time, but sometimes now I do, and I need to remind myself that it doesn't all need to be done in one day.

Reflecting on how I managed to cast 21 shows in 21 weeks from just a spreadsheet full of data, choosing a Shylock or Titus Andronicus, a lot of it was on **gut instinct and belief in people**. Belief that these actors were going to work hard over the next three days to get it ready. The trust the team put in my judgment when I advocated for people: there were a couple of times where I said to Rob, "Trust me. They will be great", and I can't think of one example where they weren't.

The theatrical world was in absolute turmoil while we were making these plays. Rob and Sarah built a team of creatives that enabled theatre to live on in a new form. They made Shakespeare an accessible and free art form, something that will live on the internet forever. I can imagine that teachers will be referring to *TSMGO* to keep Shakespeare fresh and exciting for their students for years to come. Actors may use it to prepare for auditions. I may use it if I'm casting a Shakespeare production and I need a quick refresh of the plot and the characters. It's a project for everyone.

The Use of Data in Casting (Ed Guccione)

Here, I'll do a deep dive into how data can save mental energy in order to better invest it where it's most needed on a project, discuss how this was achieved, explore the agnostic nature of data, and how designing these approaches must be specific to the challenges we want to solve for.

Casting Process

Everything we automated was done to reduce the level of complexity and cognitive load for the team, so they could put their energy into the creative process of bringing these people together. Casting in theatre normally takes weeks or even months – with *TSMGO*, casting was done in 48 hours.

Harnessing Data for Speed and Efficiency

The initial use of data on the show was all around recruitment and casting, essentially trying to make it easier to organize the input data from people who had completed a signup form for the project as a whole and to combine that data with a signup form for a given week's show.

We used a Google form to achieve this, which was connected to Google Sheets to collect the data. This works when you're not required to sift through hundreds of applications every week. I know Rob and Sarah started off doing this process manually themselves, then over time others came in to lead this area of the project.

There is a limit to the amount of information a human brain can process at once. Because the team was doing this in a very short amount of time and there was a huge amount of manual processing involved, I looked at how I could use data to take as much effort out of the sorting process as possible, so their energy was conserved for the artistic decision-making processes that were the most important to the success of the show. This simultaneously reduced human error as much as possible and made it easier for the casting process to be ethical and equitable, reflecting the values of *TSMGO* as a whole.

TSMGO was a massive project, it was really hard, and making this sustainable was a matter of survival for the project as a whole. That sustainability was something I knew I could help with.

The data mining began with very simple stuff, basically using a spreadsheet in semi-advanced ways, filtering and sorting in ways that were pretty basic. This was immediately helpful, and so then we were able to pursue other things I could do to make the process easier.

As a team, we talked about the pain points – what makes it hard and time-consuming. I work in digital technologies, as an analyst in web development, and our teams work on user needs; they speak to us about what they do and we try to create solutions for them that actually solve their problems.

Once we'd spliced the information in the recruitment form, which we accomplished by asking people to use the same email address for both forms so we had a key to combine the data with, we then started recording longitudinally who had been cast in the past, and how many times someone had applied. This was a community project, and one of the values was to make sure lots of people got the opportunity to be involved. There was a ratio of parts played vs. times applied, and we used that ratio (the number of times applied: number of times cast) to determine who rose to the top of the sheet. We're more likely to remember the people we see first, and this was an easy way of making sure the team knew who was most passionate about being involved and had yet to get the opportunity.

From there we got into filtering various things. Speaking in generalizations, and there were plenty of exceptions to this, there was a place for professionals in the show, and a place for semi-pros, amateurs, and beginners. We didn't want to depend on what people could write about themselves because amateurs might not be practiced at selling what they were good at. So we codified a system where actors declared their level of experience, and we stacked those on top of each other. So, you could go through the professionals first, then the semi-pros, amateurs, and beginners, and roughly populate out the parts by size, so people could participate without being overwhelmed.

Google Sheets has inbuilt functionality within that product that allows you to use formulas to move data into different spreadsheets, so we had one spreadsheet for professionals and one spreadsheet for amateurs. One of the reasons for this was to make sure that the product was good and that we were introducing amateurs and beginners into a professional grade performance, to provide an opportunity for them to use their skills to experience something valuable and improve.

Casting Principal Roles with Data

For principal roles, the show cast one person per part. There were two streams of information that we resolved – one was a more general biographical questionnaire and then one was a show-specific application. We didn't want to ask people to fill this information out every single week, so we stored it longitudinally for the lifespan of the project.

This was merged using a correlation ID, which was the email. It wasn't perfect, and with more time to design a system, we'd use something else as people make typos or have different emails, but we created a fixing system where we could identify "orphan" applications and match them to the initial signup form. So for these orphans, if the email had no match, the program would then try and use the name to find a match. It was fuzzy, but it was a way to ensure people weren't excluded because of technical faults.

The creative team, of course, chose what data to collect; I just managed it, but we also archived the cast each week so we could keep those longitudinal records of who had applied and who had been cast. This better enabled the team to stick to their commitment of inclusivity, because you wouldn't cast the same person every time. At the same time, it helped us remember the dedicated people who were waiting for their shot because it pushed them to the top of the pile. Doing it this way had obvious advantages over say, alphabetical order, where an arbitrary surname like Alan Aardvark means you would be seen first every week.

The next big thing was pulling images and demographic data – because actors have Spotlight pages or Backstage profiles or personal websites, you would end up accessing 350 websites to be able to see details about them that are required to cast.

Google sheets is a web-based spreadsheet program that has a large amount of functionality for collecting data from different sources. This includes the formula "IMPORTHTML"; when this formula is used with a known URL, data from these websites can be imported directly into the spreadsheet. This can include text, tables, and images. It's also possible to make these formulae dynamic and dependent on other data within the spreadsheet.

Since Google Sheets can scrape data from websites in this way, we pulled in important characteristics from those people's profiles – data they had agreed to share by nature of it being disclosed in a link they had sent us – so it was all in one place, and each actor's details were visible alongside one another, rather than on discrete pages.

Casting Ensemble Tracks with Data

The values prescribed that everyone who took part should have a meaningful experience, and as such, another key pain point was that we wouldn't cast one person per part, especially in shows where there were many parts of five lines or fewer. Trying to create ensemble tracks added a layer of complication that could quickly spiral. Combining roles quickly and manually was a challenge because of the amount of cross referencing you have to do, holding in your head what characters appear in what scenes. In the beginning, Rob and Sarah were doing this manually with some of the longest plays in Shakespeare. Even if two characters weren't in the same scene, if they exited at the end of one and the next character entered at the start of the next scene, one person would struggle to make that quick change. Even with all the diligence in the world, human error meant you might end up halfway through rehearsal before it became apparent that someone assigned a role wouldn't be able to play it. But this kind of processing is what computers are really good at, especially if you have a good, clean source of the data.

The great thing is PlayShakespeare.com had wonderfully created a data source that is machine readable in GitHub, where people store computer code. It was a brilliant tool, and it's what we used to create all that information about what scenes characters were in. This was not perfect – some characters change names when they're given a new title, and some might just be errors, but it was a much better starting point than anything else available.

I used a computer language called *R* to program a matrix that used conditional formatting to help sort ensemble tracks. To begin with, they set the number of lines that counted as an "ensemble" role, because we knew how many lines every character had. This could be 100 lines or 25 depending on the play.

Then, the sheet would populate all the characters fitting that criteria along one axis, and the number of ensemble tracks on the other. Rob or the casting director could then put an X in a box where a character would be played by a given ensemble track, and the matrix would highlight what other characters could be played by that track – eliminating characters in the same scene, or the scene before or after it.

If a mistake was made and you put an x in a conflicting character box by accident, the line would go red to indicate it was an issue. If a character was unassigned, it would be amber. Once a compatible line was assigned to someone, it went green. So in this way, the team could experiment with combining roles into ensemble tracks that worked for the production based on their creative vision, but within the limits of what was possible, by checking boxes instead of holding every character's track alive in their heads at once. This script would also output a line count per ensemble track, so Rob and the team could balance or offset line load as they saw fit based on the data; this helped to create a balanced and equitable space.

Casting Tools

Have I mentioned Google Sheets? Sheets, GitHub, the programming language R, and PlayShakespeare.com's machine-readable text were so integral to this process that they've been mentioned throughout, as opposed to being kept for this distinct section. Sorry!

Lessons Learned

This project was unique and specific in many ways:

- What the data needed to enable
- The pace
- The use of Shakespeare
- The availability of pre-made machine-readable data on the plays
- My (a data analyst's) personal investment as a best friend to the guy who created the project
- Wanting to help him live to the end of it.

None of these factors will necessarily apply to different projects. If you work in the theatre industry at a level with real resources, there may be off-the-shelf software that people can buy that will do these kinds of things for you, and if you don't, you may have to pay someone to build it for you, but there's value in doing so, and there are some principles that I think can be taken forward.

In principle, **data can reduce the effort that it takes creative teams to do their jobs effectively.** It can reduce human error rates, and it can support an equitable and ethical approach to casting. Even if you're not producing a show every week, chances are you're busy, so make it easier for yourself by investing a little bit of time in this now.

When you conserve energy by streamlining your processes, by converting manual tasks into automated ones, you gain time and energy to put your attention toward the kinds of decisions that computers can't make; you can uphold your values and focus on equitable, inclusive practices.

At my day job as a data wrangler, I don't make the decisions, I supply the data that is used to inform the decisions. That is my job there, and in some ways, it was my job here – to make the data available that allowed the team to make informed creative decisions.

There is a volunteer group called Data for Good, which helps to pair charities with data experts who can put their skills to use and do good in the world. It helps to remember that "data" is neutral. Whenever data is in the headlines it's generally because a Big Evil Corporation is using data for evil. **But data is agnostic – it's the agenda that's good or evil.**

With *TSMGO*, the data was used ethically and for good – the agenda was to cast as inclusively as possible across as many different factors of inclusion as possible. Theatre has its own particular needs, and data can help to support those needs. In my line of work, asking for photographs is not relevant to what we're asking people to do, so it can be an invitation for prejudice. In theatre, where representation is so important, you're explicit about why you're asking for that information and then delivering on that mission, those values. It allowed us to contextualize why people weren't cast – we could tell people we had 300 applications for 16 roles. It allowed us to track who was passionate and who'd been cast. It allowed us to prioritize new people. At the end of the project, we deleted all that data. We didn't store it, didn't sell it. So data can be used well if used with transparency and integrity.

Props, Costume, and Visual Identity (Emily Ingram)

Design is a crucial part of any theatrical production – whether the medium is digital or in person – and *TSMGO's* part-earnest, part-ironic homespun aesthetic is no exception. I'm going to guide you through building your own design guidelines for a digital production by exploring that aesthetic. We'll begin with a few words on imagination, screens, and Computer-Generated Imagery (CGI), and what these all have to do with DIY digital theatre.

> **Aside:** *Design, as discussed here, refers to a series of visual motifs that help to ground an audience in the world of the play, and hint at the tone of that play. These motifs come together to make up*

the set, scenery, props, and costuming of the play and can also include its lighting design.

In his guide to Shakespeare, *Shakespeare on Toast,* Ben Crystal reflects on the differences between Shakespeare's audiences and modern audiences. Crystal writes that contemporary audiences are used to regularly suspending their disbelief (p43) – theatre, film, and fiction are omnipresent in the twenty-first century – but that these same audiences have "increasingly high standards" for the visual effects they are used to seeing on their screens. Although Crystal was writing this in 2008, long before digital theatre reached the kind of mainstream attention brought on by the pandemic, his observations are hugely useful for today's digital theatremaker.

Our audiences' screens now bustle with CGI, and if we are to engage with an audience on a screen, we either need to meet the monumentally high standards for CGI and visual effects or take heed of the prologue delivered by the Chorus in *Henry V* and find simple but effective means to get our audiences' "imaginary forces" working.

Theatre – especially theatre made on a non-commercial scale – is unlikely to have the budget for high-spec visual effects, and as non-commercial work accounts for the vast majority of theatre created, I will assume here that readers will be working on a no-budget, "for-a-muse-of-fire" scale. We'll start with backgrounds and lighting and pan slowly in on the details, like props and make-up.

TSMGO's core aesthetic was very much defined by what actors had to hand in their homes during the 2020 lockdowns. The importance of this, and how it shaped our design and values, will be explored as we work through each element of design below.

Design Process

Backgrounds

There will be a greater focus on the philosophy behind our decisions for backgrounds in Chapter 5 but several key things should be acknowledged and addressed at this point since we are examining means to create a visual identity. *TSMGO* performed each of its productions on Zoom, which offers participants the ability to use a "virtual background (VBG)": an image or – if one's computer or device is powerful enough – video can be used as well. At the beginning of the COVID-19 pandemic, VBGs were the perfect thing for hiding the untidiness of one's hastily constructed home-office-kitchen-living-room. Many digital productions performed on

Zoom adopted VBGs as a way of setting the scene. Performing an adaptation of *Pride & Prejudice*? Stick a backdrop of a Regency home up as a VBG. Opening scene of *Macbeth*? Get a Google image search going for an appropriate stretch of wasteland to serve as the blasted heath.

For the reasons covered in Chapter 5 we only ever used the VBG function when "hacked" to produce alternative effects, never as intended. In the absence of VBGs, then, it's vital to find other ways to create the sense that performers are sharing the same space. Encouraging actors to find similar patches of blank white walls in their homes is one solution, but the more creative solution can be found in lighting, objects, and color palettes.

Examples of all three of these backdrop uses can be found in *TSMGO's* Christmas 2020 offering, *Shakespeare's A Christmas Carol* (Ian Doescher). The production saw Tiny Tim (played by Scottish musician and drag artist Jordy Joans, FKA Jordy Deelight) take on the Chorus role, announcing the arrival of each Ghost into Scrooge's (Wendy Morgan) bedroom.

Morgan used an up-turned table and red curtains to create a mock four-poster bed, while Deelight used a red scarf hung on the edge of their computer screen to suggest the edge of the same four-poster. Both used low lighting to create the impression of nighttime. This combination of similar lighting, similar objects, and similar colors created a unified shared space between Morgan and Deelight and allowed the audience to imagine that the Chorus really was, like Gonzo in cinema classic *The Muppet Christmas Carol*, hanging out – unseen by Scrooge – as an unseen narrator in the background of Scrooge's event night.

Lighting

One of the joys of digital theatre is that it allows creatives from across the world to collaborate with one another without the cost or environmental burden of air travel. Collaborating across time zones does present the digital theatremaker with a challenge, however. If you are trying to create the impression of a shared space, and half your actor's rooms are filled with bright daylight while the others are filled with darkness or artificial light to stave off the darkness, the illusion is quickly shattered.

Unifying your dispersed cast through a standardized lighting setup, as far as is possible with what they have available to them, can help to unify the aesthetic. If everyone in the production can be familiarized with the classic **three-point lighting setup**, it offers a very straightforward way to light both spaces and faces well. This uses a key light to light the face from one side, providing the majority of the light in the frame. A fill light then lights the face from the other side to prevent long shadows from appearing on the face, and a final back light shines on the subject from behind to prevent multiple shadows from appearing on the wall behind, while separating the subject from the background. Performers do not need expensive ring lights or film lighting kits to achieve it; desk lamps or floor lamps or, at a pinch, large torches will work just as well.

FIGURE 4.2 Three-Point Lighting Setup.

For scenes taking place under the cover of darkness, light from a laptop, computer, or tablet screen will suffice for performers with light skin, but actors with darker skin may wish to use the fill light from the three-light setup at a low level to ensure they remain clearly visible, owing to the racially biased design of many auto-adjusting apertures that have been set to correct exposure for lighter skin tones, leaving more melanated skin underexposed.

Props

In Shakespeare, propwork cannot be a last-minute thought or left to chance: a prop can change the course of an entire act or play, or alter the fate of the characters in an instant.

In *Hamlet*, poison, swords, and skulls change characters' minds and lives. In *Twelfth Night*, Viola realizes how deep a mess she's got herself into purely from picking up a ring thrown to the ground. Elsewhere in the play, Malvolio's life and reputation are ruined by a letter. In *Othello*, Desdemona and Othello's marriage, fates, and lives rest on a handkerchief.

The need for a strong props aesthetic was evident, but we could still only ask performers to use what they had to hand for props as this was all happening during the 2020 lockdowns. Cardboard, food containers, and even trash were our chosen medium as everyone – regardless of their lockdown situation – had at least some of this on hand.

As *TSMGO* moved swiftly from readings to productions of Shakespeare's work, the props design had to evolve to help lend the productions a strong aesthetic. Guides and templates were sourced or created and used as inspiration for the actors to make props at home, following principles that made them meaningful, instead of arbitrary:

Three Dimensionality: The most important thing for cardboard props was to add three dimensionality where possible to allow them to stand out on the Zoom screen. For a glorious example of this, please see Antipholus of Syracuse (Robbie Capaldi)'s sword in *A Comedy of Errors*.

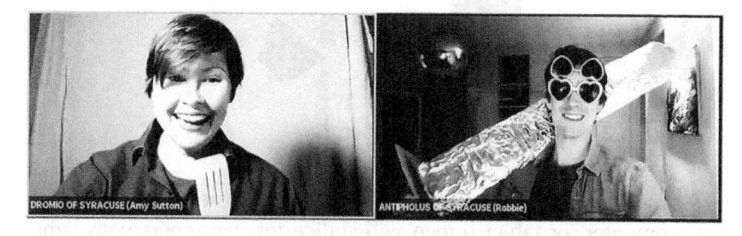

FIGURE 4.3 Amelia "Ace" Armande (nèe Amy Sutton; They/Them) as Dromio of Syracuse and Robbie Capaldi (He/Him) as Antipholus of Syracuse in *Comedy of Errors*.

Texture: Texture was vital. Silver foil used over cardboard to create the illusion of metal needed to have shadow and depth added to it (usually with black marker pen but sometimes with thick coffee grounds to add a rust effect); crowns needed marker pen patina to give the illusion of having been passed down over many generations. Age and texture allow props to tell stories, and even props that were easy to produce required little additions of texture and shadow to heighten them.

Weight: Actors were asked to consider the weight of the object their character was holding. The "severed head in a bag" they were holding might have been a birthday balloon in a carrier bag of tomato sauce but it needed to be held and hefted as though it weighed the same as a bowling ball to allow audiences to invest their imaginations in it.

Costume

Unified texture and color palettes will help to give your show a clear and consistent design. When choosing what colors to use, we considered the colors mentioned already in the play, and the colors that will contrast and complement these. Understanding how to use a color wheel (examples of which can be found easily online together with instructions for use) will help to make choices that are informed by design thinking and help colors complement or contrast one another.

Layers and detail will add visual interest and also increase the believability of a costume. Costume jewelry, waistcoats, shawls, rags, and cloaks (we frequently used a blanket or towel draped purposefully and held in place with a silver foil/safety pin brooch), all tell a story about a character's status, so we used these with abandon as the shows went on.

Make-up

Cosmetics. Grime. Sweat. In digital theatre, audiences can see these in far greater detail than they can at most large theatres, and so it was vital to get this aspect right. When performing historic plays, consider which elements of the era's make-up best serve the stories told in your play. Elizabethan aristocratic make-up is highly striking but can look unusual and distracting to modern audiences, so *TSMGO's* production of *Much Ado About Mean Girls* (Ian Doescher), borrowed only one aspect of it: very defined, cupid-bow-shaped lipstick, so that when Regina George and Cady Heron said mean things in perfect iambic pentameter, their mean words came from highly made-up, beautified mouths, to emphasize the "fair is foul" (or, at least, can be sometimes) message of Tina Fey's 2004 film. By contrast, Danan MacAleer's Parolles in *All's Well That End's Well* used regency make-up to deliberately stand apart from much of the rest of the cast to emphasize the character's foppery and duplicitous nature.

Meanwhile, in *Troilus & Cressida* and elsewhere, the actors playing Greek soldiers were encouraged to use make-up and coffee grounds to add grime to the creases of their faces, adding the illusion of age through the emphasis of the crease lines and the illusion that they have been camped out in poor conditions amid a pointless war for years. It added context to the growing restlessness of the Greek camp.

Hair

Hairstyling can help to add further three dimensionality and interest on a Zoom screen. As an actor's head and shoulders makeup the majority of what is seen on Zoom, it was important not to leave hairstyling as an afterthought, as it accounts for a large proportion of what your audience is looking at for the two hours' traffic of the screen. Silver foil coronets, plaiting or braiding, beads, grime, and back brushing (or "teasing" the hair to make it stand up) are a few ways to tell an audience about a character's status – or change of status.

Aside: *When creating or finding tutorials or inspirational mood boards for hair and make up, make sure that you are including options that are inclusive for a range of hair types and skin tones.*

Breaking the Aesthetic

Once you have established your design aesthetic, you can begin to break it. "Surprise and Delight" was a core promise of *TSMGO's* offer, and Shakespeare himself frequently established conventions in order to toy with them, to keep his audience's attention. The design expectations were subverted in key moments throughout the First Folio: Regan's use of a real broadsword to impale a servant in *King Lear* shocked audiences, after many months of cardboard equivalents. This principle was used to extraordinary effect in Kevin V. Smith's production of *Edward II*, which opened *TSMGO's* Month of Marlowe Festival in June 2021. For the first time, inspired by the films of Ingmar Bergman, the stark monochrome production was presented to an audience who had watched *TSMGO's* previous 42 productions in color. It gave the entire production a reverse *Wizard of Oz* effect, saying to the audience "we're not in Kansas anymore". Meanwhile, after months of fake blood, Edward's death – sliding sorrowfully but gently into a bath as an Edith Piaf-like figure sang to him – had a huge poignancy to it. There was no space for the audience to go "oh, that's a clever prop" or "nice use of fake blood" or "gorey!" in the YouTube chat. They were confronted very directly with the loss: Edward was there one moment and then gone, and there was no prop aesthetic to hide the emotiveness of that behind.

Design Tools

The tools used in most cases were defined by, first, what our actors had to hand and, second, how much time they could commit. The special props I created for the shows, such as Shakespeare's DeLorean, were informed by Grotowski's Poor Theatre, Blue Peter, Pinterest, and searching for cardboard weapons and cardboard props tutorials on YouTube and Google – this originally took me to stormthecastle.com, which is now defunct, but quickly leads to makers like #epiccardboardprops who do similarly impressive and detailed work from readily available materials. From there, it is a matter of using ingenuity, resourcefulness, and imagination.

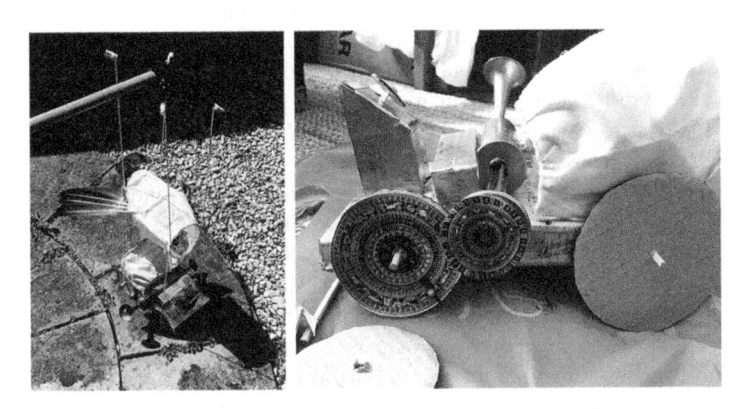

FIGURE 4.4 Shakespeare's DeLorean.

For an example of a tutorial, see this design for Clifford's arrow-through-the-neck, crafted by Ruth Page:

FIGURE 4.5 Arrow Tutorial QR Code (bit.ly/neckarrow).

Lessons Learned

Chapter 5 will address how systemizing our thinking and values helped us to make the *TSMGO* show creation process efficient. The same is true of our design process: early on in the *TSMGO* journey, we chanced upon our core aesthetic of homespun, eccentric cardboard props, and costume – partly out of necessity – but adopting this necessary design choice made us truer to our core values: Shakespeare is for everyone and this egalitarian everyone's-got-cardboard-in-their-homes-so-it-doesn't-matter-if-you-can-afford-a-real-sword-prop approach supported that principle.

In an interview with a handful of the cast and crew members of *TSMGO*, academic and theatre critic Ben Broadribb asked why – once lockdown restrictions lifted in many of the parts of the world where *TSMGO's* actors were based – *TSMGO* didn't begin to rely on slicker, purchasable props.

The answer: we had a strong aesthetic established, and we were committed to the principles of imaginative play. It could become very easy to fall into a trap of only casting actors with access to props/costume, leaving amateur performers, performers just starting out, and performers from low-income backgrounds behind. Most importantly, it enfranchised the audience as imaginative co-creators, and in line with producer Sarah Peachey's research interest in play as a creative tool for adults, it encouraged a kind of gleeful make-believe that atrophies as we age, a much-needed escape from the confines of a traumatic world event.

When considering how you might build a visual identity, effective questions to ask might include:

- What are your values, and how can these help you begin to define your production's design?
- What effect do you want your production's aesthetic to have on your audience?
- What opportunities does a choice open up, and what limitations might it impose?

Music and Sound (Adam Gibson)

Given its homespun aesthetic, music and sound were an essential way for *TSMGO* to add a sense of production value, create additional context for scenes, cue the audience as to the mood or emotional tenor of what was to come, and even help actors to represent tortured psychological states. Here, I'll explore how we developed the sound for each production, and what I'll take from this process into my wider work.

Music and Sound Process

The journey for sound design often began on Day 1, the day after the previous performance, either awaiting the details of the R&D meeting or an email with details of what to expect. By Day 2, a sound and music guide, developed by Rob and the team, was ready to provide an overall feel to the places, characters, or moods of the piece, depending on what show we were doing.

The simple truth is that I was not familiar with half of the shows, so I really needed that brief, which included a plain English synopsis of each scene and of the themes of the play, and then just a very simple, very obvious two or three words that would evoke the feeling or the purpose of the scene; things like suspense, excitement, dirge. Given the scope of the schedule, I wasn't able to go deep into all the details of each scene, and it wouldn't have been helpful to do so. Most of the sound we created happened during scene changes, so I would only have ten seconds to tell a story and set the mood for what was to come. We had to condense the genre, the emotional setup, or the geographical setting for the scene and keep the drive and forward momentum up so that we grabbed the audience's attention and prepared them for what was to come, rather than allow the energy the actors had created in the previous scene to drop.

Some shows required a lot of atmosphere, things like storms, or marketplaces, to help create a sense of place, like in radio plays. Some shows also required live vocal effects to transform voices – like the Witches in Macbeth. Once I had an understanding of the requirements of the show, I could tweak my setup to ensure I had the right configuration for what we would need to deliver.

I would also debrief on the previous week or weeks' work to assess what the audience had responded to and what hadn't really worked, so we could build on and progress our approach. Depending on the week, we would then have a two or three-hour R&D session that would go scene by scene, and would often lift out particular moments where sound could play a role *within* the scenes.

Over the next two days (Days 3 and 4), I would develop prototypes and ideas, to build the world. Often I would look at the opening, the climax of the story, and the ending to create a journey I could flesh out with the rest of the pieces. Understanding where the characters were, emotionally or even geographically, and what their journey was made it much easier to design the transitions from one to the other; it's much easier to tell the story in musical terms.

Later in the process, we extended the time frame the shows were performed in, and that gave us space for a first read-through, which was hugely helpful, as I was able to surround myself in the world and see the characters, and a rough sketch of the emotional journeys. A cue list would naturally start to emerge from that process.

Once I had a skeleton of the basic cues I would create an Excel spreadsheet, or I would build a Qlab file right away, full of empty boxes waiting to be noted and labeled as I created the work. It was useful to have a Qlab ready to go before Day 6's tech, as I could refer back to this while we built the cue list for the show, often on the night before we went live. Unlike the actors, who worked toward the night of Day 7, my peak was the night of Day 6, when we would build, test, and adjust everything so that on Day 7 I felt reasonably relaxed and in control of what I was doing.

Since things would always happen on tech day that we hadn't anticipated, it was great practice to spend Days 4 and 5 generating content or even recycling elements of atmospheres from previous shows so I had material to work from and could adjust and customize it quickly during the tech.

Sometimes on Day 6, before tech, Rob and I would meet, and he would update me with the latest cues so we could get ahead on programming. Then the show was really clear in my head and I could work my way through organizing the cue list with the script, but often that would be done on the day of the performance.

I didn't believe in doing a lot of programming in Qlab before this point, because it is much easier to populate things in order, and often in rehearsal extra moments would be discovered that called for additional cues.

One important lesson during this process was not to strive for perfection – because of the tight timelines, we couldn't predict how something I'd created would survive contact with what Rob and the actors were creating. After tech, I often had a much clearer idea of what adjustments needed to be made before the performance than I could have had working in isolation. The tech provided so much clarity on what was needed, I could then spend Day 7 (performance day) on final polishes.

Working on *TSMGO* had unique challenges – unlike a serialized TV show where the topic, the world, the characters, and the genre all stay the same, we would be completely starting from scratch week after week. TV sound designers have a big library of music they can pick from and layer in to match the emotional beats. I took inspiration from the rare exceptions: *Inside No. 9*, where all these things change week by week, and the last season of *Agents of Shield*, where they would frequently time travel and end up in different places and times, which in turn affected the genre of each episode, and consequently, the style of the music and sound. Nevertheless, they were both still working weeks ahead with big budgets and time.

When it came to briefings, I needed words that I could interpret visually in my brain very easily. Often these were to do with emotion, pace, tone, or specific instruments. "Thrilling", "driving", and "intimate" were really useful descriptions, or if we were creating a sense of place, it's easy to associate something taking place in a church with an organ. Rob frequently referred to the notion of a kettle coming to the boil to talk about how the energy would build through a play.

Directors can really help by crunching the scenes down to the minimum amount of high-value information, and the points that we really need to hit to serve the story.

Music and Sound Tools

I used a software called Logic Pro which is Apple software and one of the three main software that composers and sound designers use for mixing and engineering. That allowed me to physically make the music, with lots of libraries of orchestral sounds, the same kind of libraries that TV shows and budget films use. Occasionally I would play and record things, and on *The Tempest* we had actor-musicians send in recordings so we had an actual orchestral feel by the end of the First Folio series.

As a sound designer, I also have banks and banks of hard drives full of sound effects, and on the rare occasion that nothing was quite right, I would either go and record it or find it online. Using Logic Pro and Pro Tools you can then stitch these elements together in original combinations.

To deliver the show itself, I tried to create something as close as possible to the setup I'd use for in-person theatre. I wanted it to feel like I was operating a live show on a stage, and in person, not just hitting a couple of cues while being on Zoom. This evolved over the entire course of the project, adding new tools and equipment or stripping it back down according to the ambition of each show.

I used a mixing desk, which allows me to mix all my signals or my sound and music, because I quickly discovered it was essential to be able to adjust live during the performance, especially when using ambience under dialogue. So I would run all my stuff through a desk and then into Zoom, and run it off Qlab, which, most importantly, keeps things "live" and enables a lot of clever interventions. With vocal effects, we had to run a Zoom output into the desk and then back into Zoom through the share sound feature.

When I was doing the initial mix for the tech I would listen to the music through my professional audio setup, but also through my default laptop speakers, my phone, some cheap headphones, and a TV, to make sure

I was adjusting this to be as good as possible for every device, rather than optimizing for a specific venue or space, as you would in a theatre. Again, taking cues and ways of working from TV.

Lessons Learned

The most important thing is to **just do it**. You learn more by giving it a go. Never listen to anyone saying it'll never work. Try it. I contacted a lot of people who were industry leaders in the field to ask "how would you do this" and sometimes I would get responses asking "*why* would you do this?". In their world, these kinds of things had never been necessary, but they *were* necessary for this new medium. So I suppose one lesson is that **specialist expertise can narrow your ways of working** and you sometimes need to put your amateur hat back on and start from scratch to find the most creative solutions.

Sound has evolved hugely in the last 20–30 years, especially in theatre, but there are still very clear ways that things are done. This project was the opposite of how sound tends to work in commercial theatre – we didn't want to have control of the actors, we wanted to control the sound design in order to serve them. While in an ideal environment, we'd sit in the tech and give notes about dynamics and diction to the actors, or note the orchestra on what needs lifting out or sitting back; if we were using mics, we'd have control over those, but in this environment, because everyone is in their own homes and is using a different setup, we had no control over that, so we had to **focus on what we *could* control**.

An important lesson I learned from the unique experience of producing a new show every week was **the importance of moving on**. Good enough is good enough, and we had so much to focus on that if a piece served its purpose, that's enough. Do it quickly, then make it as good as possible, but don't get trapped trying to make it perfect.

This process also taught me to **really highlight the important things**. We needed to save our time so we had it available to spend elsewhere – an *essential* ten-second moment in the show was more worth our time than a *slightly more* evocative background atmosphere. For me, the intro was one of the most important pieces to work on because it framed the experience for the audience for the rest of the play.

Curating Guest Introductions (and Creative Producing) – Ben Crystal

For my section, I'm going to recount the journey of both the guest introductions, and of my own involvement with *TSMGO*, and how both came to serve the best interests of the project as a whole, in sometimes surprising ways. My journey was one of seeking to maximize representation, offering provocations and reflections, and serving as a first responder for the team when they encountered a sticking point.

Curating and Creative Producing Process

I came onboard *TSMGO* to curate the introductions and later as a Consultant Creative Producer.

I replied to Rob Myles' Tweet almost immediately. It was so heartening that someone felt they had the energy to kick a project like this off amidst the sudden, strange times of March 2020. The reality of a project actually continuing non-stop until November didn't really land with me; surely the pandemic would be over by the early summer at the latest?

In my reply I suggested he start it as soon as he could: these great ideas don't hang around long before it occurs to someone else (and other companies *did* do full explorations of Shakespeare during lockdown), and it felt important to start fast and lead strong.

In that first week, we agreed I would introduce the first play. This would set the tone for the play to follow and give some hooks into the story, characters, and themes for those who might be unfamiliar with this early effort of Shakespeare's, or with Shakespeare at all. I would also start reaching out to others to take a swing at the coming introductions.

As we got past *Two Gentlemen of Verona*, it was clear the merry-go-round wasn't going to stop. I began tentatively reaching out to people: can you introduce this Shakespeare play on Zoom in two days? No? Ok, no problem. Yes of course I'll try to give you more notice next time …

Academics can get nervous about a lack of lead-in time to prepare a talk. My father David Crystal's approach to giving a talk had clearly influenced me:

- Know your subject
- Know your audience
- Find out how much time you have
- Plan for less time than you're given
- Leave some things you want to say for the questions
- Talk with your audience in the moment

Prepare, Don't Plan. Or, Make It Up as You Go Along

It wasn't until we were a month in that I thought it might be time to make a spreadsheet. I wanted to see how far into the future I could schedule guest speakers.

The thing is, it was anxiety-making enough for some people to be asked to do *anything* during this stressful, worrisome time. Asking them too soon was not good. Asking them too far in advance could be even more stressful – by May 2020 it became clear that asking speakers to consider a gig on a distant Wednesday night in October was like inviting them to throw a golf ball onto the moon.

Because we were broadcasting at 7.30 pm UK time, anyone East of Moscow was a difficult ask, simply because of the time difference. The Americas, by contrast, were a much easier ask.

Curation – A Journey

I wanted to make sure the guest speakers were not all older white males. That demographic has dominated the Shakespeare industry, both in terms of practitioners and academics. I say this in great admiration of my white male colleagues, and mindful that I present as a white male Shakespearean too, as did half of *TSMGO's* core team.

To offset this historical imbalance, I sent out dozens of invitations to female practitioners and academics around the world. Most replied, and the more I gauged the lead-in time well, the more positive the response.

The curation – as in, the degree to which I was able to artistically direct and curate particular people to introduce particular plays – changed radically in response to the Black Lives Matter Movement.

The news that racial inequality made around the world in the summer of 2020 made me rethink my approach. While I'd been reaching toward diversity in gender and age and had worked hard to invite practitioners from the Global Majority, I hadn't always been successful, and so the demographic of introducers was imbalanced. I recognized I needed to work harder.

Toward the second half of the project, the Black Lives Matter Movement started to have a positive effect on the availability of Global Majority academics and practitioners – as well as actors. Global Majority theatre folk were in great demand, and our project was always at the mercy of people's real lives, which by September had thankfully started to resume in some form.

The basic mandates that came with the invitation were simple:

- You've got ten minutes
- Tell us why you love the play (or tell us why you hate it)
- Give us things in the plot or the writing to look out for
- Don't hesitate to speak from your own point of view

We had enough structure to ensure audiences were well served by the content, but enough flexibility to guarantee every introduction was unique.

The Value of an Outside Eye

As a creative producer, I wanted to be mindful of my impact.

Throughout, I kept a distance from the core team, working with them on R&Ds, but mindful of another lesson I'd learned as a young producer: you can always get *busy*: roll up your sleeves and help paint the set. **Helping to get things done is important. But so is keeping perspective on the project.**

That slight distance allowed me to help the team navigate around pitfalls – opportunities! – they couldn't necessarily foresee because they're head down and sprinting. I offered a third person, over-the-shoulder perspective, like the computer game *The Last of Us;* while the core team was necessarily in the blinkered first-person perspective of a game like *Call of Duty*, doing little other than Eat, Sleep, Shakespeare, Repeat.

As a project comes toward its final stretch, it's normal to feel exhausted beyond belief. Holding to your mission statement becomes harder the longer you're sprinting. It's important to find ways to stay creative, to give energy to lateral thinking, and still make room for blue-sky dreaming.

That distance also allowed me to see **when my help could best serve the project**. Rob and I talked about my playing a role in the show, and over the summer months, as the world opened up, I landed on Timon.

We considered how a white male playing the title role might weigh against *TSMGO*'s values and intended to counterbalance this elsewhere in the production while bringing much-needed attention to this fairly ignored part of the canon. We had talked about my playing in *Henry VIII* to shine a light on a similarly unknown play (I ended up spear-carrier-ing in that final history play and nearly jump-starting a procession 20 lines too early).

We decided to bring *original pronunciation* (the accent of Shakespeare's time) into Timon's speech as he dropped out of society. That special, unusual, shiny quality, combined with Sir Simon Russell Beale's presence, helped us attract an extraordinary group of actors from diverse backgrounds toward this relatively unproduced piece, at a time when the increase in demand for actors of the Global Majority meant they were being offered more and more opportunities elsewhere.

Lessons Learned

It's hard to single out introductions when they all had a unique offer for the audience, but some remain at the forefront of my mind.

Having just turned 14 years old, **Annabelle Higgins** was close to the age of Juliet and had taken it upon herself to draw a poster every week, encapsulating each play. Hearing a young teen's perspective on *Romeo and Juliet*, and the actions of these Elizabethan lovers, was utterly fascinating.

As one of this generation's foremost Shakespeare and pre-modern critical race studies scholars, **David Sterling Brown**'s introduction exploring *Hamlet* through the lens of whiteness is a must-watch for any classroom, and the same goes for **Sawyer Kemp**'s trans exploration intro to *Cymbeline*.

The actor **Joe Marcell**'s reflections on performing as King Lear around the world on a touring Shakespeare's Globe production felt like a real coup. And wonderfully, **Sir Simon Russell Beale** immediately wrote back with a simple *Yes!*, having invited him to introduce *Timon of Athens*. He played the part to great acclaim at the National Theatre in 2013, and his involvement was a massive boost for everyone involved – not to mention an extra incredibly powerful audience draw for an unfamiliar play.

The best lesson I've learned as a producer is **don't ask, don't get**. Rob was always excited to explore making big asks to entice ever more experienced actors to play.

And recognizing that while **don't ask, don't get** doesn't ever stop being tiring or even scary, it tends to work 25% of the time. You always have a chance of getting X to be a patron to your Theatre Company. You just gotta ask, and don't let the 75% rejection rate get you down.

Community Engagement Using Social Media (Ruth Page)

We utilized the power of social media to retain and develop our audience and enrich their experience of both the show and the *TSMGO* movement as a whole. We will explore our most effective processes before sharing my reflections on how these tools can be best used by theatremakers in the future.

Building, maintaining, and engaging with our audience was essential to the success of *TSMGO*. Without keeping the *TSMGO* flame burning bright between the weekly live streams, it would have been far more difficult to grow in the way that we ultimately did. What's more, by working online, we were presented with the perfect opportunity to have a global reach, in terms of both the creatives we got to work with and the audiences we engaged with.

Ahead of sharing our findings, it is important to note that **it is never too late to start**. I began working on *TSMGO*'s social media accounts almost two months after the project had begun. I also had limited experience in the field but was keen to support the project in any way I could. Through trial and error, research, and relentless creative problem solving, we were able to use social media platforms to our advantage, extending both our global reach as well as the imaginative world around each play.

Social media is essential to working in the online sphere. It offers an incredible platform for your creative endeavors and has a great deal of power. Consequently, it must be handled with the utmost care.

Social Media Tools

We can credit a great deal of our success to free social media and fundraising tools. As an entirely voluntary, unfunded project, we had to use everything we could at our disposal. Thankfully, many of these free platforms (each with their own limitations) worked extremely well for what we wanted to achieve. We established a presence on Facebook, Twitter, Instagram, RedBubble, and Patreon, while using Tweetdeck and Facebook Business Manager to facilitate this.

We quickly found that Facebook, Twitter, and Instagram were the most useful social media platforms for *TSMGO*'s daily engagement, offering us the opportunity to share images alongside our copy and relevant links. It also meant that most content could be easily reformatted for all three platforms. Crucially, these platforms operate based on engagement, highlighting what the people you follow are responding to, in a way that ensured our reach could grow organically, without the need for paid advertising.

We used several different platforms to raise funds for the Hardship Fund that all actors and creatives could opt into. At the time we were working, Patreon (a service that allowed people to subscribe to support creators with flexible monthly donations) and RedBubble (a custom printing service where designs could be uploaded and applied to a huge range of items) were the right fit for our model of working as a physically separated production team with a globally dispersed audience. Patreon allowed us to leverage the power of exclusive content for followers that wanted to invest in and support the project, whilst RedBubble allowed us to create global merchandising opportunities with multiple printing and distribution centers globally, with on-demand fulfillment ensuring we needn't invest anything up front, making it a particularly lean solution.

Social Media Process

An important lesson we learned is that **you can't just post and leave.** As any social media manager will tell you, it's the **engagement** that is key.

Without it, you can't expect to receive the response that you're after. So, within your social media plan, carve out a specific time to do this engagement.

The weekly tasks as Social Media and Patreon Manager included:

- Attend the R&D sessions to understand and contribute to the inspiration of the world of the play
- Begin to brainstorm exciting, relevant, added-value content and create first drafts for approval
- Receive cast headshots and short biographies to format into branded solo and group images for use on social media
- Create unique and engaging social media posts in relation to the upcoming show, such as recipes, dress codes, word of the week, cast announcements, and other highlights (e.g. countdowns, award nominations, Patreon and RedBubble promotions)
- Plan and execute exclusive content for our Patreon supporters (including, but not limited to, behind the scenes vlogs, rehearsal previews of the upcoming show, Q&As with members of the production team, prop tutorials, and *TSMGO* updates before they were publicly released)
- Communicate with cast members about engaging and sharing the content to put our name in front of their following, some of whom may have not heard about *TSMGO* yet
- Engage with audience response ahead of, during, and after the show, as well as highlighting notable reactions (such as fan art, reviews, etc)

Lessons Learned

As with all social media content, some posts worked more successfully than others. (I am defining "success" here as high engagement, in the form of likes, comments, and shares.) As part of the weekly process, it is key to note **what types of content receive the biggest reception**, and consequently, how that can be effectively used in future instances. For example, ahead of our production of *Hamlet*, we created digital newspaper headlines and articles to release before and during the show. The release of our pre-show headline (which in this context, pronounced the death of King Hamlet, later a key part of the plotline) received an overwhelmingly positive reaction. Whilst the mid-show content didn't perform as well (which we assessed was due to our followers being engaged with the show – still a good thing), we recognized **the power of setting the scene the day before** the live stream even began. When it seemed appropriate, we used this framework for shows later in the project with similar impact and reach. These posts can still be seen on our pages and remain among our best-performing content.

Over the course of our run, there was an ever-fluctuating fraction of audience members that weren't Shakespeare fans. They may have been Shakespeare-curious or perhaps have never experienced one of his plays before. Most often, they were watching or engaging to see someone in particular: someone they knew in the show or someone who was working behind the scenes. A key question that arose regarding those new, more casual audiences is: **how can you retain those one-off patrons to come back, or simply keep engaging with you online?**

As well as developing content that appeals to and engages your audience, you can develop opportunities for that audience to help promote the work. We were extremely lucky to have followers that took inspiration from the show in some way and created their own work in response to ours. From fan art to reviews to GIFs, **we established a dialogic relationship with audiences who were also creators**, generating shareable content that kept us top of mind between shows. Ksenia Nemchinova's GIF threads captured highlights from each show, from the joyful and comedic to the heartbreaking and tragic. This provided an excellent opportunity to promote the show in hindsight and drive new traffic to watch the stream on YouTube after it had aired live.

When working on something so new and ever-changing, the most valuable thing to remember is to **take everything one step at a time**. It's worth putting in the time to research, brainstorm, pitch, create, engage, and evaluate so that you can ensure a successful upward trajectory of content to run alongside your main product, which in our case, was the performance itself.

Every week, when meeting the cast at the meet-and-greet ahead of rehearsals, as "Social Media and Patreon Manager", I would be sure to say "You never know who might need *The Show Must Go Online*, but just doesn't know it exists yet. It's up to all of us to spread the word so that those people can join our community". This was perhaps the most useful thing I ever did, enfranchising those already most engaged with our work to help spread the word.

Social media, community engagement, and fundraising aren't a one-person job. Yes, it can be one person's job to create the content schedule and post, but it's up to the group (which in our case was a continually changing cast of creatives), to engage, share, and promote the project in order to grow a global reach. Throughout the endeavor, it was important for us to remind the world that even in the scariest of times where live theatre can't exist in its previous, more familiar form, there is Shakespeare here, and it is freely available for everyone.

Reinventing TSMGO for Sustainable Working – Matthew Rhodes

TSMGO Mark II was an essential part of the story for all of us, but features only in summary here, given the length of the book as a whole, and the volume of discoveries made during the initial run. Another book might well be written by the participants who came to TSMGO as part of what we described as its "franchise" stage. For now, I will look at the key changes this brought about from a strategic perspective, how these were absorbed or mitigated, and where we got to by the end of the run, so you can take these lessons forward and improve upon them further.

Once a tree has stopped growing up, it grows out.

Shortly after the First Folio series came to an end, we decided to offer a Christmas Special, and Ian Doescher offered us *William Shakespeare's A Christmas Carol*. Emily Ingram was chosen to direct, and this began a permanent shift in the scope of production, with Rob stepping back to assume the role of Artistic Director, so that emerging directors from underrepresented backgrounds could take the helm.

This new shift was evident in 2021, with productions of *Pericles* directed by Maryam Grace, John Lyly's *Gallathea* directed by Rachel "Rho" Chung, *Edward II* directed by Kevin V Smith, *Dido Queen of Carthage* directed by Amelia Parillon, *Doctor Faustus* directed by Fergus Rattigan and Emily Ingram, and a cabaret evening of new creative responses, *"Marlowe Lives"*, before concluding with the production I directed, *Two Noble Kinsmen*. 2021 was also marked by the initiation of the Groundlings' Choice Awards, produced by Ruth Page.

The production window for each project extended considerably, from weekly to around six weeks of pre-production (with the exception of the Marlowe productions, which saw the return of a weekly rotation for one month, but had different casts and creative teams attached, allowing for more pre-production time for each show, relative to the First Folio). However, instead of being contained within a small core team of five or six with some changes over time, lead creatives on the productions (directors, designers, and eventually producers) were externally sourced, with *TSMGO* core team members offering their support.

This "franchise" model utilized the templates, production practices, and performance techniques that *TSMGO* had solidified over the First Folio Series to support new productions and visions. The aim was to pass the baton of our progress to new directors to run with. Directors and other lead creatives from marginalized identities (inc. Global Majority, LGBTQIA2S+, Disabled, Emerging, etc.) were prioritized.

The franchise model was successful overall, with improvements to both organization and execution continually made over time.

Builds in Our Processes

Curation – while perhaps a minor change in the project, the move from producing according to a chronology of plays included in the First Folio to an individually curated "season" seemed to demand that there was a rationale and justification for each script selected. Directors interrogated the necessity of a given production, which led to the emergence of deeper, more personal, artistic choices as each team engaged with their respective texts.

Extended pre-production schedules – one of the most significant changes was the expanded pre-production time. Moving from a matter of days to almost two months gave directors, designers, and producers much more time for consideration, rest, and other work or projects. **Designing the pre-production period so that it accounted for other commitments improved the financial accessibility of the project.** This additional time was also used for discussions on how to continue creating brave spaces and expand our work on representation and accessibility.

However, this came with its own challenges: the perceived abundance of time and conflicting commitments between team members increased the frequency of meetings that ran long, missed communications and deadlines, and misunderstood designs and ideas. Some things continued to be rushed at the end as we filled gaps just in time. By dedicating time to share information and discoveries from meetings in accessible ways and then following up on said information, we kept the entire team engaged for subsequent productions, which improved matters as we learned to navigate the new normal. In this way, the franchise continued using each new production for constant improvement in the style developed during the First Folio Series.

Expanded teams – as we endeavored to engage with a greater number of underrepresented artists, and respect the long-range external demands on all artists involved, the size of the core production team increased. The larger team structure allowed productions to include roles and specialties as necessary for a given production, such as *Gallathea*'s embedded critic, Frey Kwa Hawking, or *Two Noble Kinsmen*'s Intimacy and Safety Consultant, Ella Mock.

One important expansion was the generosity of BSL/English Interpreter Janet Guest. Janet's commitment to attending rehearsal or watching recordings created excellent interpretations that seamlessly merged with the production, and her ability to translate throughout an entire production was similarly phenomenal.

The First Folio Series was a great collaboration of artists across disciplines, with artists building on or offering ideas outside of their discipline or responsibility, which allowed the best ideas to grow. As we continued to develop, we created artist teams on some productions to foster interdisciplinary collaboration. This helped artists build upon each other's experiences and collaborate with a shared language and understanding. Its success was seen in some way in every 2021 production, particularly in sound design, building on the Zoom expertise of Adam Gibson.

With expanded teams, we also discovered greater schedule and communication issues. Discussions between artists often didn't reach the wider team, or when they did, they were prone to misinterpretation. It also became more frequent to host meetings without some team members, which led to repeated discussions down the road. Sharing those discussions, discoveries, and decisions beyond those in meetings or group chats became even more important. Keeping those lines of communication open and recognizing the flexibility and commitment of team members helped us maintain a high standard of production.

Expanded rehearsal time – the average page count per hour covered in rehearsals dropped from eight pages an hour to a little over four pages an hour across each play, effectively doubling rehearsal time, and giving directors more time to work and run scenes.

We still only set one rehearsal for each scene. This felt important, because it continued *TSMGO's* capitalization on actors' creativity and their ability to play off impulse, but also demanded the director have a clear sense of the play from the beginning of rehearsal. The condensed schedule of the First Folio Series kept the play within the same world, while the extended schedule could cause the productions to grow and change over the additional time. This **concept creep** became a challenge at times, as some scenes were clearly rehearsed earlier or later in the schedule. To minimize this discrepancy, pre-rehearsal time was used to focus and summarize the director's vision.

Additionally, first read-throughs and dress rehearsals were introduced, first by Emily Ingram on *William Shakespeare's A Christmas Carol* by Ian Doescher. These were maintained thereafter, giving actors a first introduction to the overall shape of the play, then a private run-through under performance conditions to become comfortable and familiar with costume and set changes, technical requirements, and timing. This change relieved a great deal of nerves for performers and created more consistent and reliable performances. In this way, we became more conventional, using time-tested practices, since that additional production time made those practices more feasible.

Continuing innovation – innovation continued apace through this entire franchise model, with the core team supporting the creative ambitions of new voices with new techniques and even new software. *A Christmas Carol* introduced live video editing with Open Broadcast Software (OBS) (more discussed later), which was also used to create open captions for the 2021 productions. *Gallathea* pushed the bounds of sound design, choreo, and video. *Edward II* used the open captions to create a bilingual production, open captioning French lines into English. This was a different kind of innovation. The innovations we employed during the First Folio Series created solutions out of an *absence* of time and resources, testing them every show. As these "franchise" shows had more time but less pressure to constantly evolve, we had a chance to be more considerate; there was time to refine and hone previous discoveries. This is again reminiscent of the Pareto principle – streamlining to increase the effectiveness of each idea.

Paying people for their time, and asking the audience for a contribution – the two biggest changes we made were to request a contribution to access the production and to move from an opt-in hardship fund to an opt-out profit share.

Using a variety of pricing methods, *TSMGO* made an unequivocal statement asserting the value of its creations and co-creators. Access was granted through a mix of Patreon and Eventbrite, valued at just £5. Asking for a contribution in order to watch the performance meant that we lost some casual viewers, but it aligned with the commitment of most audience members.

Audience-generated revenue was used to compensate the artists for their time. While we must emphasize that the compensation was *not* proportional to their commitment, it *was* an important statement affirming that **art work *is* work**. While still pro bono for all involved, it was impactful for the morale of the team to be compensated in a small way.

The important balance of requiring contributions for the production to pass on to artists and wanting to limit barriers to access to art and creation was continuously interrogated during the franchise series, with various iterations of pay what you can, free archival access, and different recommended ticket prices explored.

Evolution of Our Tools

The most important tools in the production were the resources made during the First Folio Series, as you have read about previously.

Video tutorials – capitalizing on our previous success with prop tutorials and video tutorials, we expanded on this work for choreography.

Videos were an easy way to clarify the director's vision before the rehearsal calls, but more importantly, they gave the actors expectations for particular dance sequences so that they could learn and review choreography on-demand, to meet their individual needs. This focused rehearsal time on solidifying and sharpening moves and timing rather than learning from scratch. While this required time from the actors outside of rehearsal, prerecorded tutorials allowed performers to move and learn at their own pace.

Director onboarding – with each new director introduced, Rob would spend a two-hour session onboarding directors in the *TSMGO* conventions of blocking: the how and why, the tools Zoom had available, and how these had historically been deployed so that each director could make use of, flip, or evolve these conventions.

OBS – Open Broadcast Software (OBS) is a free and open-source software for video recording and live streaming, used extensively by people in the gaming community. Its use in digital theatre was pioneered by others, including alumna Victoria Rae Sook for *Food of Love* productions, but was too energy-intensive to use on the weekly schedule.

When we were no longer bound to the weekly schedule, we learned, explored, and deployed OBS on *A Christmas Carol,* to give Emily Ingram and the creative team more artistic control, particularly over Zoom tile placements. OBS was a clear artistic success with many unique effects (such as animating individual actors' tiles to enter and exit the virtual playing space by moving off the edges of the canvas, scaling them in three dimensions, colorizing the window with sepia to denote the past and more). These drew strong positive reactions from the audience, but it was clear that the time and energy requirements of undertaking this bespoke animation process for a longer show would be unsustainable.

Fortunately, Maryam Grace's desire for increased accessibility on *Pericles* highlighted the potential of OBS to support greater *accessibility* for the work, without the same level of bespoke programming required to use it artistically.

Using a technique called window-capture, we were able to pull together multiple elements from different sources and standardize a format that could be used for every show. OBS allowed us to display open captions for the scripted sections from a Word document, keep our interpreter Jan Guest in a fixed position on the screen at all times (an important bit of consistency for BSL-using audiences), and display Zoom's auto-captioning for the unscripted discussions.

While the control and malleability brought challenges such as relying on the focus, equipment, and internet connection of its operator, OBS became a key part of *TSMGO's* improved accessibility. This simplification was used to great effect however on *Edward II*, where a simple monochrome filter was added to stylize much of the piece.

Pronouns and representations – on *Gallathea*, Rachel "Rho" Chung and Emily Ingram offered artists the opportunity to share their pronouns in the press release and video description, further normalizing pronoun sharing and giving those who chose to share their pronouns an avenue to do so.

Rachel "Rho" Chung's mission to have a majority LGBTQIA2+ cast for *Gallathea* required gathering relevant information from applicants; their lived experience encouraged them to add a question allowing artists to fill in a text box with any identities they would like to be considered in their casting. This created space for artists to be able to self-identify, including identities around gender, sexuality, race, class, location, disability, neurodivergence, age, and more. Rather than fit themselves into prescribed boxes, this allowed artists to self-identify/self-describe, which amplified artist agency as *TSMGO* continued to create representative and diverse casts.

Organization tools – the longer production schedule and additional demands on larger teams meant that production requirements were easier to lose track of. While documents like the R&D document may have been easy to go back to a day or two after being created, resources eventually needed to be translated or remade into different forms for ease of communication and discussion. Additionally, new ideas discovered after the initial R&D would need to be shared and communicated in a clear way.

Tech lists for each sound cue were made for plays involving more complex sound design than just what is highlighted in the script. This was a concise list for moving through tech rehearsal.

Pinterest Boards, used on later productions in the First Folio Series, became an easy way for directors to communicate aesthetic and vision for their productions, as the production quality and artistic interpretation had more space to be stepped up.

While some tools, such as Trello, were useful for organizing processes, roles, and responsibilities, production teams often found it difficult to keep updated on completed actions. Ensuring that completed production resources were kept in a central location (a Google Drive, a director, a producer, or an email thread) was more helpful for tracking. Additionally, simply setting advanced deadlines for design elements or materials gave productions lead time and meant the time could be used for troubleshooting rather than procrastination.

Lessons Learned

While it is easier to adapt and grow by relying on single people to perform given functions, this causes problems when the situations of those people change. Our over reliance on me to operate OBS (and my stubbornness to hand the reins to others) created problems later down the line for projects. In design, this is known as a **Single Point of Failure (SPOF)**: a flaw in the design, configuration, or implementation of a system that poses a risk, because one malfunction or fault in one element could cause the whole system to stop working.

Simply put, if there is a linchpin holding things together, and that linchpin breaks, everyone is in trouble. **We should strive to design our teams and processes explicitly to avoid this problem** – especially in a pandemic world, where COVID-19 could come for anyone at any time.

Your team will be more flexible if it is able to adapt and respond to changes in circumstances *collectively*, rather than individually.

However, in seeking to spread responsibilities further afield, **handovers** were a crucial skill we needed to acquire, and sometimes pieces fell through the cracks. **If you have time, delineate and establish clear roles and responsibilities.** Miscommunications with guest speakers were made when those responsibilities were assumed to be handed off from Ben Crystal without a proper understanding of the communication, responsibilities, and expectations of the role, for example.

Opportunities found in artistic control and creation can be utilized for accessibility. **Accessibility will never be perfect and therefore must be a continuing process of improvement and refinement.** The same must be said of inclusion practices. It is an ongoing process, so do what you can, as soon as you can.

The final lesson we took away from diversifying and expanding the artistic team came from identifying what the true heart of the work was, and what core activities delivered that for audiences.

We continued to grow and succeed by honing, retaining, and democratizing the core elements of what made *TSMGO* what it was. It is easy for this to get tied up in the broader work being created, and when it does, it can feel like the success of a project is all or nothing.

Instead, creating, understanding, and maintaining **a plan that first identifies what elements are essential, and then prioritizes how to reliably achieve them,** insulates everyone from failure. This safety net gives you the freedom to then commit to your personal artistic touches and flourishes fully.

If you *do* have time, create your plan as if you *don't* have it, to ensure you achieve your most important elements first.

Key Themes and Take-Homes

Triangulation – understanding multiple perspectives on the work can clarify your own quicker than trying to originate it without a context. You are in conversation with those who came before you.

Give people every chance to get it right – when dealing with lots of people and information – clarity and simplicity, with a memorable presentation across multiple formats, will reduce error rates.

Streamlining – find every way you can to make processes lean. Every streamlined task frees up bandwidth for creativity.

Preparation breeds spontaneity – in the act of creating a detailed plan, you understand the possibilities more intimately, allowing you to better improvise when things go sideways.

Openness breeds flexibility – being too specialized can make you rigid, and rigidity can make us ask the wrong questions.

Have an outside eye on the inside – the North Star can help you navigate stormy seas only because it's in the sky, not in your pocket.

Do it, reflect, do it again – the bias to action is essential, you can always improve a work in progress.

Robust teams – no one person should be essential to success or failure: have role overlaps so people can fill in in the event of unforeseen events.

Note

1 Rob and Valerie wish to acknowledge their desire to refer to individuals according to those individuals' own preferences, which can vary. We recognize that in some cultures the preference is to use the phrase "disabled people", while in others the preference is to use "people with disabilities" instead. Here, the authors have chosen disabled people as that is more commonly preferred by those in the UK, where the majority of the core team hail from, and follows the social model of disability, in which individuals are considered to be disabled by society.

5
DIRECTING FOR DIGITAL

Digital theatre is its own medium, with its own unique demands.

There are as many different ways to create digital theatre as there are theatre companies producing digitally.

As we did in Chapter 3, this chapter will be for us to identify overarching concepts that will help directors to make meaningful and practical decisions that serve their own artistic vision and use the ways that *The Show Must Go Online* (*TSMGO*) navigated these areas to illustrate the process in practice.

The aim is always to inspire theatremakers, in the spirit of *TSMGO*, to forge their way through uncharted territory. By the time you read this, there will inevitably be new possibilities that might have entirely changed the course of how *TSMGO* operated had they been available at the time. What I hope to awaken in you is the same innovative essence that made *TSMGO* possible: the ability to think beyond tried and true practices and adapt to whatever limitations you find yourself facing.

For this chapter, we'll look at how to start practically, then run the possibilities you've generated through the prism of your values to determine what approach works best in the given circumstances. We'll also look at how **systemizing our thinking and values** helped *TSMGO* to optimize this process over time.

TSMGO transformed the practices familiar to live theatremaking by borrowing from the time-tested methodologies used in other media, including Film, TV, and Radio. When establishing what would work and how, we used a values-led approach to better navigate possibilities and tensions and stay true to our vision in a way that kept the team positively

DOI: 10.4324/9781003289906-6

motivated in service of shared goals. We hope that by the end of the chapter, you'll be able to do the same.

Before we begin to unpack some of the *practicalities* of directing theatre for a digital platform, it's important to consider *why* you want to make something in the first place. Can you answer the following?

1 *Who are you?*
2 *What matters to you? What moves you most in life? In art?*
3 *What would you want to see in the world that's currently missing?*
4 *Who do you want your audience to be?*
5 *What do you want them to think/feel/do?*
6 *Based on the answers above, what is the project?*
7 *What is the mission? What does success look like?*
8 *What are the project's values? How can you articulate the intersection between those values and the given practicalities?*

Knowing who you are, what you value, how you envision your work within the larger theatrical community (both local and global), and how you shape that work through your own personal artistic process will help determine how you address each of the challenges that will inevitably arise as you shift the storytelling practices in which you have been trained to future novel modes of performance.

For *TSMGO*, the novel platform was Zoom, which is now anything but novel after reaching ubiquitous status during the COVID-19 global pandemic.

Having a clear vision, strong values, and a well-defined aesthetic helped *TSMGO* navigate through uncharted territory and make meaningful decisions that served the series and enabled it to grow and thrive. The same will be true for you if you understand clearly what you aim to do and why you're doing it.

TSMGO was also willing to **leap in before being fully ready**; what in design thinking is known as a *bias to action*. Unlike in a typical innovation process, there was no time for lengthy research into how other digital theatre artists may have been making work. When *TSMGO* launched, we knew of **no readily available examples** of digital theatre that modeled what we wanted to create. While *TSMGO* may not have been the first to experiment with Zoom as a theatrical medium, we were starting from scratch in interpreting how this new way of working could be made to serve the dramatic purposes we intended, and we had a matter of days to do so. We did this in tandem with casting, rehearsing, and setting up for success for the following nine-month run. It may sound absurdly simple, but it can be liberating to remember that **the most important thing you can do is *start*.**

So, how do we start?

Into the Unknown – Exploring a New Performance Medium

Before you begin directing for a new medium, you'll need to consider:

- What are the unique parameters of the form/medium and how do those interface with our dramaturgical needs?
- What limitations the cast and creatives will encounter, and how might we navigate through those?
- What ancillary forms/mediums might we borrow from to help us navigate through this unknown territory?

In the case of *TSMGO*, the medium in question was Zoom. Why?

Remember, at the time this decision was made, Zoom was *not* the ubiquitous platform it is today. Sarah and Rob had some experience using Zoom as a conferencing tool in their innovation work for multinationals, and knew the platform had some basic functionality that could be manipulated. Beyond that, cursory research suggested we could either have the audience in the room with us, or we could livestream to YouTube.

We chose to livestream to YouTube so that our audience could engage with us through a platform that was familiar to them at the time; there was no learning curve on their part which enhanced our commitment to accessibility. Using YouTube had other benefits, too. As we introduced in Chapter 2 and will explore in detail in Chapter 6, YouTube would enable our audiences to engage with one another in ways that a live direct-engagement via Zoom would not. What's more, Zoom's meeting rooms limited their numbers to one hundred attendees unless using the webinar feature, which robbed us of some key ways of working. Often we had in excess of twenty cast members, and hundreds watching at home.

Let's go through the process of how we explored our options, to see how we arrived at a working model.

Drawing Context from Other Worlds

When deciding how to tackle Zoom, we took an innovation principle in hand and **sought out related worlds.**

The question was: *where else had theatre been taken out of its standard context and performed in new ways in new mediums?*

The most apparent answer to this question was **site-specific theatre.** Site-specific theatre must respond elastically to the unique properties of the space it occupies.

One of the first processes of any site-specific site visit is to audit the space:

- What are the *opportunities* – what does it *give* you?
- What are the *barriers* – how does it *limit* you?

Once you understand these opportunities and barriers, you can begin to respond to these aspects in the work, to the uniqueness of the space's aesthetic or history, and allow that to shape the way the art is made within it.

Zoom, however, has very little in the way of aesthetic or history. It is a utilitarian tool that aims to be as intuitive and unobtrusive as possible. Nevertheless, it had unique mechanics and functions that made sense to deploy in specific contexts in order to maximize our potential for creating a shared experience. These were our **opportunities.**

We had two primary elements that Zoom afforded – toggling cameras and mics off and on, and toggling between gallery view and speaker view. We could map their functions onto our existing theatrical vocabulary in order to create an experience that was at once analogous to theatre in some respects, while remaining novel from it in others.

So, we had functions that could shape **what the audience saw** and how they experienced the visuals that came onto their screens. Zoom also had functions that enabled us to shape a particular soundscape – however rudimentary it may have been, in order to control **what the audience heard**.

We quickly learned through practice how to adapt these two primary functions for our storytelling purposes: to create theatricality out of Zoom's practicality. The camera could easily be turned on and off to allow actors to make entrances and exits, and we could toggle between the types of screen views to create a particular effect. Actors could create a backstage space by keeping the microphone unmuted for moments where characters call out from the wings. Gallery view allowed us to represent multiple people in the space at the same time, turning the black rectangle of Zoom's central reservoir into the playing space.

Speaker view, by contrast, meant whoever was speaking would dominate the screen and relegate everyone else to thumbnails. We considered this view, which enabled audiences to see a speaker more prominently, as a possible standard default view. Through experimentation, we felt it relegated the other people in the scene in a way that felt undemocratic;

in-person audiences can select where to place their attention and we wanted to ensure that our digital spectators were afforded the same agency. Our experience in the theatre reminded us that in the scenes we were to create, observing the listener(s) is every bit as important to the story and the audience's experience, as focusing on the speaker. While utilizing speaker view is perfectly acceptable for business meetings and lectures, in performance it affected the dynamics differently; it meant that every speech was inadvertently given a "close-up". Speaker view deprived us of the ability to explore scaling and spatial relationships by centralizing one viewpoint.

By contrast, **gallery view** presented different barriers: the more people were on stage, the smaller they were in appearance. As a result, there was a diffusion in group scenes that actors speaking would have to fight against – the classic *forum* where speakers and their ideas must compete for attention and energy, to take and hold attention. This became a **useful problem** for actors to overcome, activating their character's *need to speak* in a way that was sympathetic to early modern performance.

When making practical decisions as a team, we (Sarah and Rob) found it necessary to view the opportunities, barriers, and their respective workarounds from multiple vantage points in order to make informed decisions; to weigh the consequences of each choice so that we aligned our decisions with our values, vision, and how we defined our process. Taking a cue from the field of commercial innovation, we built, refined, and evolved our ideas by starting with the "why" – that the "product", here the given show on a given week, was an expression of values in action. In innovation, the idea of **creating rough prototypes and iterating rapidly** comes from the notion that you learn more by *doing* – in many ways, every show was a prototype for the next. This is what's we'll referred to in this book as **"formula as a friend"**.

Like all research through practice, we were constantly reflecting and refining in real time to arrive at a decision that allowed us to move forward, one step at a time. Throughout our initial explorations, we had to consciously consider how to translate the expertise we brought with us (in this case, staging multiple live bodies in a three-dimensional space) into the two-dimensional digital arena.

For example, just as we'd discovered the complexities involved with staging groups of actors in a scene together, we discovered the opposite was also true: **when the stage emptied each individual commanded more real estate**, meaning Soliloquies – when the actor is alone with the audience – could now command the close-up. This made perfect dramaturgical sense. The soliloquy is when a character is closest to the audience, opening up their subconscious challenges and examining, heart-on-sleeve, what they should do next. Here, we judged the barriers of *gallery* view as **helpful limitations**, while the barriers of *speaker* view felt like unhelpful hindrances when viewed through the lens of early modern performance. Knowing the desired output helped us audition choices and make clear decisions on them quickly. The deciding factor was how the practicalities interacted with and helped to express our values.

To illustrate the role of values in decision-making, we include the same process of expansive possibility and reductive evaluation on another popular feature of Zoom: virtual backgrounds (VBGs).

Example Debate – Do We Use Virtual Backgrounds?

There were other options within Zoom that were attractive to the magpie sensibility in us all – the feature of Virtual Backgrounds (VBGs). VBGs in particular seemed to tempt many into its web of problems. The VBG feature allowed users to replace their actual background with an image or video from their hard drive and rear-project it behind and around them, as a kind of rudimentary green screen, which allowed for immediate possibilities to transport people into shared locations, otherworldly contexts, and add what seemed at first glance like a premium gloss of "production value".

Yet we decided never to use them in that way. Why?

Opportunities and Barriers

When experimenting with VBGs, the **opportunities** were initially enticing: one could create an immediate sense of a shared world across massive distances. It could allow for fantastic backdrops that no jobbing actor would have readily to hand. However, even this quickly seemed to collapse under its own weight of issues.

First, there was a "tearing" around the edges of the body, especially around fine details such as fingers, which were often "webbed" by the background of the room beyond as the software struggled to fill in every tiny gap. Lighting was often drastically mismatched between background and subject, making them feel disembodied in space. What's more, without going to a location, plotting where in that shared space each actor would stand, and photographing from a central point the same forest, say, from multiple angles, it would be a significant feat to create something that felt immersive or even cohesive. The idea of object permanence (i.e. that this space exists without the actors who occupy it) seemed never to be in scope. The *uncanny valley* is a concept borrowed from visual effects, in which the closer something unreal gets to photo-real, the more unsettling it becomes to us as viewers. VBG's had this same problem, with backgrounds often more high quality than the webcam resolutions of the actors in front of them.

Even if all this *could* be achieved, the **barriers** were still multifarious – it would take away camera movement, as the background would remain static and at a fixed distance no matter what the actor or their camera did. To make these backgrounds function effectively with a combination of object permanence, navigation, parallax, and lighting was more akin to video game design (or the kind of "volume" staging famously deployed in *The Mandalorian* using Unreal Engine, where a concave rear-projection screen would adjust the background dynamically in response to camera movement, to maintain relative position and create the illusion of a seamless expanse that remains "objective" to the audience), and would require time, budget, software, and hardware integration we simply did not have.

So, do we want glossy, fantastical worlds on demand or a greater number of more rudimentary tools such as proxemics, lighting, and camera movement? The values decide.

Values

When we set about to stage Shakespeare's First Folio digitally, we used the concepts of Original *Parallels*, as differentiated from the movement known as Original Practice (OP).

Original Practice is informed by and large by an attempt at historical authenticity (or an approximation of such) in performance, though different practitioners define "OP" in different ways. Theatremakers dating back to William Poel in the nineteenth century have explored how they might forge deeper connections to Shakespeare by exploring Shakespeare's performance conditions. In the later part of the twentieth century, "OP" became particularly popular after the performance experiments at Shakepseare's Globe, where Mark Rylance, Jenny Tiramani, and Claire Van Kampen were working to explore "OP" in response to the reconstructed playhouse. Others working with similar aims to recapture some of Shakespeare's performance conditions preceded Shakespeare's Globe, such as Christine Ozanne and Patrick Tucker's First Folio and cue script work with the Original Shakespeare Company. Today, we recognize "OP" productions with a number of identifiable elements: they are often all male (frequently all white) casts – though this can vary; they often feature Elizabethan costumes, historical movement, dance, and fencing practices, and sometimes feature a very different "OP": original pronunciation, reconstructed by David & Ben Crystal. "OP" looks at the parameters of the historical performance paradigm to inform how Shakespeare's plays are staged and performed today. Under the umbrella of "OP", productions might either seek faithful representations of performance conditions original to Shakespeare's acting company or make aesthetic choices that are based on and inspired by any number of elements that identify with "OP".

Original Parallels uses more interpretative methods to look at the *principles* that informed OP and how they might inform staging today. As is the case with OP, these *Parallels* can also share common principles among practitioners, who are governed by similar forces and interpret them through their own lenses.

Since collective imagination was at the forefront of Shakespeare's theatremaking ("Think when we talk of horses, that you see them"), *Original Parallels* embraces transparency and democracy throughout.

As Shakespeare's "players" could embody any gender, so today's actors need not be limited by their biological sex.

> **Aside**. We can (and did) take this further into all facets of identity, so that Shakespeare's characters can be embodied by any actor; if you are capable of making the argument, you are capable of playing the character. In the past, this has been done in both a "blind" way, where the personal identity of the actor is supposed to have no affect on the character, and then in "conscious" ways, which acknowledges the real effect different facets of identity have on the interpretation of characters. We now know that any attempts to "unsee" the personal attributes of an actor's identity essentially aims to reduce them to a white, cishet, able-bodied figure (and we would point to Ayanna Thompson's work on this subject). *TSMGO* itself began with identity-blind casting out of necessity and rapidly evolved toward more identity-conscious casting over its lifespan, in keeping with its pursuit of greater and better inclusion.

As Shakespeare himself was an innovator, using the latest technologies available in order to maximize theatrical effects, so, too, would we; like Shakespeare, we too would be shaped by the limitations we faced.

As Shakespeare's actors wore contemporary clothing, so could we. As Shakespeare aimed to capture the world around him, so would our ensembles reflect the world around us: a globalized, diversified world that "holds the mirror up to nature".

By using these and other *principles* to establish a sandbox for performance which is *in sympathy with* the original work, but not limited by the extent of Elizabethan advancements, we can innovate without having to lose the essence of what makes these plays apparently infinitely reproducible.

Where site-specific work gave us a vocabulary to interpret the digital venue of Zoom, this commitment to original parallels – to take what is useful, consider which parallels resonate and why, and deploy new equivalents in new contexts – gave us a methodology for practically staging the texts within that venue.

In the case of VBGs, we looked to the "great Globe itself", and to the work of traveling players before and since. In most early modern productions, there was little idea of a "set". While certain items may have been brought onto stage and taken away, the stage itself would remain largely as it was found, whether that stage was an inn-yard (the template for the later purpose-built theatres) or an auditorium.

Two other **values** of Original Practice, vital to how we approached things, were the principles of **shared space** and **shared light**. You may remember we identified these in our "what makes theatre theatre?" section in Chapter 1.

In Shakespeare's theatre, the audience could be seen by the actors and vice versa; the audience was a co-equal branch of the storytelling process. We believe wholeheartedly that Shakespeare works best when both the actors and their characters know the audience is there and choose to work with them; that they occupy the same space, practically, physically, and emotionally.

If this is the case, then what better way to *parallel* the properties of shared space and shared light than *being honest with the audience* and having our actors perform their pieces in their unadorned bedrooms and living rooms? The *very same place* the audience was watching from?

Our lighting was created using room lights, desk lamps, and computer screens. Our sets were bookcases, sofas, and dining tables. Our costumes were old clothes, towels, and bedsheets. Our allegiance to the principles of original parallels meant that we would expose the mechanics of our theatremaking to create a shared experience where all participants were responsible for contributing to the storytelling experience, imaginatively and figuratively. In doing so, we could acknowledge the reality in which we were telling these stories – at home, often in lockdown, and create a shared experience through our digital connection.

Finally, a critical part of our mission was also to **democratize Shakespeare and to make it** *accessible* – not only to those viewing it but also to those *making* it. It was our mission to bring together actors from around the globe, at all different levels of experience. In order to do so, it was important that people could do this simply with what they had readily available to them at home – no green screens, no expensive cameras, and no investment other than the time and passion people were willing to give.

And so, while we *did* deploy VBGs in unconventional ways – such as to create bodies of fire and ash for the fiery demons taunting Joan La Pucelle or to give Dumaine an invisibility cloak, we never used them for their intended, scenic purposes. This is another important point: just as this project had many unintended consequences, **hacking tools to produce unintended effects** is always more surprising and delightful for audiences than using them as designed. How can you use the features you can't change in ways people wouldn't expect?

Here, we see how our values, both **dramaturgically and communally**, determined the artistic output. It mattered to us that the audience knew the artists were having the same experience they were.

Our actors had homes just like yours or, perhaps, they were even more humble. Our actors had webcams and laptops and connection issues, just like yours. Our actors had limited resources, like millions of other people facing financial uncertainty as a result of the pandemic. This rawness, this deliberate and honest imperfection, spoke more powerfully to the time and circumstance of the art being made than any attempt to overcome it with gloss. Simply, creating *empathy* between actor and audience was more important than impressing the audience with flash. Our "promise of value" came not from production value, but from a real (albeit sometimes unstable) connection.

What we couldn't necessarily anticipate, but was proven true in the playing, was the powerful impact this had on imaginative co-creation. The most quoted line of Shakespeare's by theatremakers themselves is surely "let us ... on your imaginary forces work" (*Henry V*, prologue). Things like virtual backgrounds may give the art the veneer of the "premium", but ultimately forces the audience's mind to take a backward step.

We urged our audiences to step forward, "unto the breach", to return to the idea of a collective imagination. As was the case with Shakespeare's audience, our audience was critically necessary in the worldbuilding. We implored them to "piece out our imperfections", to embrace that – despite engaging in a digital medium – this was *not* film, where the world would be realistically laid out for them, but a theatre of the imagination, just as Shakespeare's had been.

In our earlier productions, we found that we relied heavily on our audience to fill in the blanks, and as we grew in confidence and skill, we experimented with more cinematic qualities, though we always strove for "freedom in your choice" for the audience. The open plane of Zoom's black rectangle, filled with characters listening and reacting, allowed the audience to check in with whatever character they felt compelled by at any time.

And thus, the fundamentals of this new space were created: on and off stage, how the playing space would be used, and what features would *not* be used in creating it.

Developing a Shared Language

Cultivating the Sandbox of Our New Zoom Space

In directing for digital, we quickly realized that identifying these fundamentals was only the beginning. Having drawn the edges of our particular sandbox, we now had to play within it. The interaction between our governing principles and each play's requirements generated new problems on an almost weekly basis; we were challenged to embody a three-dimensional, physical story within what is essentially a disembodied, two-dimensional, digital medium.

In mapping live theatre onto a digital platform, a range of questions arose:

- How do we navigate the practicality of using scripts in a performance setting?
- How do actors receive their cues; how do you simulate a backstage line of communication?
- Who on stage was a part of a conversation, and who wasn't?
- When is a character speaking to the audience, and when are they speaking to other characters on stage?
- How do we show a difference in height between characters?
- How do we create levels of staging?
- How do we fluidly create status and develop the "push and pull" of scenes?
- How do we differentiate between public and private moments?
- How do we separate locales and make them feel different?

Before we could begin to answer these, we needed to identify: how our values interact with the parameters of the platform in order to determine what we could accomplish. You will need to do the same when creating new work in new media.

Setting the Eyeline

Stoicism asks you to think in all circumstances: what *can* you do? And let go of the rest. This is an excellent mindset for creating theatre in crisis.

Perhaps the first and most important of these (an area that might be universally applicable) was resolving a functional grammar of eyelines. Our shows needed to be read to be performed, to stay true to the text in the extremely short turnaround times. In this medium, this presented an **opportunity**. Unlike traditional readings or workshops where the audience can see the script in the actor's hand, the ways in which we established the grammar of eyelines had the effect of making the script entirely invisible, which meant the piece could still be received as a performance in earnest.

Meanwhile, a standard off-camera eyeline (looking off to the side, as happens in documentary interviews and "over the shoulder" shot setups) had **barriers**. Zoom would not produce people's "tiles" in any discernible order. In gallery view, actors' images would appear differently on each person's display, which differed still from the livestream that YouTube presented to the audience. The randomization of this meant that trying to create eyelines "between frames" was impossible in all but highly specialized circumstances, without the later intervention of an intermediary platform like OBS (to be discussed in a later chapter). So if an actor decided to look off to the left of camera, Zoom may place the person spoken to on their right, so it would look to the audience like that actor was looking away from the person they were addressing. Or worse, the person spoken to could be above or below them, so the "eyeline" would never match up.

Even if it *could* be achieved, looking off-camera would then need to be done at such steep angles (90 degrees or so) that it would create a disconnect between actors and audience. The shared space would not allow for such a fourth wall.

Looking again at **related worlds**, it became immediately apparent that we were working now in the **language of the camera**. Framing, movement, and eyeline were all intrinsically more the domain of film and television, so we looked to those fields to evaluate these options.

The best solution appeared to be "on autocue" – a process of scrolling the heavily annotated script as closely to the camera as possible to maintain the illusion of eye contact with the camera (we'll talk about that annotation process later in this chapter).

The open-faced, forward-looking feel of the autocue performance method, where the camera served to represent the eyeline of the person being spoken to, put us in mind of the Coen Brothers, who often place the camera *in between* interlocutors in a scene. The classic "over shoulder" framing used in most dialogue scenes places the audience *outside*, as voyeurs of the conversation. By placing the camera between speakers, we are locked into the conversation, at the heart of the action.

Similarly, the British TV comedy *Peep Show* found success using the camera to represent the eyeline of the characters in the scene, meaning we watch the show in the first person. This very successfully created an audience complicity in the experience of the characters, going a step beyond the "fly on the wall" experience of a voyeur. The *Peep Show* audience adopted the characters' physical view, and in being spoken to *as* them, were also invited to adopt their subjective viewpoint psychologically as well.

Let us return to the values: since so much of Shakespeare is based on making an argument that appeals simultaneously to the other characters and the audience, placing the audience at the heart of the action and **inviting them to see the show from each character's perspective** (something not possible on a conventional stage) felt like it best expressed the values of the project.

Once we aligned the practicality with our performance philosophy, we considered how to use the camera, through static angles, through movement, and through the framing of objects within the rectangle the audience could see us through, to create a visual language for this new medium.

Creating Spatial Relationships and Dynamics

The first need was a system of proxemics (how space between actors assists audiences in understanding their relationships) that worked for the medium and would teach the audience rules and conventions that they could follow. As we played with proxemics, we explored what else could be defined more clearly within Zoom's limitations.

- When a character leans to one side, presses in close, lowers their voice, and eyeballs the camera, this signals the audience that what follows is an aside
- If two characters do this, we understand they are speaking to one another, unheard by others on the stage. This effect can be heightened as other characters step back in their respective frames, upping the contrast

- Tipping the camera back and placing it lower than the actor allowed them to tower high above the eyeline, making them seem tall, remote, or simply on a raised piece of staging depending on the context
- Conversely, having the camera above characters looking down helped when characters in *Titus Andronicus* fell down a hole, when Henry V faced up to the walls of Harfleur, or when emphasizing Hermia's shortness
- Our physical vocabulary enabled us to define the staging even more deliberately, and we became more adept at doing so as the series progressed
- Distance from the camera also allowed us to demonstrate shifts in relationship, whether a character was speaking publicly to a large crowd, interpersonally within a space, or privately
- A simple shifting of the weight from one foot to another to tilt the character toward one edge of the frame marked a shift in who was being spoken to – complimented by the active listener stepping forward to engage, this shift established the new connection being made

As our confidence grew and actors returned more familiar with these basic conventions, we were able to push the envelope and create fluid blocking in scenes which relied upon shared constants – door frames, sofas, clean walls, tables, and more were available in almost everyone's space and could be deployed to collapse the real distance between our actors (often hundreds or thousands of miles) to create the illusion of shared space.

As we became more proficient with the basic setups, we could explore and expand beyond our standard uses of technology and space.

Holding the laptop in what we called "pizza box" mode, with a hand supporting the base, actors were able to scroll their text with the other hand while waltzing with the camera, turning, closing in, or creating distance in time with one another to further the idea of navigating a single space together – Isabella and Angelo's interview in *Measure for Measure*, and Iachimo and Imogen's first encounter in *Cymbeline* spring to mind as clear examples of how *TSMGO* was learning to expand our use of possible staging conventions to create even more dynamic digital viewing experiences.

If you want to understand more about how we achieved our theatrical effects through a sandbox approach, you can watch a full walkthrough of the tutorial videos shared with our actors before the first rehearsal by scanning these QR codes.

134 Directing for Digital

FIGURE 5.1 Zoom Tutorial QR Code (bit.ly/tsmgotutorial).

FIGURE 5.2 Screen SetUp Tutorial QR Code (bit.ly/tsmgoscreen).

Leadership in Collaboration

Framing the Process for Actors and Audiences

TSMGO was an entirely voluntary effort from all involved, and as a result, everything on the show became about using time efficiently.

When it comes to the process of directing for digital, it is critical to develop a shared language, conventions, and skills as *fast* as possible.

In practical terms, this meant a rapid, compressed video walk-through for participants before the first rehearsal began of every key discovery that had been made to date. Once we established the vocabulary with which we would work, we found that we could streamline the introduction to this material by creating a stand-alone video that outlined all of the important components that would be integrated and utilized in a given production. The video was roughly 40 minutes long and showed where to find the tools within Zoom that we would use, how to manipulate your space and your laptop, and how to manipulate these variables to create certain effects. Everything we did would then be a variation on these themes, so we wouldn't be asking m/any actors to start completely from scratch when a complex set-piece or blocking convention came along.

We must acknowledge, this front-loading of information was by no means everyone's preferred way of working, but the necessity to save time meant that even those who had not reviewed the materials prior to starting rehearsal could be signposted to the appropriate place in the on-boarding video and instructional email as the need arose. Those who had done the prep in advance were by and large more successful because they were able to focus their attention on the performance rather than learning the "rig". Associate Producer Matt Rhodes quickly assumed the mantle of taking those who hadn't had the opportunity to check the material into breakout rooms to upskill them while rehearsals proceeded.

It was important for us to organize our time well and create efficient systems that would make working on a regular basis with limited time effective and productive. As the show evolved, we introduced a first meeting post-casting and pre-rehearsal in which we could invite initial impressions, themes, and responses to the play from the cast, and use these as a platform to discuss, evolve and workshop the ideas we had planned in the research and development phase. It was a time to unify the ensemble behind a shared vision and a shared goal, to set expectations for certain characters or scenes, and to give people a last chance to prepare anything they might need for certain sessions in the schedule.

Our convention was to host a dedicated set-piece rehearsal on a Sunday afternoon, which allowed us to summit the most complex sequences for that week's show and enabled the actors involved to maximize their prep time before performing it live for the audience.

The way we workshopped and delivered these weekly setpieces was by and large informed by the audience, who responded with enthusiasm to technical innovations, bits, and gimmicks. Part of the hook for weekly audiences was seeing how the team would tackle the especially challenging staging moments of familiar plays via the medium of Zoom.

By using an iterative, cumulative approach – again, formula as a friend with a bias to action – we were able to use the audience's expectation for us to constantly evolve how we delivered Shakespeare's growing staging ambitions as a motivation for our team.

We felt that in order to retain our audience, part of what would keep people coming back would be to create novel experiences week after week; an incredibly difficult task to try and achieve. We also knew that our audience was being trained in what to expect, and could follow the development of conventions as they evolved, piece by piece. The live chat gave us feedback on what exactly was working, and what did not, allowing us to pivot effectively, and also to defy our own conventions to create additional surprises.

Cultivating Creative Agency

Actors were asked to navigate our intense on-boarding followed by throwing themselves into an equally intense rehearsal period, with very little time to prepare by conventional standards. Our actors were volunteering their time and talent to the project; we felt it was paramount that everyone felt their work was valued and had value, to us and the audience. As such, **respect** had to be the foundational principle of working together. This is something that should extend to all collaboration, everywhere, but it bears emphasizing.

Another useful maxim we relied on was to trust the "wisdom of crowds" – in computing terms, having more processors crunching the problem would result in better answers faster than a more traditional approach in which the director stands atop a pyramid of power dynamics. Flattened hierarchies meant everyone was trusted to be responsible for their own roles, and individuals had the power to affect the specific direction in any given sequence of moments, even if the overall trajectory had previously been set by the creative team.

In a limited time, we also had to choose what to prioritize when it came to the vision and execution of a given production, which left plenty of room for individual interpretation in terms of standard modern acting questions like backstory, motivation, and so on. As these components were not conventional to early-modern theatre practices, we focused as a team on the particular challenges of the text as written, while the actors had agency in determining their character's personal history and motivation.

As a production team, we made it our mission to navigate the play's apparent dramatic intention, staying as truthful to that as we could while integrating a forward-looking, progressive philosophy.

We aimed to create a sandbox and invite the cast to play within it. What they made could be original and exciting, but it would still need to sit within the confines that held the show together and made it a cohesive and identifiable production. This process was honed as the shows went on, and we discovered what the actors responded positively to. All creativity thrives in constraint, and we were in the business of identifying helpful constraints.

In Shakespeare, a powerful tool that is often modeled by the characters themselves is the "if/then" device, which asks "if this, then what?". We used this principle to unify the actors by providing the "if", so that their individual preparation "then" responds to the dynamics of the scene.

In decision-making, we always grounded the work in the text and in conveying the sense – if choices went awry or in conflict with the sense of the scene, we would realign around this in the room, making the minimum tweaks and reframes to preserve as much ownership as possible while always seeking to serve the audience and the text first. This was a useful arbiter, as it took individual agenda out of the running. If one could explain and support a textual interpretive choice sufficiently so that most would agree, that carried the motion for how that moment would be played.

Actor Emilio Vieira described the rehearsal process as "the Octagon of ideas", where pitches could fight it out and the strongest would win. We evolved this to take the violence out of it because, while exhilarating and high stakes, the process was never combative. The magic of these times came from the fact that if anyone fought, we were all fighting for the show.

All Shakespeare is an argument (which is not, as it is sometimes taken today, synonymous with fighting), and so integrating argument as part of the *process* was an immensely useful parallel. Productive, constructive arguments, driving toward the same ambitions but from different perspectives, contexts, and clues, could unlock far more creative responses than a single top-down definitive ever could. Actor training has traditionally centered on creating actors that are pliable and responsive, a quintessential team player. While some have interpreted this as "show up, shut up, move up", or excessive agreeableness, we defined it as having space and permission to question the prevailing perspective and fight for the best version of the play. We found that a centered knowledge of the self, the skills, the context, and an acknowledgment of the value each individual brought to the table was empowering, and moreover, essential when interpreting Shakespeare and the problems inherent in early modern culture with a modern cohort of actors.

Eliminating a top-down hierarchy was particularly valuable when exploring characters from marginalized groups and ensuring the inclusion of perspectives from a variety of actors of diverse backgrounds and lived experiences. In order to hold up our value of inclusivity as a governing principle, inclusivity of perspective was essential. As such, we aimed always to create a collaborative space in which challenging the prevailing logic was not just acceptable but encouraged. This was vital to navigating many of the plays that presented difficult interpretive challenges at speed.

- Sally McLean and Miguel Perez are both veteran actors on the biggest stages in their respective countries, and when playing the leads in *Taming of the Shrew*, were given the freedom to determine their interpretations of these characters and, by extension, their interrelationship. Both found softer interpretations in the playing than some of the horrifying implications the text can be taken to, but key passages unlocked and supported this – namely, that Petruchio put himself through the same deprivations as he put Kate through during the taming, and that her resistance counter-tortured him by extension. Similarly, Sally felt Kate learned she would rather be happy than right, and that compromise is essential to all relationships. While other interpretations are of course valid and powerful, the agency of the actors was critical in a play this problematic, because otherwise actors will quickly be forced into situations that represent dangerous, triggering, and abusive spaces. To step back from these extremes in a comedy, in a pandemic, was a choice that did not ignore the problems of the play, but engaged with them in a way that offered a more sober, more mature version of the characters
- In *Measure for Measure*, Isabella and Claudio were both played by Black actors. In the play, Claudio is imprisoned and sent to execution by an extreme new leadership, which prosecutes him for extramarital sex, a "crime" committed readily by many other members of that society. This race-conscious interpretation invited the audience to draw parallels between the play's world and the very real and disproportionate imprisonment of Black people. When it came to the playing of this, I suggested that the character rage against the machine and call out the injustice, but actor Michael Ahomka Lindsay, cast as Claudio, challenged the idea. He knew how anger is interpreted differently from a Black man, and knew that his character's best chance lay in keeping that contained. It made the scene all the more real and affecting

These kinds of actor-driven debates were prevalent throughout the development of *The Merchant of Venice*. We had cast four actors from the Jewish diaspora, as well as actors from the Global Majority in key roles. The initial idea of "following the dramatic intention" led us to an attempt that kept Portia out of the worst of the Christian prejudice and

gave us *someone* to root for – the fantastical otherness of the princess in a tower on a remote island, who disguises herself to expose the corrupt nature of the law by proving at once both Shylock's rights and wrongs was a tempting one. But in the playing, it caused more problems than it solved – Portia is too inextricably connected to the malice of the Christian action in the play for her to escape. Conversations with Tiffany Abercrombie, playing Portia, Amelia Parillon, playing Nerissa, Sophie Max, playing Jessica, and David Djemal, playing Lorenzo, went late into the night as we revised our approach in light of their responses to the Trial scene. In presenting the court as corrupt and Portia as the one to expose the limitations of the law, we pulled the focus away from what Shylock had to reckon with and even felt in danger of trying to "solve racism" by simplistically laying blame on the prevailing authorities while letting individuals off the hook. We then re-played it the following day with these shifts in mind and created what David and Sophie felt was a "reclamation" of the play for the Jewish community. No community is a monolith, and others disagreed over the interpretation, but the people making the play could stand by what they performed and could therefore be confident in inhabiting their storytelling choices
- *Much Ado About Nothing* represented a teachable failure in this regard – it was the most ambitious "concept" of the First Folio run, seeing the show through a spy-spoof, espionage lens. The cast was presented with a highly developed idea of exactly how the play could align with this vision but weren't given much room to play within the sandbox owing to the scale of ambition for what we wanted to achieve in the time allotted. Consequently, many ideas felt flat or were not run with, because some actors either did not feel ownership over these choices or feel confident in their playing, and we could not help to get them to that point in time. This subsequently affected how we approached the shows that came after it

As a creative team, we set a course for a destination, and that destination was the experience we wanted the audience to have; the lens through which they would view the play. How we plotted that course and how we navigated the various challenges we encountered on the way was entirely collaborative, and *TSMGO* was so much the better for it. We came to understand that the vision of an auteur was not possible or preferable in this context and that making space for **the lived experiences and insights of others in the team as they interacted with the text had a prismatic effect**, splitting open the raw material to provide a much greater spectrum of richness and detail than a single perspective could. The art was in having the flexibility and robustness to respond to this, realign the approach, and focus all the different wavelengths in the same direction.

Maintaining this context-specific leadership provided certainty, clarity, and an evaluative lens that while not infallible, kept us moving forward together.

Thus, agency formed a basis of the approach: our textwork was forensic, notes were given fast, and actors were trusted to go away and work those notes independently. *TSMGO* engaged an expansive range of actors, who brought with them a variety of different experiences, nationalities, first languages, and access needs. Respecting agency helped us to push the needle on text accessibility considerably, while also opening people's minds to the sheer volume of creative opportunity available to an actor, as well as the sheer work to be done in interpreting and embodying this text for an audience. In this way, the notes were as much a workshop session for participants as they were performance preparation.

Leaning into the Technology – Rapid Note-Taking

Taking these notes at speed was a feat in itself. *TSMGO* worked at an incredible pace. We covered, on average, approximately eight pages an hour. We covered that material twice whenever possible.

Actors had been given textwork basics and additional resources to help them understand what their characters were saying and make some initial choices on how to say it. They were encouraged to be bold – "strong and wrong" was always better than an indistinct or tame choice.

From there, a Word document provided multifarious tools that could allow for precise annotation, if gifted with a significant capacity for working memory (which itself was strengthened week on week by the challenges of the project).

Highlighters were used to distinguish rounds of notes – yellow for first round, green for second round, and blue for third round if we were lucky enough. Where ideas were complex, notes could be made beside the text or in a comment box using the review function. These notes could even be uploaded to Google Docs for people to see the working version and remind themselves of their notes after the rehearsal session had moved on, or allow Rob to flesh out a thought in more detail for an individual without holding everyone else up.

From there, bold was used to highlight contrapuntal rhythms or missed emphases, to highlight the connections between thoughts, or the all important small words that framed the debate the character was presenting in a way the audience could follow (think of *from ... to, as ... so, if ... then ...*).

Direction was given first on an audio-only basis, focusing purely on speaking. The second round would then involve physicality and gesture, and the third round, where possible (which may take place in a breakout room) would aim to refine all this and push psychological and emotional nuances to enrich the playing.

Paper notes had too great a margin for error – you have to look away from the screen, you can't read your own handwriting, and you have to print a new, fully edited script every week. Digital tools kept everything in one place and meant there was a definitive shared record of notes that everyone could refer to, which was more economically and environmentally conscious.

Below is an excerpt of a piece of annotated text from *TSMGO*'s *Julius Caesar* that shows these tools in action – often whole discussions bloomed from a single italicized word, but this *aide memoir* allowed us to point up things we might otherwise miss, forget or skip over.

> The evil that men do lives after them, ETHOS evil good antithesis
>
> The good is oft interred with their bones; *pronounce ed.*
>
> If it were so, it was a grievous fault,
>
> And grievously hath Caesar answer'd it.
>
> (For Brutus is – an honorable man, CHEER!
>
> So are they all, all honorable men), repetition absolute CHEER!
>
> Come I to speak in Caesar's funeral. I.E NOT TRIAL ETC
>
> Para break
>
> He was my friend, faithful and just to me; PATHOS
>
> But Brutus says, he was ambitious,
>
> And Brutus is – an honorable man. CROWD SING IT WITH HIM
>
> He hath brought many captives home to Rome,

Whose ransoms did the general coffers fill; i.e public/not his own

Did this in Caesar seem ambitious?

When that the poor have cried, Caesar hath wept;

Ambition should be made of sterner stuff: a genuine internal conflict "It doesn't make sense!"

Yet Brutus says he was ambitious,

And Brutus is, – an honorable man. CONFIDENCE STRAINED CROWD CROWD NO CONTEMPORIZING **STRONGER "IS" BUT A QUESTION**

You **all** did see that on the Lupercal absolute LOGOS!!!

I *thrice* presented him a kingly crown, a huge number in context

Which he did *thrice* **refuse**. Was this ambition? VERB! CAN'T ANSWER

Yet Brutus says he was Ambitious,

And **sure** he is, – an honorable man. RIGHT? CROWD STRUGGLE TO ANSWER

SELF CORRECTION HERE – GETTING BACK ON TRACK I speak not to disprove what Brutus spoke,

But here I am to speak what I do know. Antithesis – mere rhetoric, speech can be lies

You **all** did love him once, not without cause; absolute PATHOS

What cause withholds you then to mourn for him?

CAN'T ANSWER

O judgment! Thou art fled to brutish beasts, ecphonesis not literal

And men have lost their reason. Bear with me, JUDGMENT REASON THE HEIGHT OF ROMANNESS

My heart is in the coffin there with Caesar,

And I must pause till it come back to me.

Aside. The objective here was to maximize *contrast* within the scene, between the prose, head-driven appeal we see from Brutus, and Antony's apparently heart-driven verse journey through this scene, which results in a flaming riot that runs Brutus and his allies out of Rome. The best lies are mixed with truth, and the effectiveness of *mere* rhetoric (or manipulation) relies on it being so hard to distinguish from *true* rhetoric (which depends on the genuine feeling of the speaker that they are arguing for the good). If Antony is manipulating the crowd, it must feel so earnest that they cannot tell, otherwise the crowd are idiots and the audience is not moved alongside them – we wanted the crowd to be a *conduit* to enfranchise the audience in the argument, and for the crowd's reactions to plot the audience's journey through the orations. You can see the original with coloured highlights, used as an additional aide memoir, at the QR code below, in addition to the final performance.

ANTONY.

Friends, Romans, countrymen, *lend* me your ears! Self redraft? SOFTNESS ON LEND – STATUS

I come to *bury* Caesar, not to *praise* him. **Verbs** | Antithesis-esque – conceptual distance

So let it be with Caesar. The noble Brutus SO TROCHEE

Hath told you Caesar was Ambitious; major fault back then

Para break – animate gear shift

Here, under leave of Brutus and the rest

You can see the final performance here:

144 Directing for Digital

FIGURE 5.3   Mark Antony Speech QR Code (bit.ly/JCMarkAnt).

FIGURE 5.4   Mark Antony Text QR Code (bit.ly/JCMarkAntText).

Maximizing Your Actors' Potential

These one-size-fits-all strategies left relatively little room to be able to respond to the individual and their own approach, tastes, proclivities, level of training, and what motivates them to do a great job. Great leadership should, ideally, be person-centered. To bring at least a flavor of this to the process, we relied on a few principles.

You Get Out What You Put In – This was made a tenet of the productions from very early on. Because everyone's circumstances, context, and approach is different, we could only work with what we were offered by our myriad cast members. We cast without auditions, based only on a few sentences people may have chosen to write on their application, and we had an informal "one friend" rule where, in order to maximize inclusion and meet as many new performers as possible, we would seek to work with only one actor known to the creative team prior to *TSMGO* per week. Because everyone's schedule and time zone was unique, and everyone's access needs were different, we would recommend that people do as much prep *as they could* before we got into the room and provide a briefing via email for the concept of the show and the key themes and drivers to give people a sandbox to play in. We never went so far as to *expect* this of anyone. Any progress people made individually was seen as a bonus, but the encouragement we gave stemmed from the fact that well-prepared actors invariably gave the most assured performances.

Meet People Where They Are – David Brailsford, coach of the British Cycling Team, famously sought to gain an advantage over the competition, not by transforming one element by a huge margin, but by tweaking and improving *every* element of the team's training and equipment by just 1%. Known as the *aggregate of marginal gains*, incremental changes to every individual element amounts to a huge difference to the overall outcome and performance. The same is true when working with an ensemble. Some people would come to their first rehearsal well prepped, they understood their text, they made bold choices, and they were ready to sweat the details. Others would arrive and offer a cold read; they would need help to understand what they were saying, and how to communicate that understanding through the voice. We were careful not to set a lofty standard that would create an unbridgeable gulf between those who had the *desire* to perform, and those who had the ability to do so to a professional standard. Instead, we tailored everything we did to the level that people first presented us with. If we could get actors to take two steps forward, no matter where they were when they arrived, we'd consider that a victory. With few exceptions, we were able to accomplish this in our performers and, we hope, in the experience of our participants. Those that were the most successful were almost always those who brought with them multidisciplinary ways of working, and voice actors in particular had a flare for the unique demands of this medium. **Progress, not perfection,** is what success looked like.

Everyone Gets a Cookie – As everyone who took part did so freely of their own volition and without pay, we strove to ensure the experience had a tangibly positive outcome for everyone. Because of our participants' varied experience levels, we had to achieve this in different ways for different people. Some wanted to challenge themselves in roles that were aspirational for them, others against type, and still others that they'd played before and wanted to explore again after accruing more experience. Some wanted to explore the digital terrain and familiarize themselves with how to overcome dramaturgical challenges inside the new medium. Some wanted greater familiarity with Shakespeare and an understanding of how to navigate the text competently in a short space of time. Still, others enjoyed the process of prop and set-piece making. Some simply needed to feed their vocational compulsion to "do thou work". The experience was set up to tick one or more of these boxes for each participant, and this leaves out one of the most fundamentally beneficial aspects of the project: **the replication of the conditions of the old repertory theatre**, where more experienced actors would mentor apprentices as they learned and refined their craft through a tightly packed production schedule. We were fortunate to have people of all levels of experience in the rehearsal room, which meant that the culture of the space was set by those with the bigger line loads. This in turn gave those with smaller roles the opportunity to learn from the more experienced professionals in the room.

> *Aside.* Some amateurs outshined some professionals, and turned in incredible performances. To be an amateur – to do something *for the love of it* – is the most admirable form of the work in many ways; it prevents the kind of jaded atrophy that can reveal itself when survival-scarred actors are tested in a short space of time. This vibrant mix kept everyone sharp, learning, and happy.

Through a post-production survey, *TSMGO* actors reported:

- All actors surveyed thought *TSMGO* achieved its aims (as stated in the survey)
- About 80% of actors surveyed said they learned something new
- About 50% will *do* "something professional" in "a new way" based on their experience
- 95% thought management/production was good or very good
- 100% said it was worth being involved personally
- 90% said it was worth being involved professionally

Nurture – a standard practice in innovation workshopping, we try to ensure that everyone enters the rehearsal room with a proactive perspective on building out the work. We encouraged a nurturing attitude using the improving principle of "yes, and" and the idea that other performers are constantly making bids for connection, or "offers" through their choices. These choices can be taken on and built on (a "yes") or blocked (a "no"). Whenever we as a creative team asked actors to try something, we always asked them to say "yes" first. If an actor gives an idea their best shot and that commitment doesn't yield a choice that works for the moment, we can attribute that to the fact that the choice is misaligned rather than it being due to any hesitancy or lack of commitment on the actor's part. This was another reason knowing access needs in advance was helpful, to tailor our requests accordingly, and another way in which optimizing the "rig" set up beforehand allowed us to all play using the same tools and rules. We defined what we meant by "Nurture": to take the seed of an idea, pour water on it, bathe it in sunshine, and carefully tend to it so it would grow branches – the idea we use in the show may be a single leaf on one of those branches, but we wouldn't have found it unless we cultivated the original idea. The opposite of this is "Nixing" – when you take a seed and smash it against the tarmac with a shovel before it ever has a chance to grow. This seemed to help most actors frame their approach to the creative team and to one another in a positive, proactive way.

Strong and Wrong – in Jujutsu, the practice of redirecting energy is a martial one with obvious conclusions. If someone in a grapple plants their feet and seeks to remain as immobile as possible it can be very difficult to throw them. However, if someone comes charging in with a head of steam, it's easy to pivot that energy over a hip and into the ground. The same is true (though with remarkably different results) with directing actors. Unlike jujutsu, where we point people at the ground, the aim of redirecting that strong energy with actors should be to propel them into the air to take flight. If an actor comes in rigid and low-energy, with little sense of direction or momentum of their own, generating those elements with them can be difficult and draining, especially in tight timelines. Per Newton's first law of thermodynamics, no energy is created, only transformed. So, if an actor is at a sprint with their choices made before they enter the rehearsal room, *even if* those choices run completely counter to the text, the scene, or the production, it is still easier to *transform* that energy than to try and create it from scratch. Consequently, we encouraged our actors to be bold in their interpretations and to over-play their choices in the first read-through. We would always rather shave 10% of the energy off a choice to make it read convincingly and urgently than need to dial up the vibrancy and contrast of a choice to make it read at all. We saw this work time and time again, but never more effectively than Yolanda Ovide's read of Clarence's drowning speech in *Richard III*. The first read was wonderfully light and self questioning, marveling at her own imagination. The note given was to make it a ghost story even *she* was afraid of, and the very next read, right there in rehearsal, was one of the most mesmerizing pieces of delivery of the whole series.

Similarly, those with little to no formal training or experience often plunged straight into the text with abandon, resulting in all kinds of delightful mayhem. This was brilliant! It pushed people to throw caution to the wind and shake off any ideas they may have inherited from

"Big Shakespeare" that it must be treated with reverence or declaimed in park and bark style. Even if the performance itself was unfit for our purpose, it was one of many examples of what we would call "defibrillation" – a surge of energy that enlivens and shatters the torpor that can overcome this work. From there, we were in an ideal place to begin the work of crafting the piece and harnessing that energy in service of what the scene really needed, instead of what a Shakespearean performance "should" look or sound like.

Themes and Take Homes

While every reader will take different thoughts out of this chapter and find different things useful or resonant, it can be helpful to capture key themes and practices to take forward into the future when stepping into the unknown.

Allow the possibility that some constraints can be helpful, while some are hindrances

Define the borders of your sandbox, then standardize the toys to play with

MacGyver-it: Hacking toys to create unintended effects is more fun

Encourage people to play in their own way – ownership matters

Give permission to question – engagement enlivens people, process and product

Learn by doing – to ideate and iterate is better than to get it right first time – this requires a willingness to not know the "best" or "right" answer before you start, and allow the possibility that someone else may find it in the sandbox

Progress, not perfection

When determining outcomes, be governed by values, not egos

Know what the purpose is (psst ... there can be more than one!)

Identify the opportunities and barriers

6
THE FUTURE

This book has centered on thinking differently and doing differently – on putting process first and building and engaging communities around the work. It's been about reinventing our toolkit and approach in new and unforeseen settings and circumstances.

Unlike the previous chapters, which naturally established their own limits, *The Future* is an infinite space. It falls to us, then, to first establish some useful creative constraints in shaping the conversation to follow. For the purposes of this conversation, we can start with a useful geographic limit of the United Kingdom and North America – the biggest territories in which *The Show Must Go Online* (*TSMGO*) was produced and consumed.

Within this, we will illustrate a series of **challenge areas** facing theatre's future and provide some initial stimulus for grappling with them. Then, it will be up to you to think about how the tools and approaches outlined in this book can be applied to transform these problems into opportunities for innovation. We will strive not to give answers; this is not a policy-making or proselytizing platform.

Throughout this book, we have introduced our take on a process that encourages creativity to thrive in adversity and suggested resources for generating novel solutions to new problems. Our aim here is to create a simulation space: a testing ground to explore how the techniques, perspectives, and approaches explored in this book can prepare you for the unknown, by delving into some of the most resilient challenges theatre has faced in recent decades.

Ideate solutions to these pressing issues, with some prompts to benefit from or rail against as you see fit. Throughout this process, **we want you to think beyond what's on the page**; make new connections to the challenge areas from your own knowledge and experience, using the principles of *thinking differently* and *doing differently* we established in the first chapter, *Innovation and Theatremaking*.

Part I – Warm Up

Problems and Provocations

Theatre faces a series of enduring challenges. As John Steinbeck put it, "The theater is the only institution in the world which has been dying for four thousand years and has never succumbed".

So what are the symptoms of theatre's malaise, and can you innovate new ways to treat them?

Your Role: to generate ideas that can bring theatre to new life in new ways by providing new solutions to one or more of the following areas.

To help, we have provided a **challenge area** (there are many others you could discover), an **example** *opportunity area* for how this challenge could be productively addressed (there are many others you could create), and an **example** *idea* of what that might look like in execution (there are many other possibilities). Your homework is to take this and run with it, to find new opportunities and ideas within these challenge areas, and ultimately to identify new challenge areas – ones that light your fire and that you're passionate about innovating around.

Challenge Area 1: Shakespeare

The argument in English-speaking nations has long been that too much Shakespeare is produced at the cost of developing new writers' work. What's more, Shakespeare served an imperial regime at a time of rapid colonial expansion and enslavement, meaning there are racist and misogynistic attitudes intrinsic in the writing. This aspect of the work was foregrounded as it was used as a tool of cultural imperialism throughout the Victorian era. Consequently, many of us are seeking to evolve our relationship to Shakespeare to be a healthier, more productive one.

> **Example Opportunity Area:** the value of Shakespeare for the future is extracted through **active interrogation, seen through a lens of citizenship**. It is with a debt to the works of David Sterling Brown, Farah Karim-Cooper, Scott Newstok and many others that we see the work through this lens.

Example Idea: Consider the two pivotal productions of Richard II of late: Adjoa Andoh's 2019 production at the Sam Wanamaker Playhouse, which featured all female-identifying Global Majority actors, or the 2020 serialized audio play produced at The Public Theatre in New York that featured a primarily Global Majority cast in the wake of the (#BLM) Black Lives Matter movement (conceived and directed by Saheem Ali).

A reevaluation of values, a questioning of assumptions, and a challenging of the status quo have been promoted throughout this volume. If we were to stop short at Shakespeare, it would certainly highlight a valuable limitation of the design process – that **flawed humans with biases** are responsible for interpreting and enacting it. But the process itself serves to try and make us aware of that.

Shakespeare's works have been a gateway through which to bridge antiquity and modernity, to discover lost educational values and techniques, to better understand politics and statecraft, to see through the performance of power, to engage with critical race theory in order to understand the power dynamics and structures within the plays in a meaningful way. It is a gateway not because Shakespeare represents perfection, but instead, because of its flaws, its difficulties, and its idiosyncrasies. Other works may well contain similar multitudes, but when it comes to reckoning with colonial ideology, and its continued persistence in our daily lives, it can be illuminating to return to a time close to the root of these ideas, in order to examine their persistence in our cultures.

As free, open-source material with vast resources to help anyone tackle it, it is also open for anyone who chooses to work with it. If Shakespeare's works are a tool, a hammer that has helped to forge Victorian cultural imperialism across the globe, can it also be wielded by those who seek to dismantle it? We hope so. We may be wrong.

Challenge Area 2: Money

In *The Empty Space*, Peter Brook (renownèd be thy grave) bemoans theatre prices escalating to the point where we will perform for an audience of a single millionaire. At the time of writing, this complaint – which feels so timeless as to be Shakespearean – is 54 years old. Before then, it was the Astor Place riots – raising ticket prices, instigating dress codes, and deliberately looking to alienate and exclude the working class. This too feels as though it has a timeless quality.

Example Opportunity Area: How do you **"Robin Hood"** theatre – radically redistributing the flow of money within the arts.

Example Idea: A "theatre tax" on film & streaming studios.

In seeking **stimulus** for this challenge area, the history of art is a **related world**, the relationship between art and money has never been an easy one to resolve. Perhaps the height of this tryst was the Italian Renaissance, under the Medici. At that time, billionaires (as they would now be) understood the relationship between art and politics. They, and their rivals, used art to project power, control image, and secure legacy in a way that is today rivaled perhaps only by Dwayne "The Rock" Johnson. Under original practice, we might simply seek the Elon Musks of the world to fund our projects, but under original *parallels*, we might look to see how power and rule have changed in the intervening centuries. Oligarchs like the Medici and Musk should not, in theory, have hegemony over our politics and lives. Rather, most western societies now elect rulers by consent of the governed. What would a new system – taking the ruling Medici as inspiration, but transferring rule to the populace – look like in terms of funding the arts?

Similarly, considering modern **related worlds**, we can now look to other media to which theatre provides a proving ground – many of the biggest Hollywood and Streaming stars learned their craft in the theatre. Theatres as regional training centers could redistribute opportunity to talent economically and geographically. During the times of the old rep, learning would be undertaken by apprenticeship. Learning by doing, often while receiving a wage. Paid, while failing upward in front of people. The drama school model seems to have failed in this – a relatively modern invention that has by and large siloed training into the most expensive cities in the world, and in conservatory settings, offering training on a for-profit basis. In the US, this training is often also embedded within elite universities, increasing the complex nature of accessibility. Is it time to reexamine the relationship between training, theatre, and the industries that profit from performers who earned their stripes in live storytelling? How could this help us solve the money problem, and other problems too?

Rulebreakers too can help us reimagine things – Battersea Arts Center operates a pay what you can model, while the newly launched Shakespeare North Playhouse is offering a **pay what you decide** scheme from £3. The Shunt Lounge, for its brief but exciting life, had a £5 cover charge to enter what they strove to make the best bar in London, then offered a vast array of experimental performance for free. **Inverting the relationship of bar and performance** meant that more diverse audiences were exposed, often unexpectedly, to exciting avante-garde theatre work. Another **rulebreaker** – what if venues weren't central at all to the way theatre was made and delivered? This was certainly the case during the pandemic. The large buildings tend to hoard the vast majority of available arts funding in both the UK and the US. What would an art world that decentralized the role of venues look like? In the UK, high streets have atrophied completely and many spaces remain vacant – theatre companies like Big Telly have taken over these spaces to create community art projects that aim to bring people back to the town centers and away from the malls. What would theatre look like if it moved to where people already are?

Challenge Area 3: Work Ethic

Theatre is limiting innovation through its way of working. It can **support only those who are *able* to work *within* the current system** – a system that through its own excess excludes marginalized, disabled, neurodiverse, and working-class artists who are so often unable to live up to the requirements of an unjust status quo. In creating a new sense of *belonging*, theatre cannot exclude those who don't have the privilege to already speak the secret language of the industry, already work themselves beyond breaking point, and already grew up around influential figures in the business, while those who haven't had the chance to participate in it will languish forever on the fringes.

As we write, The New Diorama Theatre in London took the unprecedentedly bold decision to **stop.**[1] They did this because in the reopening after lockdown they, as many claimed, were determined to build back better. They were unique in their admission that despite those intentions, they did *not* improve. So they stopped, to reexamine their work and their approach to the work; to try something new. The same principle in microcosm was evidenced with *TSMGO*, as our accessibility and inclusion practices progressed leaps and bounds once we stopped to meaningfully reflect on the lessons of the First Folio series.

The Show Must Go Online was **not** a sustainable working model.

> *Aside:* At one time we estimated the real-terms cost of each production. If we were to pay people *only* for the time in rehearsals, at the UK national minimum wage, *just* the personnel costs would equate to an average of £5,000 per show, or £180,000 for the First Folio series (approximately US$213,000 at time of writing). And this is at the

minimum wage, meant for entry-level, unskilled work (if such a thing exists), not at the rates of pay people would have rightly demanded and deserved were this a commercial enterprise. In short, *The Show Must Go Online* **would never have existed** as a strictly professional proposition, because that kind of money does not exist to build a community during a time of crisis, in an ad hoc fashion, simply because it is the right thing to do. Whether that money *should* be available is another question. But could we make these questions irrelevant?

The *TSMGO* team drove themselves to the brink of burnout and sometimes beyond in the name of their community, their mission, and their art. It's easy to say that this was *worthwhile*, but it was not *necessary*. The world would continue to turn. Could we have done this differently? More sustainably?

Example Opportunity Area: re-evaluate our relationship to work. Our very title – derived from what has for so long been a truism, "The Show Must Go On" reflects a culture that must be challenged. To make an accessible, inclusive theatre means creating theatre that works at a sustainable pace for all.

Example Idea: role-sharing with a doubled-up cast to halve the workload on individuals and double the imagination invested in each character (credit: Merely Theatre).

We must appreciate that the creation of the work should necessarily take longer, have more accommodations, and prioritize human efficiency over cost efficiency. The compressed three-week rehearsal, a three-week run that has somehow become the industry standard could, and should, be radically disrupted. Longer rehearsal periods with a better balance of work and respite, for a myriad of reasons, will enable artists to create superior work that can sustain longer and more popular runs. In Germany and Russia, much longer rehearsal periods are natural, and companies build a repertory of high-quality productions that can run for years, paying off the initial investment by taking a longer lens on recouping cost.

Looking at the problem from a different direction, a **Universal Basic Income**, such as the one being piloted in Ireland at the time of writing, and targeted explicitly at artists, would allow individuals to place their time and energy into projects they deem worthy of it, at a pace they can sustain, without an economic imperative driving their decision-making.

This in turn could mean very different projects come to life and thrive, because the *motivations* to make them have changed. What futures can we dare to dream that free us from these kinds of financial imperatives, away from money and toward *value*?

Challenge Area 4: Brave Spaces

Abuse of power has been widespread in theatre, perhaps for as long as it has existed. Theatre in the United Kingdom and North America has been deeply embroiled in the reckoning of the #MeToo movement, and this has shown that there is a need for radically different ways of working.

Example Opportunity Area: systems that make the work braver. While every system is subject to abuse, a strength of systems is that they can clearly establish dispassionate consequences for transgressions, while creating language and frameworks that help those working collaboratively to identify and troubleshoot those transgressions.

Example Idea: Sandy Thompson, a Scottish site-specific theatre director (as well as the daughter of a quality assurance process manager and a design engineer, and former rape crisis counsellor at Dundee Rape Crisis Centre) found it helpful in rehearsals to identify the earliest markers of abusive behavior patterns, and normalize transparent communication and early intervention. She identified distinct stages of transgressions, further defining boundary *testing* and boundary *pressing* as steps that occur before boundary *breaking*.

For the purposes of sharing a collaborative experience as we make theatre, we primarily define personal boundaries as the physical and emotional lines we draw around ourselves as we relate to others (they can encompass many different areas including our time). *Theatrical Intimacy Education* offers the slogan "Your boundaries are perfect exactly where they are" – meaning that no explanation is owed to anyone else as to *why* a boundary exists; it exists, and *must* therefore be acknowledged and respected. Boundaries must be identified at the start of the process, with the understanding that they may change. Boundaries are contextual, conditional, and revocable (*Theatrical Intimacy Education*). By establishing these boundaries, creatives in a space discover freedom to explore active and dynamic choices because they have been given explicit permission regarding the parameters in which they can engage with their partner(s) because, after all, creativity thrives under constraint. Establishing boundaries – and confirming them regularly – allows artists to thrive as they are continually seen, affirmed, and granted agency to engage in a manner that enables them.

Sandy Thompson's trajectory of boundary transgressions includes *behavioral* transgressions. Boundary *testing* refers to the act of looking for where "the line" is with individuals or groups, and boundary *pressing* is deliberately pushing that line to see what resistance is encountered – both of these steps are typically undertaken by abusers seeking to get their own way within a group dynamic.

Both boundary pressing and testing can be defined at the start of the process, and both can be identified and discussed openly *during* the process as and when they occur. This open communication shines a light on early transgressions and makes it immediately apparent that there is no way to hide the trajectory toward boundary breaking. Those individuals who engage in these behaviors may be unaware of it, and may thank you for pointing it out – it doesn't have to be intrinsically oppositional. We grow by identifying how to improve on behavior and practices that we recognize no longer serve our best interests; that is why we now wear seatbelts or helmets when it was once unheard of to do so.

By establishing these community norms, anyone who experiences or witnesses a boundary test or press is empowered to step outside the situation, name it, and report it. This helps to mitigate the escalation of behavior that leads to boundary breaking.

Boundary *breaking* occurs when an individual crosses the line that has been established regarding their collaborator's personal or emotional limits. Because these limits have been identified, shared, and confirmed, the limits must now be highlighted to reaffirm their existence. When this occurs, and it inevitably will, since we are all human, it is imperative to acknowledge this and apologize. It is also critical to acknowledge that there are actions for which an apology may not suffice for the level of harm caused and that there may be necessary legal recourse to address the severity of these actions.

Agreeing to a *system* for apology, *as* boundaries are established, provides a framework for reparation to occur. Chelsea Pace and Laura Rikard offer a system that includes stating what was done, actually apologizing for the action, and affirming how one might avoid causing similar harm in the future.

This "prevention is better than cure" approach is one way in which articulating the systems of abuse, and the systems of recourse, can reduce the instances of predatory behaviors.

As theatremakers become increasingly aware of the need to mitigate the potential for harm, some of the same design principles we have identified throughout this book have been used in the **field of intimacy.** Intimacy practitioners in theatre are helping to develop identity-aware education and practices that have expanded the definition of "intimacy" to include any element of the work that relies on an actor's lived experience. This broad definition includes all areas of an individual's protected identity traits, including gender identification, sexual orientation, race, dis/ability status, age, religion, ancestry, and more.

This expanded definition of intimacy means that harm reduction includes supporting individuals from marginalized groups when they are in creative spaces; providing education and support for the entire creative team so that a marginalized individual is not burdened with the additional emotional labor of educating everyone else in the space. The commitment to cultural competency around productions that share the stories of those who have been Othered helps to promote an environment in which individuals are seen, supported, and respected. As we write this book, we are witnessing massive changes in the fields of actor training and rehearsal practices that demonstrate shifts in the previously established practices and provide hopeful glimpses of the changing landscape of our field.

Challenge Area 5: Hierarchies in the Making Process

The auteur director has the whiff of fascism about it – the charismatic strong personality with a certainty of purpose and a clear-cut sense of what "right" looks like. Marcus Aurelius, one of the so-called "five good Emperors" of Rome, would not have been seen as such by those in Germania. Similarly, actors working to deliver a vision they have no part in authoring often groan under the weight of such responsibility, without the commensurate rights.

> **Example Opportunity Area: Redistribute rights and responsibilities in the rehearsal room.**
>
> **Example idea:** Create a "pitching" noticeboard where ideas for the show can be shared by anyone, for any part of the production.

While *TSMGO* maintained the role of the director as an active decision-maker responsible for guiding the trajectory of the piece, the systems-led thinking that created the values, and the articulation of "what success looks like", help to sideline ego and create a sandbox in which everyone knows the aims, and is empowered to "pitch" creative contributions.

In talkbacks, actors repeatedly described this freeing opportunity as "best idea wins". Participants could generally see how someone else's pitch better fulfilled the aims and values, and would happily adopt it.

A facilitative leadership style – which aims to lead from below, troubleshooting areas of difficulty each participant encounters, discovered by both the participant and the director as they produce their work – can further help to bring the best out of individual contributors. But how can this be taken further? Devising the values and practices, the limits of the sandbox, together from the outset is an immediate improvement. Principles of devised theatremaking and ensemble theatremaking can also be brought to scene work with an established text.

The simple breakdown of **goals and roles** is essential to ensure that individuals are not burdened by responsibilities they did not consent to take on, or impinged upon by the exertion of others' right to authorship over what is their responsibility to perform.

There may be people in the room for whom working on their character is the only contribution they wish to focus on, whereas others may wish to contribute beyond that. Some may welcome others' input and some may not, and this may change at different times in the process. Can we make space for responsibilities to be distributed equitably, in an opt-in way? What would need to change in order that anyone could co-author a moment, a character, a scene, or a work? How would they?

Challenge Area 6: Tradition

You can't be innovative in a vacuum. What is innovative is only so because it responds to "tradition", and in some way disrupts it. "Tradition", in a sense, is inevitable. But it is also the machine we rage against to make progress.

The valid question being asked right now, including by your authors, is *whose tradition*? What if work was made in a way influenced by other cultural norms, practices, or by new-minted processes that are forged by groups that have a more reflective make-up of the community being served?

Tradition can and does stifle innovation. When Shakespeare finished his run of plays, the playhouse where much of his work originated and was performed burned to the ground. Under our guiding idea of *original parallels*, it's hard not to heed this as an inspiration.

The main problem commonly encountered by the perennially "emerging" theatremaker is that innovation is a by-word for risk, and the more resource-scarce an industry, the more risk-averse it becomes. Theatre so often defeats itself by playing safe. How do we encourage a healthier relationship with risk?

Example Opportunity Area: Make work to play, not to succeed.

Example Idea: companies guarantee funding for one risk-taking "emerging" production per season, often from teams that don't fulfill the usual requirements for production on the main stage.

Looking at **related worlds**, play happens perhaps nowhere more than at Lego. As a business, its tradition is to maximize profits. Yet within their corporate structure, they have protected innovation funding that *must* be spent on experimentation, and crucially, with *no* imperative to succeed commercially, or even succeed at all. The department's Key Performance Indicator – the measure by which it is deemed successful or otherwise – is "to gather data on an idea".

This is similar to how science funding is designed to work. Curiosity-driven discovery, without the need for a direct and immediate application. In exploring the most extreme conditions of the universe, NASA has created hundreds of innovations that have found practical commercial applications here on earth but were discovered in pursuit of something on the edge of what's possible.

Can art serve a similar function? With the dawn of so-called metaverses in virtual and augmented reality, could we create ring-fenced funds for artists to explore the limits of emerging technologies and in doing so, push them in ways that result in commercial applications down the line?

Tradition also informs **who money goes to**, and *this* stifles innovation significantly. The *X Prize* famously offered a cash prize to whoever could solve the problem of cleaning up oil spilled in the oceans, and a semi-finalist for that prize was a tattoo artist who sketched his idea on the back of a Las Vegas napkin with no ecological or engineering background. In conventional funding settings, he would never even have been considered.

Aside: The problem with prizes, however, is that they remain exploitative despite the apparently egalitarian veneer. Hundreds, or even thousands of people burn time and energy to compete for the chance for their idea to become a reality, and only a tiny fraction are successful. That's millions of wasted work hours. And that's before you take into account intellectual property ownership, and so on ... how could we solve these issues, while keeping the barriers to entry open?

If we want to see innovation in theatre, **we cannot award opportunities only to those who've already "proven" they can do it.** That ensures the *same kind of work* is continually produced. For the reasons outlined in "Work Ethic" above, we *must* open opportunities up to those who might not yet have proven they can do it. This is because many *can't* prove anything within the current system, which is set up to require huge levels of overwork with very little remuneration, condensing the work into as intense a space as possible, making it impossible for people with many different access needs to perform at their peak.

What's more, there are real problems with the way **hiring and appointments** work within theatre. In the vast majority of cases, these require artists to promote a predetermined, singular vision. As things stand, **you can't go to a theatre and pitch a** *process* where the outcome is uncertain. Innovation is still synonymous with risk, and the scarcity model under which the system operates means this must be minimized. The bigger risk is decaying away slowly, but entirely, like the apocryphal frog in the pan of water that gradually boils. What other guarantees or assurances beyond the norm *could* institutions and enablers use to award funding and appointments?

Challenge Area 7: Media Diffusion Is Killing Theatre

Nothing will ever beat the visceral *feel* of the embodied experience, the mass gathering, but the world is changing. New avenues are opening. It was once innovative to put a *roof* over a theatre – we see no difference between going inside and going online.

And yet, many theatre productions seek to compete with cinema and streaming *on their terms*, placing an emphasis on a type of production design that represents their principle strength, and with which cash-strapped theatre can rarely compete. How do we stand apart as a medium and remind people what we do that cinema and streaming cannot?

Opportunity Area: Differentiate the offer theatre makes to audiences.

Example Idea: Immersive theatre experiences.

Beyond luminaries like Punchdrunk, who have created large-scale environments in which to feel like you're *in* the experience, and companies like Secret Cinema that have created pop-up Universal Studios style environments in which to watch films, there are alternatives to large-scale production design. Clown shows like Red Bastard and yes, Shakespeare, frequently make use of audience participation and interaction – something impossible in conventional screenwork.

The proscenium arch is a Victorian convention that has flattened the stage into a screen – practitioners of early modern work, or any work taking place in traverse, in the round, in thrust, know the value of disrupting this convention. After all, having the whole audience pointing forward at a focal point is what a movie theatre is for – and it can offer scale and immersion at a level theatre simply can't. **The Bridge Theatre** in London, created by Nicholas Hytner, is a brilliant example of innovation in *use of space*. It can be used proscenium, thrust, in the round, or "immersively" with a yard similar to the Globe, where plinths are raised in various orientations to give the actors a clear playing space. This sandbox structure excites untold possibilities for storytelling in three dimensions, right next to the audience, effectively leveraging the many advantages of in-person performance against the ease and comfort of streaming services.

Challenge Area 8: Theatre Takes Too Long to Get Made

What makes theatre *theatre* must be constantly re-examined with each new production and by each new maker in order to have a hope of it surviving.

The big questions we have to answer in funding applications are essentially "Why this? Why now?" The problem is that due to the turnaround time involved in the grantmaking process, *"now"* **was actually three-to-six months ago** in a best-case scenario. In reality, many ideas struggle through development processes to find an audience over a span of years.

"The moment" is more momentary than ever. The pace of our society moves faster than ever, and our ability to respond by mounting productions that resonate with the zeitgeist must simultaneously be more responsive than ever. Yet all the ways in which we conceive of, rehearse, produce, and fund projects stand in the way of being truly responsive to the moment.

> **Example Opportunity Area:** facilitate radical, rapid, responsive productions that are in keeping with the flow of *Kairos* – doing the right thing at the right time.
>
> **Example Idea:** a rep company responsible for raising a new production of an existing show in the canon based on the week's or month's events, per *Last Week Tonight*.

Back to Brook again. In *The Empty Space,* he speaks of an opera that took place in the bombed out remains of an Austrian opera house. The lesson was that the arts are an act of defiance against the forces that oppress us. But through this lens, it becomes apparent that art can be most vibrant when it is at its most *responsive*. How can we envision a future for our art that responds to oppression with performance, and in so doing, relates injustice to the public consciousness, and perhaps even activates the audience to appeal to its own interest?

Everything created in lockdown was by necessity *truly* responsive – to time and place, to community problems, and to creative challenges. Creators had to start from the ground up with every piece they created. What if we did this every time we created something? What if we addressed real challenges honestly, as if for the first time, and in revolutionary ways?

Challenge Area 9: Is Theatremaking Inherently Unsustainable?

We've talked about a more sustainable theatre for makers and audiences. But the planet is dying. So we should at least attempt to address that, too. Theatre is a uniquely transitory experience – while the scale of production is smaller than other entertainment industries, the impact of the worldbuilding process in theatre is experienced by a vanishingly small number of people compared to other forms of entertainment. We must ask hard questions about whether the investment of resources in theatre that cannot be repurposed in the future is a responsible use of those resources given the climate crisis. As *Just Stop Oil* put it at the time of writing: there can be no art on a dead planet.

Example Opportunity Area: creating environmentally restorative theatre.

Example Idea: a promenade outdoor production in which rewilding seeds are sewn as part of the story.

Theatre is far from the top of the most polluting industries in the world, but it will take improvements everywhere to right our current course, especially as those industries that *do* pollute the most, appear to be doing the least. This kind of race-to-the-bottom-thinking has never been our ethos, however. During the pandemic, we said: what *can* we do? The climate crisis continues, so the same question applies.

The Theatre Green Book is a first step toward optimizing our practice for sustainability. This series of recommendations has been developed with sustainability consultants, with a focus on reducing consumption, waste, and carbon emissions.

The pandemic and lockdowns have taught those who created work over this period that restraint, creative imagination, repurposing, and efficiency can become essential at any moment. By creating a more sustainable theatre, we may incidentally help optimize our practice to be more resilient when these principles are *essential* to creating *anything*.

Moreover, the drive toward a more circular economy will teach us valuable lessons about purposeful and lasting *design*. How do we create pieces that will be used again and again in new contexts, to represent different items? Many theatre departments are already extraordinarily resourceful in this regard, but part of the messaging is certainly about reframing audience expectations away from new-is-best, and toward finding joy in the response to the challenge of creative repurposing. What if we adopted, as Jamie Lloyd has, virtually bare bones stages, and returned to a theatrical paradigm like Shakespeare's: a celebration of the imagination?

Challenge Area ∞: The Unexpected

All of the above are problems we know about, problems you will likely be familiar with, and problems you just as likely may already be exhausted by. If we flip that script, and you're reading this book at a time when all of these problems have been elegantly solved, theatre still won't be a utopic artform that requires no evolution. That will simply never be the case. There will always be new problems to solve, and those that have the greatest opportunity, the most energy hidden within them, will be the problems we can't anticipate, just like the pandemic. Here, you've seen an example of a project that successfully encountered and overcame an unexpected problem, and now you know how to do it yourself. So do it yourself.

Part II – Over to You

Who Are You Waiting For?

> "Our deepest fear is not that we are inadequate,
> Our deepest fear is that we are powerful beyond measure.
> It is our light, not our darkness, that most frightens us.
> It's not just in some of us; it's in everyone.
> And as we let our own light shine, we unconsciously give other people permission to do the same".

Aside: *this (abridged) excerpt from what was once widely accepted to be a passage from Nelson Mandela's emancipation speech was in fact first authored by spiritualist Marianne Williamson. Regardless of its provenance, it speaks to the truth.*

There will always be challenges to be tackled. There will always be new art to be made. There will always be new forms for it to take and new things to say with it. Who are you to contribute a rock to the pile of progress? Who are you *not* to?

Lindsey Turner asks student directors to answer an important question for themselves before they start a project: **from where do you derive your authority?**

If you still have no other answer, **then let *this* be your authority: your own unique perspective, context, and creativity, and this toolkit.**

In formal design thinking, there are two cardinal crimes, according to Karel Vredenburg, Director of IBM Global Design Leadership, Culture, & External Programs:

- Having ideas but never actually *making* something.
- Making something with no sense of who it's *for*.

You have to make it, and it has to be for somebody. In Peter Brook's terms, a thing must happen, and someone must witness it.

So to Time we leave it. And to you.

Note

1 https://newdiorama.com/news/a-season-of-no-shows

APPENDICES

APPENDIX A

SAMPLE "YOU'VE BEEN CAST" EMAIL DOCUMENT

Hi everyone!

First of all, congratulations! You've been cast in our next show **TSMGO: Macbeth on Wednesday 7 October at 7 PM BST!**

Please find attached to this email some more information on **how to work with Zoom**. I've also included the **Track Sheet** which shows which scenes your characters appear in. Please note the ensemble tracks are subject to change as we work on the script later this week.

The **Script** will be coming at the end of the week. We will be using the version of the text from playshakespeare.com if you'd like to start familiarizing in advance! Please note we may make some minor edits – we will send you the Master Script at the end of the week which you will need to use for the show.

Before the first rehearsal, **please do the following:**

1 **Read through your scenes,** and make some choices to bring with you. We don't have much time together so we need everyone to be familiar with their parts before we start
2 Read the Zoom Theatre Guide PDF *in full* attached
3 Watch the TSMGO Digital Theatre Tutorial *in full* here: <LINK> and Zoom Setup Guide here: <LINK>

The show will be very technically ambitious! So we need you all to be up to speed on this.

A **Briefing Guide** will be coming in a separate email later this week. This would be a meeting in normal life, but as we have to prepare at such a pace, we have created as many resources as possible to help us all strive for slickness together and maximize the juice we can wring from our limited rehearsal time!

Section 1: Casting Details!

Please find in the table below the part(s) you'll be playing, and the contact details for the rest of the cast. This will be invaluable in creating opportunities to rehearse with those you share scenes with. While Rob will be running as much as he can, you'll want to run stuff together, work notes, etc. in breakout rooms for sure.

PLEASE CAN YOU EMAIL name@email.com BY 11 AM BST TOMORROW TO CONFIRM THAT YOU WILL BE TAKING PART.

In your reply, PLEASE ALSO INCLUDE your LOCATION (to identify time zones) and RE-CONFIRM ANY AVAILABILITY CONFLICTS you have Saturday 3rd to Wednesday 7 October.

Please see below for the present casting:

CHARACTER	ACTOR	EMAIL	PRONOUNS
Macbeth			
Lady Macbeth			
Malcolm			
Macduff			
Ross			
Banquo			
First Witch			
Lennox			

(Continued)

(Continued)

CHARACTER	ACTOR	EMAIL	PRONOUNS
Duncan, King of Scotland			
Second Witch			
Third Witch			
Lady Macduff			
Ensemble 1			
Ensemble 2			
Ensemble 3			
Ensemble 4			
Ensemble 5			
Ensemble 6			
Ensemble 7			
SWING 1			
SWING 2			

SWINGS: swings are an invaluable addition to the team – they are our last line of defense in the event of technical difficulties or personal emergencies. Consequently, swings may have to jump in at any point in the play to cover any character, which is why we like to cast experienced, safe-pairs of hands in these spots. Previous swings have read in during rehearsals for others who can't make it, expertly covered on the live show, and are favorites amongst audiences when they do appear! We remember swings in future applications, with the intention of giving swings another role down the line.

Rehearsals

Please see below the rehearsal timings as they currently stand. You may not be needed for all rehearsals (leads will be needed for most). Once we have everyone's confirmed availability conflicts and time zones, we will build a schedule bearing these in mind as best we can.

(All Times BST)
SATURDAY: tutorial, home read-through, prep, etc. | 17:00–18:00 **MEET & GREET (ALL CALLED)**
SUNDAY: Zoom Rehearsal 11:00–12:00 | 13:00–15:00 | 16:00–18:00 | 19:00–22:30 **SETPIECES WITH FIGHT/MOVEMENT DIRECTOR**
MONDAY: Zoom Rehearsals 16:00–18:00 |19:00–22:30
TUESDAY: Zoom Rehearsals 16:00–18:00 |19:00–21:00 | 21:00–22:30 **TECH RUN (ALL CALLED)**
WEDNESDAY: Zoom Rehearsal 14:00–16:00 and LIVESTREAM 18:30–22:30

REMINDER: North American actors won't be expected at the UK morning rehearsals.

We also encourage you to arrange time outside of these slots to work on notes with your scene partners.

IF YOU ARE TAKING PART: please email **associate producer Ruth Page** at name@email.com by **Thursday 1 October** with:

1 Your Twitter/Social handle
2 Your web-res headshot
3 A 140 character bio including Twitter/Social handles of the three biggest companies you've worked for e.g. Globe, RSC, Mischief, BBC (doesn't have to be heavyweight institutions – everything is relative!)

All this helps hugely in drawing casual viewers to the project, and helps us to promote the show and your involvement!

Thank you so much! We look forward to getting started.

Best wishes

Sarah & Rob
TSMGO

Appendix A1. Sample "Briefing" Email

Hi everyone!

First of all, we now have a full cast, hooray! Please see the final cast list at the bottom of this email. We're so looking forward to working with you all.

Here is your briefing for the next few days. This is an email that should be a meeting!

In order to maximize the very limited rehearsal time we have together, please can you make sure you've **done all of the following ahead of Sunday's first rehearsal**:

1. Watch the TSMGO Digital Theatre Tutorial *in full* (link sent in the first email) and the Zoom setup guide
2. Read through the Zoom for Theatre Guide PDF (sent in the first email)
3. Read through the Macbeth Briefing Guide PDF *(attached) in full*
4. Check through the cast track Excel *(updated version attached)* sheet to ensure you know which parts you are playing
5. Read through the Master script *(attached)* to familiarize yourself with your part(s), make some choices, and annotate it with entrance/exits, and mic/camera on/off, etc.

Please check the cast track to see the scenes in which you appear. Ensemble can also use this to note character name changes in the script.

You'll want to spend some time calibrating your preferred set-up, practicing entrances and exits, etc. before Sunday, so we can all hit the ground running. The rehearsal room below will be live until we do the show, so do drop in to orientate yourself.

The Zoom Links

Rehearsal Room (open until 16:00 BST Wednesday): <LINK>
Password: Password

Performance Space (different Zoom link) (CALL TIME 18:30 BST Wednesday): <LINK>
Password: Password

Rehearsals (All Times BST)

I'll share the proposed rehearsal schedule later in a separate email – please make sure you take note of your call times. We also encourage you to arrange time outside of these slots to work on notes with your scene partners.

A reminder that ALL ARE CALLED for the Meet & Greet on Saturday at 5 pm BST and the Tech Run at 9 pm BST on Tuesday. Sunday 7–10.30 pm BST is when we work all setpieces (i.e. physical business/fights/special effects, etc.).

Props

We'll be sharing guidance on props, costume, and setpieces (which we'll rehearse Sunday night) by tomorrow. Our Master of Props, Emily Ingram (cc'd), will be putting together tutorials for some of the props you'll need. You will find these here: <LINK>

Socials

If you don't already, please follow us on socials and help us promote the show by sharing, posting, and retweeting!

@TSMGOnlineLive (Twitter) @TheShowMustGoOnline (Instagram & Facebook)

Cast List

CHARACTER	ACTOR	EMAIL	PRONOUNS
Macbeth			
Lady Macbeth			
Malcolm			
Macduff			
Ross			
Banquo			
First Witch			

(Continued)

(Continued)

CHARACTER	ACTOR	EMAIL	PRONOUNS
Lennox			
Duncan, King of Scotland			
Second Witch			
Third Witch			
Lady Macduff			
Ensemble 1			
Ensemble 2			
Ensemble 3			
Ensemble 4			
Ensemble 5			
Ensemble 6			
Ensemble 7			
SWING 1			
SWING 2			

Here's the link to the show which you can share far and wide! <LINK>

We'll be following up later with a list of props, costumes, and setpieces.

Thanks all!

Sarah

Appendix A2. Sample "Briefing" Guide

TSMGO: *Participation Briefing*

Please read this briefing in full. This will allow us all to move forward faster together.

As I'm sure you can appreciate, there are a lot of you all around the world, and we have three days to make magic together. Every detail you pick up now is more time spent making the read the best it can be!

There are four sections to the briefing:

1 Preparation
2 General Notes
3 Text
4 Rehearsals

Read and absorb all these, and you'll be fully set up to hit the ground running for the rest of the week! Huzzah!

1) Preparation

Remember, above all we are looking to **entertain each other and our audience**. We want this to be **fun and joyful**. It WILL be a little anarchic. Mistakes will be made.

We're not looking for perfection, but we ARE striving together for slickness.

Hopefully, by now you've seen one of the shows, and you'll know they're built around some core values: **pace, energy, clarity, resourcefulness,** and **ingenuity**.

Theatre, to me, is ultimately a transfusion of energy from us to the audience. At this time, it is having a truly profound effect.

Here are some resources to get you started:

A summary of the play
A list of characters and their descriptions
A graph of character relationships/interactions

Please take the time to read and understand your part(s), and make some choices.

Everyone's experience is different, so reach out if you want help.

If you come across anything unfamiliar in the language, chances are it will be covered at shakespeareswords.com, a great online resource that Ben Crystal has generously provided **FREE** access to for the cast and crew!
   Login: name@email.com
   Password: Password

2) General Notes

PICKING UP CUES: because of the slight time delay in the transmission, we have to be hyper-conscious of snatching off the end of the person's line as we speak. When they are saying the last syllable of their last word, you want to be starting. If we have even a small pause after each line, over the course of the play, that creates 20 minutes of silence and pulls the wind out of the play's sails. This is something to be conscious of while rehearsing. In Richard III this was mastered in scenes for the first time, and the audience commented on what a transformational effect it had – the impact of this subtle trick on bringing things to the "next level" can't be underestimated.

FLOWING LIKE A RIVER: don't break up the text. The text wants to flow, and by flowing with it, you contribute to the momentum and intensity of the play and make it easier for the audience to connect the dots in difficult/complex thoughts.

Everything you say is important, and on YouTube, like the groundlings of Shakespeare's day, we have to fight to grab and hold onto the audience's attention.

Imaginary Forces: because you'll be sitting or standing in your living room giving a bravura performance of Shakespeare, it really helps to do imaginative work on worldbuilding and character, so you 'project' this into the minds of the audience. How are the five senses being activated in each scene/moment, what is the wider context (the moment before you came on stage, your character's life experiences up to the play beginning, are they hungry, have they been running?)

Text work basics: count the syllables – there are plenty of accented "eds" to be pronounced in order to fit the rhythm. It's a great practice to underline the verbs in your text and try to inflect them with a vocal quality that brings their meaning to life – verbs give the illusion of action and things happening.

We may make additional cuts as we go along. This will solely be with the quality of audience experience in mind.

If you are a **SWING**, it's of course up to you how much preparation you do, as you may be called in mid-stream if someone drops out due to connectivity problems, or something else unforeseen happens. As such you're an invaluable addition to the team and our last line of defense should anything go awry!

3) The Text

Please use The Master Script provided.

Everyone using the same version guarantees we are all singing from the same hymn sheet.

It's an editable document, so you can also mark up your script in any number of ways to set cues for microphone and camera, underline emphases, and so on. This is really valuable in building a sleek and streamlined experience for yourself.

Please have the script open on your screen throughout. If you attempt to read from a printed copy, you will cast your energy downward, and we'll lose your face while you're talking, meaning the audience will spend a lot of time looking at the tops of heads.

- **Tip:** Consider collapsing the "page breaks" so you have a continuous stream of text
- **ACT and SCENE character lists:** In the act and scene headers, you will see in brackets a list of characters. This tells you everyone who is in the scene throughout. ONLY THOSE DESCRIBED BELOW THIS with ENTER ... actually enter at the start. The rest have entrances mid-scene. Only this initial entrance will be read live, for the rest, you'll need to enter on your cue
- **ENTRANCES AND EXITS:** Please mark your personal entrances and exits clearly (I use large font size and highlighting) to ensure you don't miss them

PROPS AND ACTIONS: We have marked in the script where there are actions that take place in the play, and where you might require props. These are our opportunities to be inventive and have fun! Audiences love this stuff so much, and it's a brave new medium we're playing in.

Look at the color coding in the script – props are in blue, and actions are in red. When it comes to props, the more inventive and resourceful the better, and Emily Ingram, our Associate Stage Manager, will help you with these. We are trying to recreate movie magic in our living rooms. Purple is for sound cues.

If you'd like any advice on fashioning props, please contact Emily: name@email.com

4) Rehearsals

REHEARSAL ROOM (open until 16:00 BST Wednesday):
https://us02web.zoom.us/j/81513845528?pwd=eWM1ZHRJVDJESUc4KysxekOxWDZidz09
Password: MACBETH

The digital rehearsal room will be available 24hrs a day until it closes before the show.

This is available for you to get slick with operating Zoom, and to run scenes.

Please **coordinate with one another** using the emails in the casting announcement, and get together to run scenes.

I will do everything I can to be available to you during the next few days, so do feel free to request my presence. As you are donating your time and talent, I will of course endeavor to support you as much as possible!

Similarly, if you discover any actions in the course of working either with me or with one another, **please communicate the business you discover to your scene partners.**

NORTH AMERICA ACTORS: the idea is that you would join the afternoon/evening rehearsals BST. Please don't deprive yourselves of rest!

PERFORMANCE SPACE (DIFFERENT ZOOM LINK) (CALL TIME 18:30 BST Wednesday):
<Zoom Link>
Password: Password

Please join at this time to check your setup is working and do final checks and prep before we go live at 19:00 BST.

4) Rehearsal Timetable (All Timings Are BST)

REHEARSAL TYPE	DAY	TIME
MEET & GREET (ALL CALLED)	SATURDAY	17:00–18:00
SCENES	SUNDAY	11:00–12:00
SCENES	SUNDAY	13:00–15:00 | 16:00–18:00
SCENES (SETPIECES)	SUNDAY	19:00–22:30
SCENES	MONDAY	16:00–18:00
SCENES	MONDAY	19:00–22:30
SCENES	TUESDAY	16:00–18:00
SCENES	TUESDAY	19:00–21:00
TECH RUN (ALL CALLED)	TUESDAY	21:00–22:30
SCENES	WEDNESDAY	14:00–16:00

Appendix A3. Sample Conversation Email Document

Hi all!

We'll use this thread for notes, updates, availability for rehearsals, answering questions, and for you to have productive discussions in prep for Weds.

Please do not reply to the rehearsal schedule thread.

Thanks!

Sarah

Appendix A4. Sample Props, Costume, and Setpieces List

1) Setpieces

Some of these will be rehearsed with Janet Lawson our fight coordinator.

We currently have:

1.1 Witches
1.3 Witches dance and chant
2.3 Duncan murder revealed
3.3 Murder of Banquo
3.4 Banquet & ghost of Banquo
4.1 Cauldron spell
4.1 Apparitions
4.1 Witches dance
4.2 Murder of Macduffs
5.1 Sleepwalking scene
5.7 Young Siward & Macbeth fight
5.8 Macduff & Macbeth fight
THANK YOU EVERYONE!
Rob, Sarah & The TSMGO Team

2) Props

Thane of Cawdor pin – Ross, Macbeth
Torches – Banquo, Fleance, Servant
Belt & dagger – Banquo, Fleance
Crown – Macbeth, Lady Macbeth
Notebook & pen – Doctor of Physic
Macbeth's head – Macduff
Letter – Macbeth, Lady Macbeth
VBG of blood-covered Banquo – Banquo
Scarf/Neckerchief – Macbeth
Candle – Lady Macbeth
Daggers x 2 – Macbeth, Lady Macbeth
Hatchet/axe – Murderers
Wine & wine glasses – all in 3.4
Baby – Lady Macduff
Hand-rubbing effects – Lady Macbeth
Branches x 2 – all in 5.6
Swords – Young Siward, Macbeth
Tutorials and guides for props will be added to the props folder: <LINK>

3) Costume

Character group names taken from the Shakespeare's Words Graph – see page 3 of briefing guide

PLEASE CONSIDER STATUS, PERSONALITY, etc. in putting together an outfit – be creative! Please bring along to rehearsal on Tuesday for the Tech Run

Use the Pinterest board as reference material (hover over each image to see Rob's comments): <LINK>

Duncan – Robe + Crown

Macbeth – Armor + Kilt (as Thane) Robe + Crown(as king)

All Warriors – shoulder kilt with signature pin on one shoulder, pauldron on the other

Witches – hair braiding, either gold (1st), bronze (2nd) or brown/green (3rd) colors and headdresses: 1st horns, 2nd trees, 3rd worms)

Lady Macduff & Lady Macbeth – medieval head dress, constrained. Lady M had no headdress once queen/after the first banquet

Servants + Children – cloaks/kilts pinned to one shoulder, no armor

Doctors – high/tight scarf on neck, perhaps whole head wrapped tight, black/gray

Appendix A5. Sample Rehearsal Schedule Email

Hi all!

Looking forward to seeing you all today at 5 pm BST for the Meet & Greet!

Below is the rehearsal schedule for this week. This has been created taking on board all the notes on availability that we've been sent, and time zones wherever possible (for North Americans, the earliest you should be called is 8 am your time).

If there's anything we've missed, please give me a shout asap.

We have a very tight schedule! So please check through it carefully and make a note of all the times you are called (cross-check your scenes in the Excel cast track, and write the times in your calendar, set reminders on your phone, or write on a note next to your laptop, etc.)

Here's a handy time zone calculator if you need it: https://www.worldtimebuddy.com/

Please can everyone be on Zoom ready to start at the call time – we recommend jumping on five mins before. We'll send a call sheet out ahead of each slot to give you a rough idea of what time we'll need you, and a reminder of who is called.

With the setpieces, please note these are very unpredictable in terms of timings, so please be prepared to start earlier/later than noted in the schedule. Your flexibility and patience are hugely appreciated!

For details on setpieces, see the list in TSMGO Macbeth Props, Costumes & Setpieces pdf (this will be sent by later today)

ALL TIMES BST	SUNDAY	MONDAY	TUESDAY	WEDNESDAY
11 am–12 pm	1.7 / 2.2	N/A	N/A	N/A
1–2 pm	1.5 / 4.2	N/A	N/A	N/A
2–3 pm	4.1*	N/A	N/A	AVAILABLE
3–4 pm	N/A	N/A	N/A	AVAILABLE
4–5 pm	5.1 / 5.3	2.4 / 5.4 / 5.2 / 5.5	AVAILABLE	N/A
5–6 pm	5.6 / 5.7 / 5.8 / 5.9**	2.1 / 3.2	4.3	N/A

(Continued)

Appendix A   **181**

(Continued)

ALL TIMES BST	SUNDAY	MONDAY	TUESDAY	WEDNESDAY
7–8 pm	3.5 / Setpieces in 4.2 / 5.1	3.1 / 3.3	3.4	SHOW (call 6.30 pm)
8–9 pm	Setpieces in 1.1 / 1.3 / 4.1	2.3	1.1 / 1.3	SHOW
9–10.30 pm	Setpieces in 3.3 / 3.4 / 2.3 / 5.7 / 5.8	1.2 / 1.4 / 1.6 / 5.9 for Ross	**TECH (ALL CALLED)**	SHOW
*No Banquo	**No Ross			

Quick reference for the rehearsal link: <LINK>
Password: Password

If anyone would like to have some additional time with Rob to run speeches, etc. he can make himself available Mon/Tues 1.30–3.30 pm BST (please drop me an email to book). We will use the Wednesday slots as spillover for anything that needs running again.

Please **don't reply to this thread** – instead use the "**Conversation**" thread (to follow) for discussions and questions, so we can keep this as a quick reference for everyone.

Remember: we encourage you to arrange times to run scenes with your scene partners outside rehearsal times, or ask for a breakout room in the Zoom chat if you want to run something while we're running another scene in the main space.

The rehearsal room is open 24/7.

Thanks!

Sarah

Appendix A6. Sample Rehearsal Call Sheet

Macbeth TSMGO Dir: Rob Myles	Rehearsal Schedule	Sunday, Oct 4, 2020 11 am–12 pm BST
PLEASE REMEMBER TO SHOW UP READY TO WORK FOR YOUR CALL TIME (recommend 5 mins)		
Time (BST)	**Work**	**Called**
11–11.30	Act 1 Scene 7	MACBETH ( ) LADY MACBETH ( )
11.30–12	Act 2 Scene 2	MACBETH ( ) LADY MACBETH ( )

Macbeth TSMGO Dir: Rob Myles	Rehearsal Schedule	Sunday, Oct 4, 2020 1 pm–3 pm BST
PLEASE REMEMBER TO SHOW UP READY TO WORK FOR YOUR CALL TIME (recommend 5 mins)		
Time (BST)	**Work**	**Called**
1–1.25	Act 1 Scene 5	MACBETH ( ) LADY MACBETH ( ) MACBETH'S MESSENGER ( )
1.35–2	Act 4 Scene 2	MESSENGER ( ) ROSSE ( ) FIRST MURDERER ( ) SECOND MURDERER ( ) SON TO MACDUFF ( ) LADY MACDUFF ( )
2–3	Act 4 Scene 1	MACBETH ( ) LENNOX ( ) FIRST WITCH ( ) SECOND WITCH ( ) THIRD WITCH ( ) FIRST APPARITION ( ) SECOND APPARITION ( ) THIRD APPARITION ( ) BANQUO ( )

Macbeth TSMGO Dir: Rob Myles	Rehearsal Schedule	Sunday, Oct 4, 2020 4 pm–6 pm BST
PLEASE REMEMBER TO SHOW UP READY TO WORK FOR YOUR CALL TIME (recommend 5 mins)		
Time (BST)	Work	Called
4–4.30	Act 5 Scene 1	LADY MACBETH ( ) GENTLEWOMAN ( ) DOCTOR OF PHYSIC ( )
4.30–5	Act 5 Scene 3	MACBETH ( ) SERVANT ( ) DOCTOR OF PHYSIC ( ) SEYTON ( )
5–5.10	Act 5 Scene 6	MALCOLM ( ) MACDUFF ( ) SIWARD, EARL OF NORTHUMBERLAND ( ) YOUNG SIWARD ( ) SOLDIER ( ) SOLDIER ( )
5.10–5.25	Act 5 Scene 7	MALCOLM ( ) MACBETH ( ) MACDUFF ( ) SIWARD, EARL OF NORTHUMBERLAND ( ) YOUNG SIWARD ( )
5.25–5.45	Act 5 Scene 8	MACBETH ( ) MACDUFF ( )
5.45–6	Act 5 Scene 9	MALCOLM ( ) ROSS ( ) MACDUFF ( ) SIWARD, EARL OF NORTHUMBERLAND ( ) ANGUS ( ) LENNOX ( ) CATHNESS ( ) MENTETH ( )

Macbeth TSMGO Dir: Rob Myles	Rehearsal Schedule	Sunday, Oct 4, 2020 7 pm–10.30 pm BST
PLEASE REMEMBER TO SHOW UP READY TO WORK FOR YOUR CALL TIME **(recommend 5 mins)**		
Time (BST)	**Work**	**Called**
7–7.15	Act 3 Scene 5	LENNOX ( ) LORD ( )
7.15–8	Set Pieces 4.2 (murder of the Macduffs)	FIRST MURDERER ( ) SECOND MURDERER ( ) SON TO MACDUFF ( ) LADY MACDUFF ( )
	Set Pieces 5.1 (Sleepwalking)	LADY MACBETH ( ) GENTLEWOMAN ( ) DOCTOR OF PHYSIC ( )
8–9	Set Pieces 1.1 (Witches)	FIRST WITCH ( ) SECOND WITCH ( ) THIRD WITCH ( )
	Set Pieces 1.3 (Witches dance and chant)	FIRST WITCH ( ) SECOND WITCH ( ) THIRD WITCH ( )
	Set Pieces 4.1 (Cauldron)	FIRST WITCH ( ) SECOND WITCH ( ) THIRD WITCH ( )
	Set Pieces 4.1 (Apparitions)	FIRST WITCH ( ) SECOND WITCH ( ) THIRD WITCH ( ) BANQUO ( ) FIRST APPARITION ( ) SECOND APPARITION ( ) THIRD APPARITION ( ) MACBETH ( )
	Set Pieces 4.1 (Witches dance)	FIRST WITCH ( ) SECOND WITCH ( ) THIRD WITCH ( )
9–10.30	Set Pieces 3.3 (Murder of Banquo)	BANQUO ( ) FIRST MURDERER ( ) SECOND MURDERER ( ) FLEANCE ( ) THIRD MURDERER ( )
	Set Pieces 3.4 (Banquet and ghost Banquo)	MACBETH ( ) ROSSE ( ) LENNOX ( ) LADY MACBETH ( ) LORD ( )

(Continued)

(Continued)

		BANQUO ( ) SERVANT ( )
	Set Pieces 2.3 (reveal of Duncan murder)	MALCOLM ( ) MACBETH ( ) ROSSE ( ) LENNOX ( ) MACDUFF ( ) LADY MACBETH ( ) BANQUO ( ) DONALBAIN ( )
	Set Pieces 5.7 (Young Siward vs Macbeth)	MACBETH ( ) YOUNG SIWARD ( )
	Set Pieces 5.8 (Macduff vs Macbeth)	MACBETH ( ) MACDUFF ( )

Macbeth TSMGO Dir: Rob Myles	Rehearsal Schedule	Monday, Oct 5, 2020 1 pm–3 pm BST
PLEASE REMEMBER TO SHOW UP READY TO WORK FOR YOUR CALL TIME (recommend 5 mins)		
Time (BST)	**Work**	**Called**
1–1.30	Speeches	LADY MACBETH ( )
1.30–2	2.3	PORTER ( )
2–3	Speeches	MACBETH ( )

Macbeth TSMGO Dir: Rob Myles	Rehearsal Schedule	Monday, Oct 5, 2020 4 pm–6 pm BST
PLEASE REMEMBER TO SHOW UP READY TO WORK FOR YOUR CALL TIME (recommend 5 mins)		
Time (BST)	**Work**	**Called**
4–4.15	Act 4 Scene 2	ROSS ( ) LADY MACDUFF ( )
4.15–4.35	Act 2 Scene 4	ROSSE ( ) MACDUFF ( ) OLD MAN ( )
4.35–4.45	Act 5 Scene 4	MALCOLM ( ) ANGUS ( ) ROSS ( )

(*Continued*)

(Continued)

		LENNOX ( ) MACDUFF ( ) SIWARD, EARL OF NORTHUMBERLAND ( ) SOLDIER ( ) YOUNG SIWARD ( ) MENTETH ( ) CATHNESS ( )
4.45–5.05	Act 5 Scene 5	MACBETH ( ) SEYTON ( ) MACBETH'S MESSENGER ( )
5.05–5.35	Act 2 Scene 1	MACBETH ( ) SERVANT ( ) BANQUO ( ) FLEANCE ( )
5.35–6	Act 3 Scene 2	MACBETH ( ) LADY MACBETH ( ) GENTLEWOMAN ( )

Macbeth TSMGO Dir: Rob Myles	Rehearsal Schedule	Monday, Oct 5, 2020 7 pm–10.30 pm BST
PLEASE REMEMBER TO SHOW UP READY TO WORK FOR YOUR CALL TIME **(recommend 5 mins)**		
Time (BST)	**Work**	**Called**
7–7.30	Act 3 Scene 1	MACBETH ( ) SERVANT ( ) ROSS ( ) LENNOX ( ) LADY MACBETH ( ) FIRST MURDERER ( ) SECOND MURDERER ( ) BANQUO ( )
7.30–8	Act 3 Scene 3	BANQUO ( ) FIRST MURDERER ( ) SECOND MURDERER ( ) FLEANCE ( ) THIRD MURDERER ( )
8–9	Act 2 Scene 3	MALCOLM ( ) MACBETH ( ) ROSSE ( ) LENNOX ( ) MACDUFF ( ) LADY MACBETH ( ) BANQUO ( )

(*Continued*)

Appendix A 187

(Continued)

		PORTER ( ) DONALBAIN ( )
9–9.20	Act 1 Scene 2	MALCOLM ( ) ANGUS ( ) ROSSE ( ) LENNOX ( ) DONALBAIN ( ) KING DUNCAN ( ) SERGEANT ( ) ATTENDANT ( )
9.20–9.40	Act 1 Scene 4	MALCOLM ( ) ANGUS ( ) MACBETH ( ) ROSSE ( ) LENNOX ( ) BANQUO ( ) DONALBAIN ( ) KING DUNCAN ( )
9.40–10	Act 1 Scene 6	MALCOLM ( ) ANGUS ( ) ROSSE ( ) LENNOX ( ) MACDUFF ( ) LADY MACBETH ( ) BANQUO ( ) DONALBAIN ( ) KING DUNCAN ( )
10–10.30	Act 5 Scene 2	ANGUS ( ) LENNOX ( ) MENTETH ( ) CATHNESS ( )

Macbeth TSMGO Dir: Rob Myles	Rehearsal Schedule	Tuesday, Oct 6, 2020 11 am–12 pm BST 1–3 pm BST
PLEASE REMEMBER TO SHOW UP READY TO WORK FOR YOUR CALL TIME (recommend 5 mins)		
Time (BST)	**Work**	**Called**
11–12	Dagger Tech	MACBETH ( )
1–2	Speeches	MACBETH ( )
2–3	Act 1 Scene 5	MACBETH ( ) LADY MACBETH ( )

Appendix A

Macbeth TSMGO Dir: Rob Myles	Rehearsal Schedule	Tuesday, Oct 6, 2020 4 pm–6 pm BST
PLEASE REMEMBER TO SHOW UP READY TO WORK FOR YOUR CALL TIME (recommend 5 mins)		
Time (BST)	**Work**	**Called**
4–5	Act 3 Scene 4	MACBETH ( ) ROSSE ( ) LENNOX ( ) LADY MACBETH ( ) LORD ( ) FIRST MURDERER ( ) BANQUO ( ) SERVANT ( )
5–6	Act 4 Scene 3	MALCOLM ( ) ROSSE ( ) MACDUFF ( ) ENGLISH DOCTOR ( )

Macbeth TSMGO Dir: Rob Myles	Rehearsal Schedule	Tuesday, Oct 6, 2020 7 pm–10.30 pm BST
PLEASE REMEMBER TO SHOW UP READY TO WORK FOR YOUR CALL TIME (recommend 5 mins)		
Time (BST)	**Work**	**Called**
7–8	Act 4 Scene 1	MACBETH ( ) LENNOX ( ) FIRST WITCH ( ) SECOND WITCH ( ) THIRD WITCH ( ) FIRST APPARITION ( ) SECOND APPARITION ( ) THIRD APPARITION ( ) BANQUO ( )
8–8.10	Act 1 Scene 1	FIRST WITCH ( ) SECOND WITCH ( ) THIRD WITCH ( )
8.10–9	Act 1 Scene 3	ANGUS ( ) MACBETH ( ) ROSSE ( ) BANQUO ( ) FIRST WITCH ( ) SECOND WITCH ( ) THIRD WITCH ( )
9–10.30	TECH	All Called (Please keep in mind this rehearsal may run late, please let us know if you are not able to stay past 10.30 pm for any reason)

Appendix A7. Sample Zoom Theatre Guide

Getting Started

- Download and test Zoom app ahead of time (see Zoom instructions on the next page) – grant permission for it to use your webcam and microphone. During the reading, contact Emily using the chat box if in need of support
- Screen set up at eye level in a well-lit, quiet room with a plain background (nothing branded or offensive). Laptops strongly preferred – if you need to use a mobile, rotate to landscape. Ensure your device is on mains charge
- Sit in front of your screen, facing the camera, so head and shoulders are visible, and you remain close to the mic. Please check your sound quality and use good headphones where needed
- Have the script open on screen so you are facing the camera. For mobiles, prop it up so the script (ideally on screen) is in your eyeline to avoid talking down to the table or to the side
- Stay on mute with videos off when not in a scene. If you are in a scene but don't speak for a period of time, please ensure you remain quiet with no background noise
- Pay close attention to the script – when 3–4 lines away from your cue to enter the scene, unmute and get ready to turn on video

Internet Connectivity

In order to ensure you have the strongest internet connection possible, there are some steps you can take to reduce lag/blurring/freezing:

- Set up as close as you can to your router so the signal is strong
- If you live with housemates/family, ask them nicely if they wouldn't mind downloading any films they plan to watch ahead of time, so they can play them locally on their device, rather than streaming during the show
- Take your mobile/cell off the wifi
- Close your internet browser so nothing is refreshing in the background
- If your connection is really poor, you could try restarting your router
- As a backup, find a local Zoom number on this page https://zoom.us/u/ab1Z3dtqcT and you can join with audio using your phone (you should be asked when you join the meeting whether you are using audio from your computer, or dialing in by phone)

If you happen to lose your connection entirely during the show, and can't use the Zoom chat, please send an email or use the WhatsApp group.

If the worst should happen, one of our Swings will be ready to step in and take your place for the remainder of your scene. If you're able to reconnect, you will join at your next entrance.

Timetable (All Timings Are GMT/BST)

	What We'll Be Doing	What You'll Need
18:30	Zoom call opens – tech set up	ALL CAST CALL – time to set up and run mic checks. All props/costume to be set
18:45	Final preparations and discussions	Final prep and check-in before we go live
19:00	We go live, with an introduction to the play	All stay on mute & videos off while the host gives welcome and our guest speaker introduces the play.
19:15	We start the read	All stay on mute and videos off – for those in the first scene, be ready to turn on when Rob calls out the play and music begins
INTERVAL	A five minute break to use the facilities, refresh drinks, discuss impressions so far	We will still be live while the production team and guest speaker take questions from the groundlings. Actors take a break, please keep videos off and stay on mute (please direct support questions to Emily via the chat box)
Approx. 21:00	We continue, reading Acts 4–5	All stay on mute and videos off – for those in the first scene of the second half, be ready to turn on when music starts
Approx. 22:00	The reading concludes, all players are introduced, and we take questions from the audience.	After everyone is called back on screen, please turn on your videos with mic on but stay quiet except when speaking. We will let you know when we are offline.
22:30	FINAL CLOSE & AFTER PARTY	

The Protocol

- OFFSTAGE = Camera OFF, Mic OFF
- ONSTAGE = Camera ON, Mic ON
- [within] or similar = Camera OFF, Mic ON

Appendix A8. Sample Final Show Prep Email

Hi everyone,

Looking forward to tomorrow! Thank you SO much for all your hard work, it's looking EPIC!

A few key final technical bits to check/prep ahead of the show (please go through all points):

1 **Boost your internet connections** – ask everyone in your home if they can download any films/TV shows they want to watch, so they're not streaming them. Other than the one you're using for the show, disconnect all other devices from WiFi. Make sure all browsers/tabs are closed to save on bandwidth – the only things you should have open are your script and Zoom
2 **Sound quality** – we'll do a final sound check before the show to adjust volumes. If you've been experiencing issues, please ask Matthew to check tomorrow before call time
3 **Lighting** – check your lighting to make sure we can see your lovely faces, and importantly your eyes:) Avoid backlights (including windows), and direct light on your face – it's better to bounce it off a wall in front of you. Bear in mind the time of day we'll be performing – for those in UK it will get darker during the show, so best to block out natural light so it's consistent. PLEASE CHECK THE LIGHTING STATES LIST and mark in your scripts when you're meant to be in darkness
4 **Entrances/Exits** – please double-check you have these noted for every scene and highlight them clearly in your script. Mark in MIC ON/OFF and CAMERA ON/OFF at the appropriate points so you don't miss them. Please email Emily to confirm any remote camera kills you are expecting
5 **Props/Costumes** – have these ready and set in the positions you need them before the call time at 6.30 pm BST. Any final help you need, please reach out to Emily Ingram
6 **Naming** – a reminder that the format is CHARACTER (Full Name). For those who have to change your character name mid-show, make sure you change it after your exit so it's ready to go for your next scene (you should only have one character at a time on screen). Note these changes in your script. For Witches please write the word "FIRST" in the character name, not "1st"
7 **Swing** – we'll go over the swing protocol with everyone when we meet at 6.30 pm BST, but one key thing is that if for any reason we have to

remove you from a scene (e.g. if you missed an exit, or your camera froze) you will be invited to restart your video. Please hit **LATER** so you can turn your camera on at your next entrance

8 **Notifications** – please make sure you have turned off all notifications on your devices so that you don't get "pings" coming through during the show

9 **Sound Cues** – during the show, unless you're meant to be talking over background music mid-scene, please wait for sound cues to finish before speaking, else you won't be heard

And finally that all important **link for the performance (DIFFERENT TO THE REHEARSAL LINK – call time is 6.30 pm BST** – the host has to start the call first, so don't worry if you can't get in before this): <LINK>
Password: Password

Any last questions/concerns on setup, please give me or Emily a shout.

Thanks all!

Sarah

Appendix A9. Sample Green Room Email

Hi everyone,

BRAVO!!! What an absolutely stellar team you've been this week – you've all worked super hard in pulling together what is Shakespeare's arguably most ambitious production, and put in beautiful performances to boot. We can't thank you enough for your energy and commitment. It was a joy to work with you all.

Here are some social bits for you:

We have a Facebook Alumni group for continued chats and merriment! Please go to the link below and request to join: <LINK>

Thank you so much for all of your interactions with our social media platforms. You helped to create awesome momentum throughout the week. But, we still need your help!

Please continue liking, sharing, and interacting with our content, and if you see anyone posting about missing live performance/looking for recommendations, please tag us in the conversation. Helping us spread the word about The Show Must Go Online and the fact that "Shakespeare is for everyone" will make such a big difference, and mean more people will see your brilliant performances!

Below is a reminder of where to find us on social channels – we'd welcome audience reviews on FB too!

https://www.facebook.com/TheShowMustGoOnline/
https://www.instagram.com/theshowmustgoonline/
https://twitter.com/TSMGOnlineLive

We have an IMDB page which the brilliant Matthew Rhodes will be updating: https://www.imdb.com/title/tt12063532/ This will be updated soon, so do check back once the show is up to make sure your links are correct.

A quick note on the Patreon – the funds run monthly so I will be in touch with everyone from the September shows in the next week about how to opt in for their share.

And finally, the link to the show for you to share far and wide:) <LINK>

Take care all!

Best wishes

Rob & Sarah

APPENDIX B

LIST OF CREATIVES INVOLVED IN TSMGO

Aarushi Ganju
Andrew AB
Adam Boyle
Adam Bruce
Adam Courting
Adam Gibson
Adam Parker
Adam Pelta-Pauls
Adam Turns
Adam Woodhams
Ahd Tamimi
Ailis Duff
Alec Bennie
Alec Stephens III
Alex Andlau
Alex Britt
Alex Pearson
Alex Phelps
Alexander Hopwood
Alexandra Bandean
Alexandra Bennett
Alexandra Kataigida
Alexia Moyano
Alexis Danan
Alice D Bloomer
Alice Langrish
Alice Merivale
Alice Osmanski
Alicia Berard
Alix Dunmore

Allie Croker
Ally Poole
Amelia Parillon-Samuel
Amit Khanna
Amy Sutton
Andrea Smith
Andrew Brown
Andrew Mockler
Andrew Nesbitt
Andrew Pawarroo
Andrew Yabroff
Andy Mcleod
Andy Pacino
Angel Dumapias
Angela Bull
Annabelle Higgins
Anthony Michael Martinez
Arden Fitzroy
Aruna Clinch
Ash Pryce
Ashley Byam
Audrey L'Ebrellec
Aurora Nicole Kim
Austin Tichenor
Azaan Symes
Ben Crystal
Ben Galpin
Ben Gilbert
Benjamin Chandler

Benjamin McFadden
Bennett Pologe
Bernard Soubry
Bess Roche
Beth Burns
Beacon Bowman
Bill Bingham
Bill Glaser
Blioux Kirkby
Bonnie MacBird
Brandi Adams
Brandon Dodsworth
Breanne Weber
Brian Eastty
Brian Gillett
Bryony Reynoldsg
Callum Lloyd
Cameron Varner
Candace Leung
Candice Handy
Carla Della Gatta
Carlos Drocchi
Carly Sponzo
Carol Harvey
Caroline Basra
Carys McQueen
Charlene V. Smith
Charles Sloboda-Bolton
Charlie Clee
Charlotte Coles

Appendix B **195**

Charlotte E Tayler
Charlotte Ellen
Charlotte Harvey
Charlotte McEvoy
Charlotte Vaughn Raines
Chi-Chi Onuah
Chloe Wigmore
Chris Garner
Chris Pearson
Christine Atieno
Christopher Marino
Christopher Paddon
Christopher Poke
Christopher Smart
Claire Richardson
Claire-Marie Hall
Claire-Monique Martin
Clark Alexander
Clay Sanderson
Clive Keene
Colin Hurley
Comfort Fabian
Constanza Ruff
Corinna Brown
Curt Himmelberger
Dafydd Gwyn Howells
Dan Beaulieu
Dan Blaker
Dan Blick
Dan Wilson
Dana Demsko
Daniel Cech-Lucas
Daniel Cordova
Danielle Farrow
Dannan McAleer
Danny Adams
Dathan B Williams
David Collins
David Djemal
David Ellis
David Johnson
David Martinez
David Sayers
David Sterling Brown
Debra Ann Byrd
Derekk Ross
Disa Andersen
Doireann May White
Dominic Brewer
Drew Linson
Drew Paterson

Duncan Hess
Ed Guccione
Eduardo J Pérez-Torres
Edward Daranyi
Eifion Ap Cadno
El Neylon
Eleanor Shannon
Eleanor Wilkinson
Elena Pavli
Eliza Jayne Gilroy
Elizabeth Dennehy
Elizabeth Lancaster
Elizabeth Tavares
Leo Mock
Elliott Bornemann
Elloise Thomson
Elsa Tuxworth
Emer McHugh
Emilio Vieira
Emily Beach
Emily Beck
Emily Carding
Emily H. Gilson
Emily Ingram
Emily Millwood
Emma Wilkes
Emma Zadow
Enric Ortuno
Eric Rasmussen
Esmonde Cole
Eugenia Low
Eva Yacobi
Evangeline Dickson
Evie Hargreaves
Ezra Jackson-Smith
Faiza Qureshi
Felix Beauchamp
Fergus Rattigan
Fiona Tong
Fleur de Wit
Flinn McManus
Fran Cattaneo
Francesca Baker
Fred Arnot
Freddie Hill
Frey Kwa Hawking
Gabriel Akamo
Gabrielle Sheppard
Gah-Kai Leung
Gareth Balai
Gareth Turkington

Gary Boulter
Gemma Miller
Genevieve Levin
Genie Kaminski
Geoffrey Mamdani
George Jones
Georgia Andrews
Gethin Alderman
Gillian Barmes
Gilly Kelleher
Gina Atkinson
Giulia Rose
Grace Ioppolo
Grace MacDougall
Grace Kelly Miller
Green and Gray Audio
Gregory Jon Phelps
Guido Garcia Lueches
Hailey Bachrach
Hannah Balogun
Hannah Roze-Lewis
Hannah Young
Harley Jane Kozak
Harriet Sharmini Smithers
Harry Boyd
Harry Brierley
Harry Farmer
Harry R. McCarthy
Hasna Haidar
Hayley Mitchell
Hector Bateman-Harden
Heidi McIver
Helen Millar
Henry Charnock
Henry Jenkinson
Holly Ashman
Honey Gabriel
Ian Blackwell Rogers
Ian Doescher
Imelda D'souza
Isabel Adomakoh Young
Ivan Doan
Jack Baldwin
Jack Lancaster
Jackie T. Hanlin
Jacqueline Youm
Jake Runeckles
James Dawoud
James Drake
Jamey Grisham
Jamie Gould

196 Appendix B

Jamie Richard-Stewart
Jan Guest
Jan Zálabák
Jane Elsmore
Janet Lawson
Jason Adam
Jason Blackwater
Jed McLoughlin
Jed Resnick
Jeff King
Jeffrey Weissman
Jemma Geanaus
Jemma Alix Levy
Jenn Deon
Jennifer Glover
Jennifer Shakesby
Ren Ruidi
Jenny Rowe
Jenny Wills
Jeremy Mortimer
Jes Gislason
Jess Vince-Moin
Jessica Erin Martin
Jim Trimmer
Joanna Clarke
Joanna Harte
Joanna lucas
Joanne Randle
Joe Penczak
John Chapman
John D. Huston
John DeFilippo
John Spilsbury
John-Otto Phike
Jonathan Cobb
Jonathan Oliver
Jordan Lillie
Jordy Joans (formerly Deelight)
Joseph Marcell
Josh Tucker
Joy Tan
Joyce Branagh
Judith Quin
Julia Giolzetti
Julia Stemper
Julia Walker Wyson
Julie Baber
Julie Martis
Justin Skelton
Karim Hadaya

Kate Donnachie
Kate Roche
Kate Sketchley
Katerina Ntroudi
Katharine Bubbear
Katie Forster
Katie McKenna Mestres
Katie stimpson
Katie Tranter
Katrina Allen
Katrina Michaels
Kavita Mudan Finn
Kay Guccione
Keagan Carr Fransch
Kelly B. Jones
Kevin V. Smith
Kim Cincotti-Seldon
Kim Durham
Kirsten Foster
Kirsty Cox
Kit Brenson
Kit McGuire
Kristin Atherton
Kristin Duffy
Kwinten Van De Walle
Lachlan McCall
Lane Graciano
Larissa Oates
Lauren Ash-Morgan
Lauren Wilson
Laurent Winkler
Laurie Ogden
Lebogang Fisher
Lee Heinz
Lee Ravitz
Leo Atkin
Leonard Cook
Lesley Wilcox
Lewis Allcock
Liam Alexandru
Lindsey Huebner
Lindsey Row-Heyveld
Lisa Hill-Corley
Liza Graham
Lois Abdelmalek
Lottie Davies
Louise Lee
Louise Oliver
Lucy Aarden
Lucy Aley-Parker
Lukas Brasherfons

Luke Barton
Luke Farrugia
Luke Heys
Luke MacLeod
Luke Rhodri
Lydia Bakelmun
Lynn Favin
Lynsey Beauchamp
Lynwen Haf Roberts
Maanuv Thiara
Mairin Lee
Maise Carter
Mallory Shear
Manish Gandhi
Margaret Katch
Margo Hendricks
Mari Hayes
Maria Graciano
Marina Smith
Mark Burghagen
Mark Hammersley
Mark Holden
Mark Laverty
Mark McMinn
Mary Ion
Maryam Grace
Maryanna Clarke
Mary-Jayne Russell de Clifford
Matt Richardson
Matthew Crawford
Matthew Khan
Matthew Minicucci
Matthew Rhodes
Maya Cohen
Meg Hodgson
Megan Jarvie
Megan Montgomery
Meg Robinson
Mehmet Ozbek
Melanie Lam
Melanie Leon
Melissa Rojas
Mercedes de la Torre
Meredith DiPaolo Stephens
Micaela Mannix
Michael A Lake
Michael Ahomka Lindsay
Michael Bertenshaw
Michael Downey

Appendix B   **197**

Michael Eriera
Michael P. McDonald
Michael Padgett
Michael Perez
Michael Skellern
Michael Witmore
Michah Weese
Michelle Kelly
Miguel Perez
Mike Perrott
Miriam Kerzner
Misha McCullagh
Miztli Rose
MJ Lee
Molly Keogh
Montgomery Sutton
Muhaddisah
Murphy Hickey
Myra Lee Bell
Nadia Lamin
Nadia Nadif
Naila Mansour
Nancy Linden
Naomi Denny
Nat Kennedy
Natalie Ann Boyd
Natalie Boakye
Natalie Chan
Natalie Harper
Natalie Winter
Nathan Everett Patterson
Nathania Bernabe
Nayia Anastasiadou
Neelaksh Sadhoo
Nerrisa Makgakga
Niamh James
Nicanor Campos
Nicholas Halliwell
Nicholas Waters
Nick Leos
Nicky Allpress
Nicole Miners
Noelle Fair
Olaf Raymond Eide
Olga Blagodatskikh
Olive Fannie Gates
Ollie Corchado
Owen Horsley
Patricia Akhimie
Patrick McHugh
Paul Carpenter

Paul Foulds
Paula Brett
Pedro Araújo Santos
Peter Rogers
Philippa Hammond
Phoebe Elliott
PJ Barner
Quinn A. Hendel
Rachael Bellis
Rho Chung
Rachel Goodman
Ramona Von Pusch
Raphael Corkhill
Rebecca Brincat
Rebecca Brough
Reneltta Arluk
Rhiannon Willans
Richard Hand
Richard Stranks
Roanna Lewis
Rob Myles
Robbie Capaldi
Robert Chisholm
Robert Cohen
Robert Daoust
Robert Lightfoot
Robin Hellier
Roger Carvalho
Roger Parkins
Ross Bailey
Ross Ford
Ross Martin
Rowland Stirling
Ruben Espinosa
Rupert Sadler
Russell Proctor
Ruth Page
Sakuntala Ramanee
Sally McLean
Sam Benjamin
Sam Charney
Samantha Wendorf
Samuel Nunes de Souza
Samya De Meo
Sanjukta Nath
Sanna Javed
Sara Hymes
Sarah Freia
Sarah Gruber
Sarah Ingram
Sarah McCourt

Sarah Peachey
Sasha Wilson
Sawyer Kemp
Scarlett Archer
Scott Ellis
Seb Yates Cridland
Seeta Indrani
Seyan Sarvan
Shakira Searle
Shalyn Bass-McFaul
Shamiso Mushambi
Sharon Eckman
Shona Struthers
Sian Eleanor Green
Simon Balcon
Simon Willshire
Simone Chess
Simone Ellul
Siobhan Richardson
Sir Simon Russell Beale
Sojourner Hazelwood-Connell
Sophie Max
Soumya Mishra
Stefano Guerriero
Steph Ferreira
Stephanie Crugnola
Stephanie Stevens
Stephen Connery-Brown
Stephen Leask
Stephen Moss
Stephen Schnetzer
Stephen Charrett
Steve Connor
Steve Purcell
Steven Jensen
Stuart Vincent
Sulin Hasso
Stellan Knowles
Susan Benninghoff
Susan Bush
Sven Maertens
Swachata Sanjiban Guha
Sydney Aldridge
Tahir Ashraf
Tamara Ritthaler
Tamara Theisen
Tamsin Lynes
Tania Gasa
Tanvi Vivirmani
Thomas Miller

Tiffany Abercrombie
Tim Green
Timothy Weston
Toby Trimby
Tom Vanson
Toni "Bones" Benedetti
    Martin
Tony Pisculli
Trevor Lin
Tricia Mancuso Parks
Tyler Moss
Tyler Nowakowski
Valerie Andrews Bauer
Vanessa Corredera
Dr Varsha Panjwani
Veera Suomi
Verna Vyas
Victoria Howell
Victoria J Valliere
Victoria Rae Sook
Wayne Lee
Wendy Lennon
Wendy Morgan
Whitton Frank
Will Block
Will Gillham
Yaiza Freire-Bernat
Yarit Dor
Yoky Yu
Yolanda Ovide
Yvonne Riley
Zach Livingston
Zoë Land

APPENDIX C

LIST OF TSMGO PATREON PATRONS

Reynold Buono
Margaret Billington
Lauren Ash-Morgan
Monica Sharp
Austin Tichenor
James Nysse
Nathan Young
Erin Sullivan
Imelda D'souza
Rose Lippard
Mari Hayes
Charlotte Webb
Paul Hart
Frank Hollander
JT Stocks
Alice
Dyani Johns Taff
Dan Wilson
Caroline Kraft
Andy Kesson
Alexandra
Kelsey Linberg
Will Fisher
Susan Edgren
Nick Brush
Margo Louise Kolenda-Mason
McHarg-Rhodes Family
Stuart Ian Burns
Maryam Grace
Claire-Monique Martin

Lisa Hill-Corley
Elizabeth Evanna Morris
Patty Clark
Eduardo PÃ©rez Torres
Ollie Corchado
Eric Mauro
Justin Bai
Blake
Kate
Jason Blackwater
Michael Price Nelson
Sabrina Senior
Sharon Heath-Schug
Stephanie Hickey
Natasha Kinsman
Christina Brouwer
Stephanie Shirilan
Mika Haugen
Steve Garde
C
Tricia Mancuso Parks
Wendy Lennon
Alix Dunmore
Amy Lunn
Tom Coley
Yvette Flower
Janeks Babidorics
Liam Alexandru
Raphael Akamo
Whitney Conti
Jack Fairley

Elizabeth Akamo
Manu Das
Doireann May White
Dominic
Becksie Chandler
Sonalee Rau
Laurie Ogden
Jack Shear
Alex Dabertin
Bolaji Akamo
Rebecca Jukes
Sanna Javed
Charlotte Allan
Jeanette McClellan
Helen Pearson
chungclan
Madeleine MacMahon
Veronica C Kerkel
Maveric Garde
Lola
Melisa
Helen Corbett
Natasha McCloy
Anne Morgan
Giulia Elena Xuereb
Monika Sobiecki
Stefan Kahlstorf
Hannah Soulsby-Phillips
David Pieragostini
Andreas Buchtrup
Andersen

200 Appendix C

Micaela Mannix
Riwa Saab
Sophie Maule
Claire
Lorna French
Darryl Hackett
Shannon
Catherine & Graham
   Ingram Smith
Daniel Eilon
Liza
Ben McEwen
Victoria Watts
Nancy E Smith
Lucy Farrar
Leanna
kroberts
Pilar Lueches
Adam Bicknell
Caroline Eustace
Carys Griffiths
Gemma Allred
Chris Chua
Dan Poppitt
Christine Dillon
Brenda Foulds
Eileen Myles
Amy Finkbeiner
Giles
Gill
Sean Mohoganogan
Emma Love
Nathan Patterson
Hasna Haidar
Peter Oskarson
Emilio Vieira
Elizabeth Dennehy
Alex Brinkman-Young
Andrew Yabroff
Mary Whitcomb
Fiona Tong
Juliane Sattler
Tobias Christopher
Honey Gabriel
Mark Dixon
Hannah
Tyler Nowakowski
Cally
Stephen Higgins
Lynsey Beauchamp
Noel Bickford
Kathrin Franke
Brian Kinsley

Benjamin Broadribb
Ally Poole
Gabi Arnold
Debra Rae Cohen
Walter Kailer
Mark Keeler
Perter Brine
Katie Jones
Gaudi Daamen
Rachel Brock
Alix McKenzie
Courtney Herber
Brendan O'Neill
Rob McConeghy
Maurice Kessler
Saffron Vickers Walkling
Rebecca Pauling
Per Hols
Maggi
L Jay H.
Iain Farrell
Naomi Parkin-Tyrie
Levi Hardin
Janet Murphy
Meghana Duggirala
Amanda J McCarthy
Michael Lesh
Ros Burdett
Beth Senturia
Elizabeth Hardy
Lalitte Stolper
David Bowman
Martin Fisher
Bennett Pologe
Marianne McAleer
Pamela Kelly
CafÃ© Noir
irtadb
Kerstin
Macaulay Gallacher
Alexandra Simone
Nate Smith
Kathryn Burke
Daniel Cordova
Paul Carpenter
Derek Lords
Matthew Berrigan
Zach Waddington
Duncan Keene
Tamara Ritthaler
Lynn Dolan
David Sterling Brown, PhD
Alister Downie

Peter Binkley
Clyde & Kathy Wilson
Joseph Stephenson
Courtney Glazer
Lucy Aley-Parker
Ffion Jones
David Sieracki
Jacqui Morrison
Emily Carding
Karen Yacobi
Eugenia Low
Heather Dean
Dika Ryan
Jenn Deon
David Lynn
Elaine McHarg
Gillian Barmes
C Denoon
Emily
Lynne Weiss
Dr. Eric Rasmussen &
   Dr. Victoria Hines
Jenny Boyd
Elizabeth Lancaster
Don Carlson
Rosanne Gillis
Dominic Klyve
Stephanie
Lucy AP
Louise R
Spencer
Colleen Davis
Debra Workman
Margaret Minsky
Patrick Gordon
Lynn Freitas
Sarah Hoare
Anne Butler
Deirdre Ryan
Kristen Soule
Alison W
Sheila MacDonald
Lisa Farrington
Barbara Moss
Daniel Abrantes
Olga Blagodatskikh
Richard Peachey
Denise Yates
Amanda Freeston
Gerry & Helen Macdonald
Gill Page
Brian Eastty
Eleonora Alei

Appendix C **201**

Tony Wakeford
Jenny Rowe
Fr. Defenestrato
Shari Schutz
Miriam Kerzner &
  Robert Chisholm
Alex Mechanic
Kris
Margaret Aleks
CLC1000
Susan Rowland
Danielle Farrow
Woodlandmaples
Alex Benarzi
RJ M
Chloe B
Jen Sloan
Louisa Murphy
Ash
Gareth
Ange Lane
Mitch Albala
Charlotte Reese
Karen Girling
John Wells
Douglas Lanier
Clive Cubitt
Christine McCarney
`movyshoes
Christopher Thorpe
Derryn Snowdon
Elena
Robina Bamforth
Catherine Brewer
Carol Dover
Alister Downie
Thomasin Ringler
Jeremy Mortimer
Mary Jane Brett
Catherine Hope
Matthew Rhodes
Kelley
Scott Manchin
Mark Lively
Nick Dunnett
Rachel Muers

Justine Griffith
Christopher Pearson
Julie Baber
Ian Doescher
Ken & Sally Lawton
Janet Lawson
Adriana Barreiros
Johan Richter
Claire
Joey Hopkinson
Violet Mackintosh
Matt Risby
Gemma Lise Thornton
Rebecca Wood
Katherine Lange
Natalie Shoham
Sara Rhodes
Hayden Williams
Linda Healey
Jo Hopkins
Heidrun Atherton
Agathe Majou
Michael Cawley
Cynthea Frongillo
Kenneth Whyte
Mark McMinn
Ashley Hirons
T. Schwartz
Zena Thornton
Tekla Rae
Julie Balen
PJ Schoff
Christopher Green
Lynn Kutner
Ruth Lotero
Garrie Powers
Maria S Hind
Linda Keuntje
Mattias Carlborg
t y
Esther Levin
Emma Barraclough
Debbie Gilpin
Theo Clarke
Amber D'Albert
Agnes

Matthew Darroch-
  Thompson
aa
Natasha Kay
Ellise P Mayor
Emily Oldroyd
Priya
Phyllis Kathleen Koons
Jo Woodworth
Rosee Hadden
Zoe Land
Jennifer Vernon
Carrie Sorensen
Judith K.
Tim Padmore
Jeffrey Kaplan
Jo-ann Turford
Deborah Sutton
Sarah Warburton
Hui Hua Chua
Luke Barton
Eileen M McCarthy
Geraldine Pelletier
Clive Butler
Simon Bolland
Anneke vd Stege
David Rawlins
Mary Paul
Ksenia Nemchinova
Laura Stephen
Jennifer Koons
Ian Myles
Eva Forsom
Marie Rosenthal
Gillian Bailey
Elizabeth Marchant
Sally Lawton
Caroline Campbell
Eva-Luise Schwarz
Amy Danson
Shelby C
Amber Elby
Victoria Rae Sook
Bonnie MacBird
Gillian P. Cusack

APPENDIX D
LINKS TO TSMGO PLAYLIST

FIGURE D.1 TSMGO Playlist QR Code.

bit.ly/tsmgoplaylist

INDEX

Aarden, Lucy 52, 196
Abercrombie, Tiffany 139, 199
accents, or dialects, homogenization of 48
accessibility and inclusion 20, 50, 113, 116–9, 123, 140, 153
Agents of Shield 102
Airbnb 18, 19
Aldridge, Sydney; Casting A Show A Week 82–7
Ali, Saheem 151
Andoh, Adjoa 151, xiii
apology practices 57–8, 61
Apple 18, 103
Armande, Amelia "Ace" (nèe Sutton, Amy) 96, 194
Astor Place riots 11, 151
audience focus 16
audience, financial support of (*see* Patreon)

Bard City, *Shakespeare In A Week* 68
Bate, Jonathan 78, 80
Battersea Arts Center 152
Beale, Sir Simon Russell 107–8, 197
Beaulieu, Dan 78, 195
Big Telly 153
Black Lives Matter Movement 67, 106, 151
Bottom's Donkey Head 25, 74
boundaries, breaking of/pressing/testing of 155–6

Brailsford, David Sir; British Cycling Team 18, 145
brave spaces 62, 113, 155–7
Brewer, Dominic 59, 78, 195
Bridge Theatre, The 161
British Cycling Team 18, 145
British Sign Language, interpretations of 61
Broadribb, Ben 34, 100, 200
Brook, Peter 151, 162, 164
Brown, David Sterling 10, 108, 150, 195, 200

Call of Duty, videogame 107
Capaldi, Robbie 96, 197
Carding, Emily 59, 195, 200
casting 3, 15, 44, 49, 51, 64, 69–70, 75, 78–9; actor gender 83–4, 117, 127, 157; conscious practices of 3, 44, 49, 83, 117, 127; data driven practices of (*see* Guccione, Ed) 87–92
Chung, Rachel "Rho" 44, 112, 117, 197
Clear, James 18
clues 7, 13, 15
Colbert, Stephen 57
community: code of behavior within 49–51; cultivation of 53–5; finding focus 43–4; finding people 45–9; informed consent

204 Index

50, 62; intentional 44–5; key pillars of 52; niche identification 47; safeguarding of 50–51
community agreements 60–61
community engagement, via social media (see Page, Ruth) 2, 10, 15, 20, 52–5, 108–111
community, leadership of: metaphorical roles 56
community needs, identification of 49
Conniff, Sam 7
creativity, constraints and deadlines under 137, 148–9
Crowds, wisdom of 3, 19–20, 136
Crystal, Ben 22, 127; Curating Guest Introductions and Creative Producing 104–8; *Shakespeare on Toast* 93
Crystal, David 105, 127
Csikszentmihalyi, Mihaly, *Flow* 45
cultural competency 157

Data for Good 92
design thinking: action bias 121; empathy map 44
Dido Queen of Carthage 112
digital theatre: discovering your values 126–130; imagination 36, 92, 127, 129; maximizing actors' potential 144–8; performance medium considerations of; practicalities: eyelines, cueing scripts 131–2; practice as research 124; shared language 114, 130, 134; spatial relationships 132–4; systemizing thinking 36, 55, 65, 67, 76, 78, 79–80, 88, 118, 120, 132, 135, 157; tool hacking 129, 148; tutorials 70, 166, 170; Virtual Backgrounds (VBG) 93–4, 125, 128–9
digital theatre, directing of 121; shaping audience experience 131
Djemal, David 139, 195
Doctor Faustus 112
Doescher, Ian 52, 59, 195, 201; *Much Ado About Mean Girls* 97; *Shakespeare's Star Wars* 2, 28–9, 81; *William Shakespeare's A Christmas Carol* 94, 112, 114

Dr. Martin Luther King Jr. 59
earned media 52
Edward II 98, 112, 115, 117
empathy map 44
Empty Space, The (see Brook, Peter) 151, 162
epiccardboardprops 99
ethos 40–43

Farrow, Danielle 59, 195, 201
Fey, Tina, *Mean Girls* 97
First Folio Series 2, 73, 103, 112–7, 153
Floyd, George, murder of 67
Food Of Love 116
Foundation for Intentional Community, The 45

Gallathea, TSMGO production of 44, 112, 115, 117
Game of Thrones 67
Geller, Charlie, and McKay, Adam; film *The Big Short* 68
Gibson, Adam 114, 194; Music and Sound 99–104
Gilpin, Debbie; Mind The Blog 59, 201
GitHub 90–91
The Good Place 49
Google Drive, use of 117
Google Sheets 86–7, 89–91
Grace, Maryam 112, 116, 196, 199
Guccione, Ed; The Use of Data in Casting 87–92
Guest, Janet 113

harm reduction 157
Hawking, Frey Kwa 113, 195
Henry VIII 107
hierarchies, flattening of 60, 136, 157–8
Higgins, Annabelle 59, 108, 194
hunches 7, 13–20
Hytner, Nicholas 161, i

IBM Global Design Leadership 164
ideas, capture of 14, 17, 27, 157; generation process 20, 28, 79, 114, 135, 137, 150
ideation 19, 26, 33
if/then 137
IKEA 46–7
immersive theatre, experiences of 160–1

Index **205**

incremental changes/improvements 12, 23, 76, 145
Ingram, Emily 12, 73, 112, 114, 116–7, 171, 175, 191, 195; Props, Costume and Visual Identity 92–100
Ingram, Sarah 52, 197
innovation principles: drawing from other worlds 122; prototyping 23–7
innovation process 4, 7, 76
Inside No. 9 102
intimacy, definition of and protected identity traits 157
Iron Man 22
Italian Renaissance 152

Joans, Jordy (FKA Jordy Deelight) 94
Johnson, Dwayne "The Rock" 152
Joy (the Joy Mangano story) 18
JSTOR 80

Kairos 10, 52, 161
Kamprad, Ingvar (*see* IKEA) 47
Karim-Cooper, Farah 150
Kate Morley PR 52
Kemp, Sawyer 108, 197
Key Performance Indicator (KPI) 159
Kingdon, Matt 7
Knives Out, storyboards 22
Kondo, Marie 14

Last Week Tonight 161
The Last of Us, videogame 107
LeBillon, Jonathan 10
LEGO 22, 159
Lindsay, Michael Ahomka 138, 196
listening in action 50–1
LitCharts "Shakescleare" 70, 78, 80
Live Chat (*see* YouTube Chat)
Lloyd, Jamie 163
Logic Pro, software 103
Low, Eugenia 59, 195, 200
Lyly, John (*see Gallathea*)

MacAleer, Danan 97
Mandela, Nelson 39
Marcell, Joe 108, 196
market, gap opportunities 18–19
Marlowe Lives 112
Max, Sophie 139, 197
McLean, Sally 138, 197
Medici family 152

Merely Theatre 154
MeToo Movement 51, 155
Miller, Gemma 77, 195
Mock, Ella 113
Morgan, Wendy 94, 198
Much Ado About Mean Girls 97
The Muppet Christmas Carol 94
Musk, Elon 152
Myles, Rob: Read and Edit The Play 77–9; Research and Develop The Production 79–82

NASA 46, 159
Nemchinova, Ksenia 59, 111, 201
New Diorama Theatre, The 153
Newstok, Scott 17, 151

O'Brien, et al; *Culture is Bad for You* 44
Open Broadcast Software (OBS) 116
opportunity, areas of 150, 27, 79, 100, 123, 125, 149
optimization 31, 65–6
Original Parallels 37, 127–8, 152, 158
Original Practice ('OP') 68, 126, 152
original pronunciation 107, 127
Original Shakespeare Company 126
Orson Welles' *War of The Worlds* 54
Ovide, Yolanda 147, 198
Ozanne, Christine 126

Pace, Chelsea 156
Page, Ruth 69, 99, 197; Community Engagement Using Social Media 108–11
pain points 11, 13, 88
Pareto principle 66, 115
Parillon, Amelia 112, 139, 194
Patreon 2, 54, 75–6, 109–11, 115, 193, 199–201
Peachey, Sarah 1, 7, 8, 78, 100, 197; worked at ?What If! Innovation 7; Producing A Play in a Week 69–77
Peele, Jordan 16–7
Peep Show 132
Perez, Miguel 138, 197
Pinterest Boards 98, 117, 179
PlayShakespeare.com 70, 78–80, 81, 90, 91, 166
Poel, William 126
possibilities, imagining of 17–19
pronouns, inclusive use of 58, 70, 117, 167–8, 171–2

prototyping 7, 22–3, 26
Public Theatre, The 151
Punchdrunk 36, 160
purpose architecture 46–7
purpose vector 46–7

Qlab 102–3
Quirk Books 2, 59, 65

R, programming language, use of 91
racially-biased lighting adjustments 95
Rasmussen, Eric 78, 80, 195, 200
Rattigan, Fergus 112, 195
Red Bastard 160
reframing failure 28, 58
rehearsal periods, Germany and Russia 154
Repertory Theatre conditions 146
Research & Development, organization tools 80, 117, 140
Rhodes, Matthew 62, 69, 72, 73, 135, 193, 196, 201; reinventing TSMGO for sustainable working 112–9
Rikard, Laura 156
Ritthaler, Tamara 59, 197, 200
Robben Island Shakespeare 39
Robinson, Ken 17
RSC Complete Works 78
rule breakers 13, 14, 64
Rylance, Mark 126

Sam Wanamaker Playhouse 151
Saturday Night Live (SNL) 64, 67
Schur, Michael: cornerstone questions 49–50; *How to Be Perfect* 49, 51, 57–8
Screen Skills 82
Secret Cinema 160
Shakespeare's *A Christmas Carol* 94, 112, 114
Shakespeare Birthplace Trust, The 2, 52
Shakespeare North Playhouse 152
Shakespeare, arguments within 127, 132, 137, 143
Shakespeare's Globe 4, 108, 126, 128, 161, 169
Shakespeare's Star Wars 2, 28–9, 81
Shakespeare, William - Plays Of: *All's Well That Ends Well* 97; *Comedy of Errors, A* 37, 96; *Cymbeline* 26, 67, 108, 133; *Hamlet* 55, 85, 95, 108, 110;

Henry IV, part I 59; *Henry VI*, part I 84; *Henry VI*, part II 84–5; *Henry V* 36, 93, 129, 133; *Julius Caesar* 81, 141–4; *King John* 26, 78; *King Lear* 4, 35, 37–8, 98, 108; *Macbeth* 4, 81–2, 94, 101, 166–9, 170–2, 178–88; *Measure for Measure* 133, 138; *Merchant of Venice, The* 3, 83, 138; *A Midsummer Night's Dream* 25, 66, 86; *Much Ado About Nothing* 139; *Othello* 3, 10, 95; *Pericles* 112, 116; *Richard II* 85, 151; *Richard III* 147, 174; *Romeo & Juliet* 74, 85, 108; *Taming of the Shrew, The* 82, 138; *Tempest, The* 23, 103; *Titus Andronicus* 24, 87, 133; *Troilus & Cressida* 97; *Twelfth Night* 82, 95; *Two Gentlemen of Verona, The* 1, 23–4, 105; *Two Noble Kinsmen, The* 62, 112, 113
Shunt Lounge, The 152
single point of failure 118
site-specific theatre 12, 123, 128; barriers 123; opportunities 123
60 hour Shakespeare 68
Slap Chop 18
Smith, Kevin V. 112, 196
SnapCamera, use of AR app 25, 74
social media: Facebook 52, 59, 73, 109, 171, 193; Facebook Business Manager 109; Instagram 52, 109, 171; Patreon 2, 54, 75–76, 109–111, 115, 193, 199; RedBubble 109; Tweetdeck 109; Twitter 10, 54, 69, 105, 109, 169
social media, lessons learned 110–11
social media, strategies of; building presence 107–8
social media tools 109
Soliloquies, staging of 124–5
Sook, Victoria Rae 116, 198, 201
Sponzo, Carly 59, 194
Stigner, Jack 13
Stoicism 131
Stoicism, negative visualization 68
systemization: productivity 66; starting with 'why' 66

Systems Thinker, The 55
technical innovations: window capture
  116–7
The Theatre Green Book 162
theatre, pain points 11, 13, 88;
  problems and provocations
  150–63
theatremaking: environmentally
  responsible practices 141, 162;
  facilitative leadership style
  55–6, 63, 158; hierarchies
  within 3, 60, 136, 157
Theatrical Intimacy Education xiii–iv,
  57, 155
Thompson, Ayanna 127
Thompson, Sandy 155
Tiramani, Jenny 126
transgressions, stages of (Sandy
  Thompson) 155–6
Trello 117
triangulation 78, 119
TSMGO: accounting practices:
  Patreon, Survey Monkey,
  Zoom, Mailchimp 75;
  aesthetics of 92–4, 96, 98, 100;
  appointment viewing 21, 67;
  awards 2; costume, governing
  principles of 97–8; design
  elements 93–100; design
  inspirations (Grotowski's Poor
  Theatre, Blue Peter, Pinterest,
  YouTube and Google tutorials)
  98–99; digital groundlings 53;
  Dramaturgy; Editing Processes;
  Embodied engagement;
  example of actor notes
  140–44; Final show prep
  checklist 72, 191
  (see Appendix A8); first
  followers 52, 59; 'franchise
  model' 112–3; Groundling's
  Choice Awards 58;
  Groundling's Choice Awards
  apology 58; guest
  introductions 21, 104
  (see Crystal, Ben); Hardship
  Fund 2, 44, 54, 109, 115;
  legacy of 2, 20, 53, 62;
  Lighting 80, 94–5, 125–6,
  128, 191; major media
  coverage of 2, 52; makeup,
  cosmetics 97; media; mission;
  Moderation 55; Month of
  Marlowe Festival 98; motto
  (Shakespeare for Everyone,
  For Free, Forever) 1, 46;
  onboarding processes (for
  directors) 116; Performance
  paradigm, philosophy of
  127–132, 163; post-
  production survey 146;
  Production Pain Points 88;
  Production Process
  (see Peachey, Sarah;
  Producing a Play in a Week);
  props 1, 28, 65, 70, 71, 72,
  78, 80, 92–3, 95–6,
  98–100, 171–2, 175, 178,
  180, 190, 191; Rehearsal
  room practices 72–3, 146,
  170, 175–6, 181; research
  and development processes:
  opportunity map 80; response
  to *Hamlet* commentary 55;
  rituals of participation 53–4;
  scheduling complexities 71;
  Shakescleare translation use
  of 70, 78; SNL parallels to 64,
  67; stage management
  responsibilities and checklist
  74; staging devices (see Zoom,
  staging conventions);
  streamlining time zones 71–2;
  strong and wrong 140, 147;
  system for note taking (use of
  highlighters, systematic,
  layered feedback) 15;
  systemization and time
  allocations 65, 72, 76–7,
  114, 135, 168, 175–6;
  templates - see Appendices
  165; 3-point lighting set up
  94–5; values of shared light,
  shared space 128; visual
  identity 92–3, 100; weekly
  production schedule 65
Tucker, Patrick 126
Turner, Lyndsey 164

Universal Basic Income, Ireland pilot
  154–5

Van Kampen, Claire 126
Venkatrathnam, Sonny 39

Vieira, Emilio 195, 200; octagon of ideas 137
Vredenburg, Karel 164

Williamson, Marianne 164
Wilson, Jeffrey 2–3
The Wizard of Oz 98

X Prize, The 159

"yes, and" 19, 146
YouTube algorithm 48
YouTube Chat 20, 29, 49, 53, 55, 59, 74, 136

Zoom functions, speaker view, gallery view 123–5
Zoom, staging conventions - 36, 123, 127, 130, 133, 135